Bangkok's Foodscape

Dear Professor Moss,

How lovely to reconnect!
I hope you and your colleagues
enjoy this book.

All the best,

Gail Yasen

June 30/2008

Studies in Contemporary Thailand

Edited by Prof. Erik Cohen, Sociology Department, Hebrew University, Jerusalem

Studies in Contemporary Thailand No. 16
Series Editor: Erik Cohen

Bangkok's Foodscape

Public Eating, Gender Relations, and Urban Change

Gisèle Yasmeen

White Lotus Press

White Lotus Co., Ltd
G.P.O. Box 1141
Bangkok 10501
Thailand

Tel.   (66) 0-38239-883-4
Fax   (66) 0-38239-885
E-mail   ande@loxinfo.co.th
Website http://thailine.com/lotus

Printed in Thailand

Designed and typeset by COMSET Limited Partnership

ISBN   974-4800-89-5   pbk.   White Lotus Co., Ltd., Bangkok

Contents

Contents

List of Tables, Figures, and Field Note Entries

Tables

Figures

Field Note Entries

Preface

This study examines public eating in urban Thai society. The book provides a "thick description" of the recursive relationship between society and space by advancing the concept of foodscape. The focus is the widespread habit of purchasing prepared food in Bangkok. Three interrelated questions form the heart of the research effort:

1. How can one represent and interpret Bangkok's food-system? What are its past, current, and future trends?
2. How is Bangkok's foodscape gendered? Is it possible to typologize eating establishments *vis-à-vis* gender relations in urban Thailand? What are the different roles played by women and men in the culture of public eating? Are gender relations complementary, hierarchical, or antagonistic?
3. What are the spaces associated with the sale of cooked food in Bangkok, and how are these being affected by rapid urban development? How are food-shop owners adjusting to the socio-spatial changes? How is space conceptualized with respect to gender and food-systems in Thai society? Are private/public spheres relevant in the Bangkok case?

Women dominate the sale of prepared foods, particularly at the level of small and micro-enterprises. What is fascinating about the Thai case is the presence of women in this sector, making them a firm part of the public sphere. By looking at the mutual interrelationship between food-systems, gender relations, and urban spatial phenomena, I establish why and how public eating is gendered and how small food shop (eating establishment) owners are adjusting to the rapidly changing environment of Bangkok.

The theoretical pivot is that urban space is gendered with respect to the food-system in unique ways that intersect with discourses of "public" and "private." Through recourse to relevant literature, statistics, and empirical research, I construct a portrait of Bangkok's foodscape. The methods used include participant-observation, formal and informal interviewing, and a quantitative survey of the Victory Monument Area in Central Bangkok. The result is a hybrid between ethnography and more traditional approaches to urban geography. A self-reflexive use of field notes and interview transcripts creates a grounded representation of place focussed on the field research encounter.

Chapter 1 unearths the foundations of the research project. First, a sketch is provided of the subject matter to introduce the central questions this study addresses. The study of food and foodways[1] is justified and the bodies of literature briefly commented on that have conditioned my view of urban foodscapes, a concept introduced in the first chapter. The study's theoretical "hook" is outlined in greater detail in Chapter 2, which draws on the work of Smith, de Certeau, and cultural geography to advance the notion of foodscape and how it can be used to interrogate public/private sphere models. Chapter 3 introduces the methodological approach, ethnography broadly defined, and illustrates through examples how I went about reaching conclusions and gathering data. The Victory Monument case study area is also presented. Chapter 4 outlines the basic structure and function of the Thai food-system and couches it in wider Southeast Asian foodways. Chapter 5 focuses on Thai and Southeast Asian gender relations in the food-system and introduces the results of the quantitative survey. In Chapter 6, the study's principal informants are introduced and their daily lives profiled. Daily routines and operating budgets are presented and analyzed. Chapter 7 weaves together the factors that enable cooked-food sellers to open a business. The necessary and contingent relations present in different locational environments and the changing real-estate market and role of the local state are also explained. This chapter also introduces the important topic of the foodscape's encounter with globalization and the rapidly changing local-global dialectic. Chapter 8 summarizes several years of work examining the impact of the Asian economic crisis, and subsequent, gradual recovery, on the food-system of Thailand.

The final chapter serves as a *quo vadis* with commentaries on the situation found in Bangkok in the first few years of the new millennium. This book's final chapter illustrates some of the major changes affecting Bangkok's foodscape in the turbulent years following the devaluation of the Thai baht in 1997 and the subsequent Asian economic crisis. It also outlines the need for organizing strategies within the prepared food sector to improve the social and economic capital of Bangkok's thousands of micro-entrepreneurs.

Conclusions identify the socio-economic, ideological, and spatial factors that explain the public eating phenomenon and its gendering. It reflects on the heuristic considerations of an ethnographic *bricolage* and the advancement of the foodscape concept. The meaning of public/private spheres as evidenced in Bangkok's food-scape is clearly different from that of neighboring South and East Asian societies. Changes in the Bangkok food-system studied in the mid-1990s point to the blurring of boundaries between home and work, formal and informal enterprises, as well as "tradition" and "modernity."

Acknowledgements

Some three years and the contributions of many people have been needed to turn a PhD dissertation completed in 1996 into this highly revised work. Those to whom I owe the greatest thanks are the people in Thailand who so kindly opened their world to me both during my research and since. The anonymous informants described in this study therefore the first to be acknowledged. Heartfelt thanks extend to Diethard Ande of White Lotus Press who saw the manuscript through to completion and was extremely patient over the years, gently reminding me that the book was overdue. Series editor Erik Cohen also provided useful suggestions for revisions and John Stape is commended for his fine editing job as well as his work on the preparation of the index. Edward M. Stauffer is to be thanked for diligent attention to the final typesetting and proofs.

While undertaking doctoral research from 1991–96, I had the good fortune of working under the supervision of Professor Terry McGee at the University of British Columbia, Vancouver. It is an honor to count Professor McGee, a scholar and gentleman, as a friend who has been a source of constant encouragement both in my student days and in the many years since. Fellow McGee students provided stimulating conversations and companionship over the past decade.

Post-doctoral research conducted under the auspices of the Development and Security in Southeast Asia (DSSEA) project funded by the Canadian International Development Agency (CIDA) allowed me to collect the supplementary material during 1997–99 that informs the last chapter of this book. Many thanks to DSSEA co-directors Professors David DeWitt and Carolina Hernandez, who guided me over those two years. My subsequent work as a consultant for the United Nations Food and Agriculture Organization (FAO) facilitated data collection in 2000–02. I am indebted to Olivio Argenti and Michael Wales of the FAO for having engaged my services and for sharing their extensive knowledge of food-systems in the South.

The work of numerous scholars of Thailand has informed this study. Although there are too many individuals to be named, I should like to acknowledge the invaluable advice of Charles Keyes, Jacques Amyot, Jim Glassman, Charles Greenberg, Amara Pongsapich, and Nurul Amin. Narumol Nirathron deserves special recognition for making arrangements to update some of the food statistics. Marilyn Walker passed on valuable data from her survey of food habits in Thailand and accompanying dissertation, and her friendship and support have played an important role for a decade. I have been extremely fortunate to get to know Irene Tinker, Professor Emeritus of the University of California at Berkeley and former Director of the international street foods study widely cited here. If it were not for the encouragement of Claude Comtois, now at the Université de Montréal, I might have never undertaken graduate work.

My Thai language instructors at the Southeast Asian Studies Summer Institute (SEASSI) at the University of Washington deserve special mention. Dr Peansiri Vongvipanond and *Ajaan* Kannikar Chanprasert provided valuable information for this thesis. Thitiya Paobthong's coaching in Thai has saved me numerous times as my Thai becomes rusty.

I am indebted to the Social Sciences and Humanities Research Council, the International Development Research Centre's Young Canadian Researcher's Travel Grant and the Northwest Consortium for Southeast Asian Studies. The Canada-ASEAN Centre and the Canadian Universities Consortium UBC-AIT Partnership Project generously provided travel funding.

Lisa Kwan is the first to be thanked for her top quality maps and floor plans. Catherine Griffiths and Mark Yaolin Wang designed excellent graphics. Cyndia Pilkington, Keith Taverner and Wendy Cooper helped with editing and formatting. Thanks go to Meg Andersen for entering part of the Bibliography. Jessica North kindly assisted with the Glossary.

Khap khun maak to Kamolrat Sa-Ngeam (Morn) and Arporn Somjit (Kapook), my dedicated assistants in Bangkok. Morn has continued to play an *ex officio* research assistant role over the years, and it is an honor to have her as a close friend. I have benefited from her advice, hard work, and companionship. I should like to express gratitude to Arthur and Marianne, Vespry who were there during my doctoral research when I needed them in Bangkok as "surrogate parents."

Betty Valdez Diamsay's care-giving to our baby, and other related duties, made submitting the revised manuscript possible. Finally, my mother Marie Antoinette

Martineau's enduring love and support has made the arduous journey of over a decade of research in Asia possible. She cared for me when I was discouraged and egged me on.

Lastly, my husband Iskander Ahmed has been a source of strength over the past five years. I dedicate this book to him and our young son Marcel who has put up with mommy's being on the computer during much of his first years of life.

Chapter 1

Public Eating and Bangkok's Foodscape

Any visitor to Thailand's cities, particularly Bangkok, will notice the preponderance of food stalls, street foods, restaurants, and other examples of the popularity of purchasing prepared or take-away food outside the home and eating-out in street cafés and restaurants. In addition, one of the things that stands out in Southeast Asia in general and urban Thailand in particular compared to cities in the neighboring regions of East and South Asia is that selling prepared food is overwhelmingly an occupation dominated by women. Add to this the fact that women are extremely represented as consumers of prepared food and as restaurant and food stall customers in Thailand.

The scenario just described is one of the distinguishing features of everyday life in Bangkok. How did this phenomenon come about? How does this particular aspect of the food-system function? *Bangkok's Foodscape* attempts to provide some answers to these questions by painting a portrait of certain aspects of the city's "geography of public eating" as it presented itself in the boom period of the pre-crisis 1990s. The bulk of this study addresses the period from 1992 to 1994 with a concluding chapter providing a "snapshot" based on research done on the impact of the economic crisis on the food-system after the devaluation of the Thai baht in 1997.

This book is therefore primarily about "public eating" in Bangkok, how this foodscape is gendered, and the myriad ways in which the food-system experienced socio-spatial change as a result of rapid economic growth in Thailand prior to 1997. Three interrelated topics and bodies of literature are therefore examined: (1) Thai and Southeast Asian food-systems; (2) sex-gender systems in the region; and (3) studies of urban socio-economic relations in Bangkok. The primary problem—to explain how and why public eating is gendered and how, specifically, large numbers of women come to use public space to sell and consume food—is situated at the conceptual interface of gender, food, and spatial systems (see Fig. 1.1 for a model).

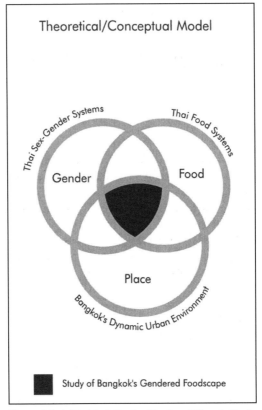

Figure 1.1 A Model of Gender, Food, and Place to Study Bangkok's Foodscape

Studying Urban Food Habits

Food and foodways can be used as a "lens" to focus on many other aspects of human existence. Like the concept of landscape, which is a view of space from a certain perspective, a *foodscape* can be thought of as a point of view on a given place (Appadurai 1990; Cosgrove 1984; Daniels and Cosgrove 1993). It is therefore a type of representation or an "aid to vision" that pays particular attention to the spatial relations in the "food-system."

The study of eating habits interfaces with other social spheres such as agricultural systems, religious beliefs, kinship patterns, and medical practices and is a solid province of anthropology and history (Arnott 1976; Barrau 1983; Camporesi 1993; Fenton and Owen 1981; Mennel 1985; Montanari 1994). Social hierarchies are often reinforced, and contested, by and through food praxis (Douglas 1984; Goody 1982; Van Esterik 1992; Walton 1989).

By studying eating habits from a geographical perspective, the role that food plays in the production of space and functioning of urban places becomes apparent (Sorre 1952). When this research was first undertaken in 1991, the study of food by geographers was virtually unheard of. At that time, there were a handful of people in the discipline who had studied food and eating habits from a spatial perspective (Simoons 1991, 1961; Drakakis-Smith 1990; Walton 1989; and Watts 1983). Carl Sauer in *Seeds, Spades, Hearths, and Herds* (1963) and parts of other volumes (1952) presented a macro-historical treatise on food and agricultural history. Several decades later, there were a host of studies of food examined by geographers (Bell and Valentine 1997; Cook and Crang 1996; Crang 1994; Cwiertka and Walraven 2001; Law 2001; Warde and Martens 2000).

There are two bodies of literature that this study resembles more substantively. The work of McGee and his colleagues spawned several studies of urban labor markets and petty commodity production in the "Third World" and has paved the way for my own enquiries into the urban food-system (Guerrero 1975; McGee and Yeung 1977; MacLeod 1989; McGee et al. 1988).[1] Similarly, Tinker and her collaborators at the Equity Policy Center conducted comparative research, from a feminist perspective, on street foods in various provincial towns in southern Thailand providing considerable comparative data useful for this study (Chapman 1984; Cohen 1986; Tinker 1987).

Feminist geographers and others exploring "the geography of gender" have a particularly useful contribution to make to the exploration of *foodscapes*. A few have taken on the challenge as a subject worthy of study on its own or as part of enquiries into housing or community development initiatives and related social activism. As a gendered activity, the daily course of buying, preparing, selling, and consuming food in many ways defines, distinguishes, and modulates the life-worlds of women, men, and children (Bowlby 1988; Charles and Kerr 1988; Giard and Mayol 1980). The performance or non-performance of food-related work is also instrumental in defining culturally meaningful ideologies of femininity and masculinity.

The spatialization of motherhood and femininity in Southeast Asia, particularly in Thailand, is not as "housebound" as in traditional Western, Southern, and East Asian cultures. Could this be somehow related to Thai relationships to food, as evidenced by the prevalence of public eating, which indicates a more flexible cultural valuation of the "home cooked meal"? If one compares these practices with traditional Mediterranean or South Asian societies, this seems plausible. The book draws considerably from non-Thai examples, as well as from some non-Southeast-Asian cases, to explore these questions further.

This study examines "public" eating in Bangkok by studying the habit of selling and consuming prepared food outside the home. Street food vendors, outlets in food centers, and catering networks serve urbanites meals for consumption *in situ* or as take-out or delivery to homes and offices. These small, usually family-based establishments comprise what I have labelled as Bangkok residents' everyday food strategies. Medium-scale and larger establishments catering to the middle-classes and the wealthy serve a more exclusive clientele. This elite foodscape is compared and contrasted to mass-based every-day strategies. The boundary between the two systems is far from clear, the distinction between them being an analytical choice rather than an empirical reality. Indeed, typologizing food establishments, a fairly complex activity, is one of this book's objectives.

Although public eating has drastically increased in the past twenty years following Thailand's rapid industrial and urban development and subsequent crisis and recovery, many of these patterns have historical roots related to gender relations prevalent in the region. One of these is the long-standing presence of women in food vending and small-scale commerce, a wider Southeast-Asian phenomenon (Manderson 1983; Van Esterik 1982; Tinker 1992). Rural markets and travelling merchants selling both raw and prepared food are an important part of Southeast Asian folklore and of the ethnographies of the region, many of which were produced by women anthropologists fascinated by the apparent power and autonomy of Southeast Asian women (Djamour 1959; Firth 1966; Geertz 1961). "These women (and their male colleagues) were struck by the participation of indigenous women in economic life, and the extent to which this afforded them autonomy, power and authority" (Manderson 1983: 2). A writer from the 1950s summarizes his perception of the high status of Thai women:

> The social position of the Thai peasant woman is powerful: she has long had a voice in village governmental affairs; she often represents her household at village meetings when her husband cannot attend; she almost always does the buying and selling in the local

markets. (It is so unusual for a Thai male to do this that it elicits comment if he does.) Through their marketing activities Thai farmwomen produce a sizeable portion of the family cash income, and they not only handle the household money, but also usually act as the family treasurer and hold the purse strings (de Young 1955: 24).

Women in many societies, including East and South Asia, manage family finances. Southeast Asian women add to this role by actually earning the money and often by doing so while occupying the public sphere.

Of additional importance in the case of Siamese[2] society is the historical importance of "restaurant culture," a hybridized offspring or *luuk kreung* of the indigenous market-stall tradition and Chinese shop-house commerce (Skinner 1957).[3] This is partially an outcome of the historical alliance between entrepreneurial Thai women and migrant Chinese laborer merchantmen, who met, married, reproduced, and created a new cuisine and way of life in urban Thailand beginning in the late-nineteenth century (Keyes 1987; Van Esterik 1992a; Skinner 1958).

To a certain extent, this hybridization resembles the development of *Peranakan* (mixed Chinese-Malay) culture in Malaysia, Singapore, and Indonesia (Hellwig 1994). Unlike the "pluralistic" society of colonial Malaya described by Furnivall (1939), Chinese immigrants to Siam are thought to have integrated somewhat more smoothly into mainstream Thai society, although this is now considered an exaggerated representation of their experience (Chan and Tong 1995; Szanton 1983). Bangkok is still a city with strong Chinese influences, and the pivotal role of the Chinese and Sino-Thai in Bangkok's food-system is referred to throughout this volume.[4]

Thai gender relations are central to the way urbanites have negotiated access to public space in order to sell and consume prepared food. In the case of rural ethnic Thais, particularly those from the North and Northeast, these relations are predicated on matrilineal kinship patterns, bilateral or cognatic inheritance systems, and residence patterns often matrilocal or at least neo-local following marriage. Urban dwellers, many of whom are migrant women from the North and Northeast selling cooked food, retain some of these rural social relations.

Women entrepreneurs dominate the sale of cooked food and also play an important role as consumers. Men play key roles as food suppliers, customers, and as co-owners/managers of the enterprises. In larger, more profitable restaurants, men account for nearly half the employees. The food-system is undergoing many transitions in terms of gender relations and spatial organization as Bangkok continues to experience rapid socio-economic change. This study examines some of

Gisèle Yasmeen

these changes in reference to Thai urban society at large through a case study of a central neighborhood in Bangkok.

Public eating is important for several reasons. First, it is a significant branch of the urban life-support system by supplying a primary need—food—to the population. Small-scale vendors and shopowners are part of an efficient inexpensive mechanism for distribution of commodities in the mega-cities of "developing" countries (McGee and Yeung 1977).[5] For most urbanites, food must remain affordable, hygienic, and geographically accessible. Secondly, a widely used cooked-food retailing structure provides a source of employment for micro-entrepreneurs and their assistants. In Bangkok and other Thai cities, this represents a significant share of overall employment opportunities for women. An interrelated and more important result of convenient prepared food is that its spatial and economic accessibility lessens the burdens of domestic work related to shopping, cooking, and cleaning up. Although Thai men are known to participate in household duties, women tend ultimately to be responsible for food-related work in the home.[6] Public eating is hence a convenience for the female consumer employed outside the home. Single men also benefit. Thirdly, there are a host of externalities to the consumption of food in public spaces. An active street life creates a vibrant city (although civic authorities seldom share this view). A significant part of Bangkok's lively street scene is associated with its foodscape. People are found in public places cooking and purchasing prepared food for on-site consumption or "take-out" twenty-four hours a day. Related to this is safety associated with having "eyes on the street" that provide an informal civic patrol (Jacobs 1961). When streets are populated both by women and men, benefits include the actual and perceived security of women and children in public. Finally, the spaces of food consumption can also serve as informal community venues where information is exchanged and children cared for.

The Culture of Public Eating in Thai Society

> Most middlemen who control traffic in large expensive goods are male, while those who deal in local produce in daily markets are usually women, who are referred to as *maeliang* (mother-nurturer).

> C. F. Keyes, *Thailand: Buddhist Kingdom as Modern Nation-State* (1987)

The origins of Thai public eating are evidently complex and will be unpacked in this study as an economically, culturally, and socially crucial aspect of the Thai urban

6

lifestyle: "It was reported that in Bangkok, 90% of the population goes out a *majority of the time for meals outside the home*" (FAO 1989: 8; emphasis added). Household budget data from the mid-1990s indicated that 50.4% of monthly food expenditures were spent on prepared meals in the Greater Bangkok Metropolitan Area (National Statistical Office 1994: 43).[7] This represented a 5% increase over 1988 data (NSO 1994: 43–44). In 1962, only 30% of the food budget was spent on prepared food in Greater Bangkok (NSO 1963). Given that the extended metropolitan region had a population of nearly nine million in the mid-1990s, the prepared-food industry is clearly an important part of the local and regional economy.

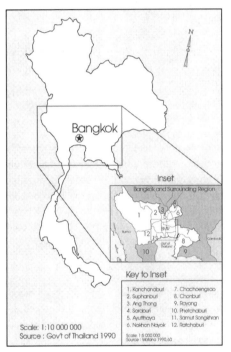

Figure 1.2 Locating Bangkok in Thailand

I begin by defining and describing the "culture of public eating" in Bangkok. The peculiarities of the Thai situation are compared to the literature on other Southeast Asian cities, especially Singapore, where public eating has shifted to government and private "hawker centers," "eating houses," and other types of food centers. The

7

"pure competition" associated with the less regulated environment of Bangkok is fruitfully contrasted with the formalized and hyper-regulated prepared food sector of the island state. The cleavage between the two, as well as the convergence, facilitates the discussion of key concepts of "formal and informal" or "traditional and modern" sectors in the food-system. These comparisons appear toward the end of the book.

The majority of cooked-food producers are women, forming 82% of small-scale vendors (Amin 1991). Unlike the situation found in much of Indonesia, a balance of male and female customers for both eat-in and take-out food is evident.[8] Women and men roam much of Bangkok with relatively equal ease. This gendered access to urban space is a stark contrast to the traditional "place" of women and men in other societies where it is or was common for women to be secluded in the home while men dominate(d) the "public" sphere. Engaging public/private sphere models and critiquing their relevance to Thai and Southeast Asian urban society is one of the theoretical objectives here.

Stalls, Restaurants, and Food Centers

Small restaurants, food centers, and larger more expensive establishments play a crucial role in Thai urban eating habits. Over the past twenty years, the typical "market stall" and floating market restaurant have been replaced by the curry and noodle shop. One can still buy *kwayteow reua* or "boat noodles" in the city where customers typically buy beef noodle soup from a shop in a boat on dry land (Pranom 1993: 37). This is a nostalgic reminder of a bygone era in Central Thailand where "canal culture" once prevailed (see Fig. 1.3). Van Esterik explains the historical importance of market food in Thai cuisine:[9]

> Noodle dishes, snacks, and other market foods were very mobile in Bangkok. Market foods were brought directly to the homes of the wealthy as well as of the middle-class and poor, by peddlers who sold their dishes up and down the lanes and canals of Bangkok. Pushcart vendors gathered near schools to sell meals and snacks to children. In the sixties, Thai department stores featured food pavilions where Thai and foreign foods could be purchased to take home or consume on the spot. (1992: 181)

Today, the canals have for the most part been paved, but the selling and eating of prepared food continues to take place on streets, lanes (or *sois*) twenty-four hours a day and includes both mobile and stationary vendors. Increasingly, public eating

Figure 1.3 Photograph of a Typical Market Stall and Floating Restaurant selling Noodles in Damnoen Saduak

occurs in indoor or semi-indoor (covered) places such as office buildings, university cafeterias, vaguely Singaporean food centers, and shopping plazas.[10]

Some "traditional" eating-establishments are in decline whereas others continue to attract business. The juxtaposition of "tradition" and "modernity" in the foodscape is illustrated by Figure 1.4. In this Hong Kong Bank advertisement, two wealthy Chinese men are seen sitting in a simple traditional food shop. They are wealthy as evidenced by the Mercedes Benz parked in front of the restaurant and the way they are dressed. "Everything has changed except the relationship and the barbecued duck," says the ad. The photograph and message could be applied to many parts of urban Southeast Asia where the middle-classes are asserting their cultural origins and traditions often through food habits. This is a direct *remise en question* of Westernization.

Defining "cooked-food shops" (or simply "food shops") versus restaurants is not a simple affair. The term "food shop" is a direct translation of the Thai *raan ahaan*, which refers to any stall or restaurant where prepared food can be obtained. The word is informal and used in everyday speech. Expensive eating establishments are often referred to as *pattakarn*, a more elegant expression that has a more literary use and is invoked to attract customers. There is a whole spectrum of eating establishments in Bangkok ranging from street-stalls to the largest restaurant in the world. Both ends of the continuum can be conveniently referred to by the term "food shop" in Thai. The only fixed criterion seems to be that the establishment should provide seating to qualify as a *raan ahaan*, whether these are small stools or lavish and expensive furnishings is immaterial though an expensive up-scale establishment can also safely be referred to as a *pattakarn*.

Historically, the only grand eating establishments in Bangkok were Chinese, hence for some the term *pattakarn* implies a Chinese restaurant even today. The boundaries become even more blurred with food centers and other hybrid establishments. One of the objectives of this research is to negotiate through the fuzzy terrain associated with public eating. In exploring these positions and spaces insights into the workings of the food-system can be gained.

There is a great deal of *convenience* for the consumer in this food-system. In Bangkok, prepared food is generally available at all times—particularly in areas where young single people live—resulting in a more active nightlife. Working women stop at roadside and shopping-center food shops on their way home to purchase food for the family. Curries and side dishes are typically placed in plastic bags. The proverbial "plastic bag housewife" (see Van Esterik 1992) who has made her appearance on the Thai urban stage in the past twenty years is a testimony to the

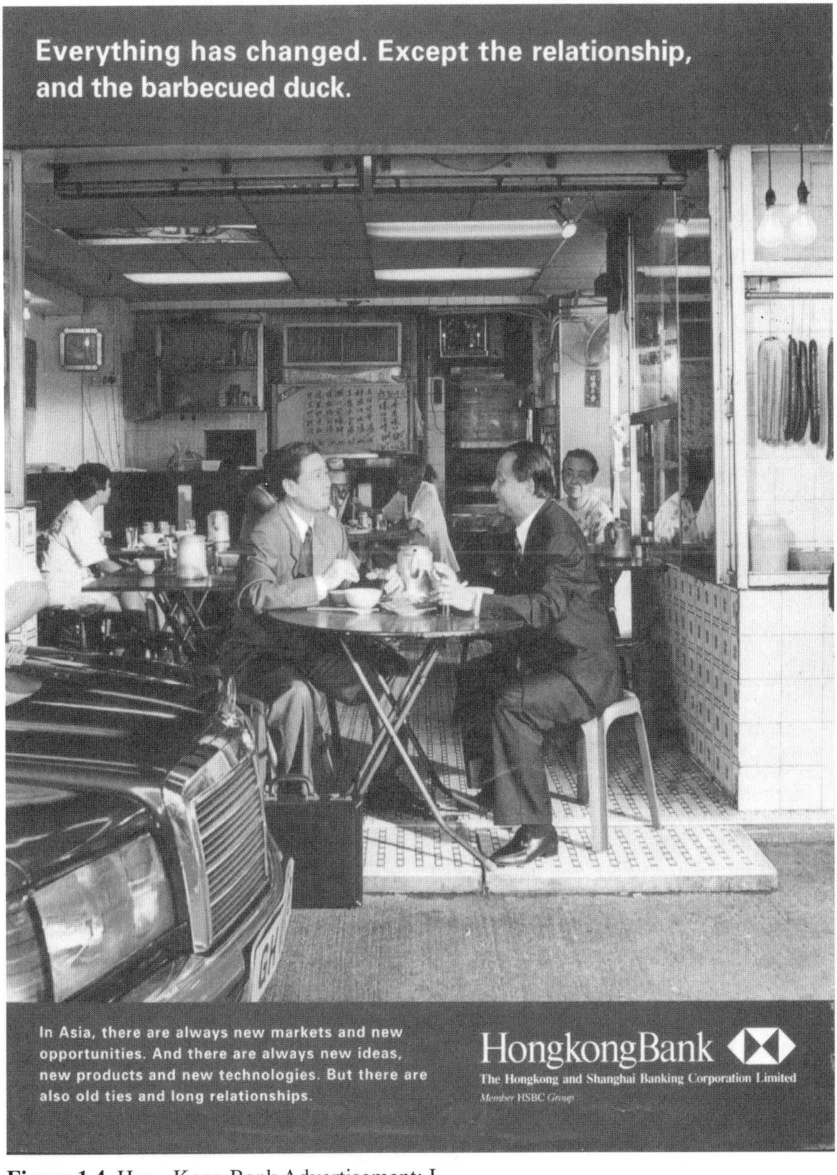

Figure 1.4 Hong Kong Bank Advertisement: I

contracting-out of domestic work to micro-entrepreneurs. Nurturing behavior (Thai = *liang*) is commodified and displaced from the household to the public sphere but remains mostly a woman's domain.

Thai urbanites "contract-out" of food preparation. This initially attracted my attention to the Bangkok food-system as a potentially liberating strategy in the sense described by Dolores Hayden (1981) with respect to community cooking and dining. It is now clear to me, however, that this system is possible due to the great divide between rich and poor in Thailand. Thai society is a highly hierarchical system; small-scale cooked-food sellers tend to be carefully circumscribed within the food-system as subordinates. There are social, health, and environmental costs associated with this inexpensive and convenient system, notably for the producers of prepared food. This book goes into detail about patterns of (self-)exploitation in the prepared-food distribution system. Nevertheless, neighboring countries and regions with a similar level of poverty do not exhibit the same degree of public eating or, more specifically, their women do not participate in public eating to the same extent or in the same, visible ways.[11]

Food Habits and Urbanization

> In Dublin's fair city
> Where the girls are so pretty
> It was there that I met my sweet Molly Malone
> She wheeled her wheelbarrow
> Through streets long and narrow
> Singing "Cockles and Mussels Alive, Alive O"

Traditional Irish folk song

Not long ago, women "micro-entrepreneurs" could be found selling food in many cities of Europe and North America as the above folk song suggests (Bowlby 1988). Women clearly had a place on the streets as micro-entrepreneurs as well as consumers. It was at this time in North American history—the late nineteenth and early twentieth centuries—that women in cities began formally to defend and demand their access to the public sphere and ask for this access to extend to the formal political sphere (Ryan 1990). The turn of the twentieth century also witnessed the birth of the planning profession, which significantly altered the previous use and design of public space. The concomitant and later activities of developers led to the massive construction of suburbs, the ultimate privatization of space and women (Mumford 1961; Hayden 1981, 1984).

A number of studies have touched upon some aspect of food habits in relation to economic and spatial transformation (Drakakis-Smith 1990; Konvitz 1987; Lam 1982; McGee and Yeung 1977). More generally, Engels observed in the nineteenth century that home-based production was gradually edged out of the market with the development of industrial capitalism and that this, along with the rise of private property, resulted in the economic and social marginalization of women (Engels 1972). Engels and his school have not been without their critics (see Bryson 1992). Mies (1986) in her discussion of "housewifization" challenges Engels by arguing that the nuclear family itself was a product of capitalist accumulation. The housewife and the related creation of the private sphere were outcomes of this development. Certainly this was the case in North America and Europe until economic restructuring in the past twenty years resulted in the emergence of new home-based businesses (many owned by women) and industrial home-working (MacKenzie 1987; MacLeod 1986).

Southeast Asia's rapid industrialization and urbanization have resulted in an explosion of small home-based enterprises selling prepared food. These businesses reduce the costs of reproducing labor, and serve the interests of large-scale industry by freeing up labor, especially that of women. The widespread availability of cheap food both facilitates and is an outcome of this labor force participation and "subsidizes capital" by making low wages economically possible (Chua 1994). Combined with local cultural practices, this is a partial explanation of the preponderance of buying prepared food in Bangkok. Since the Southeast Asian industrial strategy is based on high rates of female labor force participation, it seems unlikely that Mies' housewifization is an inevitable outcome of economic change there (see Bell 1992). This may be one step toward explaining the resilience of the Thai "public" sphere evidenced in the foodscape.

Thai and Southeast Asian Urbanization

Night stalls and eating outside the home are traditional aspects of Southeast Asian society. The growth of urbanization and industrialization has contributed to the rapid development of the prepared food sector (Drakakis-Smith 1990; Lam 1982; McGee 1967; McGee and Yeung 1977). As Van Esterik (1992) and the references of early travelers to the kingdom explains, the "market tradition" included many stalls selling prepared food and snacks for sale or barter.

In the case of cities like Singapore and other colonial agglomerations, the importation of laborers from China and India fuelled the demand for prepared food sold by street hawkers. The workers who migrated to these entrepôt cities were mostly men who could not cook for themselves due to lack of knowledge and facilities. Male hawkers ended up responding to this need and women sometimes acted as business partners in family enterprises (Lim 1982). Bangkok, too, was the destination of many migrants, especially from China. This resulted in the institution of a similar food-system albeit one that evolved differently (see Fig. 1.5). In Thailand, the hybridization of Thai and Chinese ways fused to the point that the eating habits and cuisines transplanted by Chinese immigrants were assimilated into Thai urban culture along with the creation of a hybridized Sino-Thai identity and behavior patterns (Skinner 1958, Keyes 1987).

Figure 1.5 A Chinese Hawker in Bangkok, Late 19th or Early 20th Century

As early as the 1940s, when Singapore was still a British colony, efforts began to eradicate the "scourge" of street food vendors, which was quite a typical municipal response at the time (McGee 1971). The island began to transform the spatial economy of food hawking by proposing to relocate mobile and stationary vendors in government operated hawker centers. By the 1980s, the process was complete and the last "real" street vendor was relocated. As Chapter 7 explains, the only street restaurants that exist today in the city are in gentrified areas that attempt to recreate the ambience of "Old Singapore." They are expensive and poor imitations of the coolie stalls of the past and mostly serve middle-class consumers and tourists. These public-eating institutions can be compared to restaurants in Vancouver's Gastown or in Old Montreal. The Singapore case provides a fascinating contrast to Bangkok.

Studies of Eating Habits and Street Foods

In addition to the IDRC street vending studies from the 1970s and EPOC's street foods project from the 1980s, there are interpretive studies of urban eating habits that touch on the issues addressed here. Prominent work has been conducted by anthropologists who have compared and contrasted society's engagement with food in "traditional" versus "modern" situations (Douglas 1984; Goody 1982; Mead 1964).

The anthropological study of food in Thai society has resulted in fascinating theses (see Bhavivarn 1993; Formoso 1989; Walker 1991), books (Krowolski and Simon-Barouh 1993) as well as scholarly articles (Muecke 1992; Van Esterik 1986, 1992). Those in the field of public health as well as the more traditionally situated "informal sector" studies have also begun to pay attention to the importance of public food distribution systems and the practices associated with the sale of prepared food (Naruemol and Oudin 1992; Napat and Szanton 1986; Sunanthana and Sriprat 1993). This book complements what is a growing literature on similar themes in the rest of Southeast Asia (Guerrero 1975; Jellinek 1977 and 1991; Klopfer 1993; McGee and Yeung 1977; Murray 1991; Turner 2002; Yasmeen 2001b).

With a wider historical and geographical sweep, the *Annales* School has studied the breadth and depth of food habits (Forster and Ranum 1979), much of it with reference to the city and its spaces of consumption (Aron 1989; Leclant 1979). This work has usually been based on archival and/or ethnographic methods that interrogate the meanings and practices associated with food and foodways.

Methodologically, the approach of these aforementioned authors is more closely related to the one here. There is, however, a quantitative side to this approach, which complements the qualitative data gathered through in-depth interviews and participant-observation.

Other work relevant for this study treats the emergence of working-class eating establishments as well as those of urban elites (Amdur et al. 1992; Klopfer 1993; Rouffignat 1989; Shelton 1990; Valée 1989; Walker 1991; Walton 1989; Zukin 1991.)[12] This appears to be a novel development that focuses attention on the recursive relationship between foodways and place. Many studies are framed within a discussion of social hierarchies or economic restructuring. On a larger scale, the impact of industrialization and urbanization on the British food-system and associated gender roles is examined by Goodman and Redclift (1991). They examine the relationship between the changing roles of women, particularly increased labor force participation rates, and the ways and places in which food is prepared, distributed, and consumed. Similar work has been conducted on the role of fast food and the effects of "McDonaldization" on the family (Schlosser 2001; Reiter 1991).

> The food consumed by the household has increasingly, in the past half-century, become processed and prepared outside the home, in the food manufacturing sector, service industries and, through a growing sophistication in household food preparation using new domestic technologies (Goodman and Redclift 1991: 7).

Women form the majority of employees in food processing and food services both in "post-industrial" and industrializing economies (Employment and Immigration Canada 1990). This is partly due to the gendering of certain skills and the stereotyping of women as "nurturers" as well as the flexibility, ease of entry, and low pay associated with the industry. Similar reflections were made by Hartmann, who critically examined the impact of industrialization on women's lives in the United States:

> The sexual division of labor reappears in the labor market, where women work at women's jobs, often the very jobs they used to do only at home—food preparation and service, cleaning of all kinds, caring for people, and so on. As these jobs are low-status and low-paying, patriarchal relations remain intact, though their material base shifts somewhat from the family to the wage differential, from *family-based to industrially based patriarchy*. (1986: 25; emphasis added)

Another factor that explains this division of labor is that women are considered to be a disciplined, malleable, and docile labor force. These are the same "qualities" that are associated with women workers in export-processing zones (Enloe 1989; Ong 1987; Wolf 1992). Although not "innate" feminine characteristics, employers believe these stereotypes and the success of their enterprises depends on the exploitation, consent, and vulnerability of their employees. Another interpretation would be that women's traditional abilities, learned through gendered socialization, are marketable, money-earning skills.

There are parallels as well as differences between the food-system in Europe and North America and the situation found in Bangkok. "Western"[13] food-systems have, *grosso modo*, undergone transformations that involve the capital intensification of food-processing and displacing formerly home-based activities into factories (staffed by women).[14] Economic restructuring over the past 15 to 20 years, however, includes the return of small-scale entrepreneurialism, much of it home-based and performed by women entrepreneurs (*Better Meals* 1995; *Simple Salmon* 1995). Examples include the rise of the "pizza by the slice" eatery. Alternative food preferences and critiques of the "industrial palate" have materialized in Western cities in the form of co-ops, natural food shops, and restaurants, and the resurrection of farmers markets (Belasco 1989; Farm Folk/City Folk 1995).

In contrast, the Thai system has been characterized by increased micro-entrepreneurship and the maintenance of a labor-intensive system although domestic and foreign capital already plays an important role in the food processing industry, largely for canned fruit and seafood, packaged noodles, snack foods, drinks, and some Thai foodstuffs for domestic consumption (curry pastes, sausages, and poultry). There is also, similar to recent Western developments, a growing interest in pesticide-free organic foods and a return to lost Thai culinary traditions (see Chapter 4). This activity is largely fuelled by the educated Thai "new" middle-classes.

Like the Western situation, Thai domestic meal preparation is partly displaced and is performed by micro-entrepreneurs who locate in public space (streets, lanes) or in privately owned spaces with public access such as shopping centers, food centers, and office complexes. Could it be that the Thai cooked-food distribution system is a manifestation of service-based patriarchy in addition to one based on industrialization? Feminist authors have argued that women's integration into factory employment has, to a certain extent, marginalized them by subordinating female workers to paternalistic discipline (Ong 1989; Wolf 1992). The service sector, including the sale of prepared food, may appear to be liberating Thai women

Chapter 2

Public/Private Spheres and Thai Food-systems

This chapter begins by laying out the conceptual, historical, and most of all the geographical foundations of the inquiry into Bangkok's *foodscape*, an exploration framed in three themes: gendered access to space, women's work, and the impact of socio-economic transformation on eating habits. The research forms a building block in the exploration of the "politics of location," a deeply contested and complex cross-cultural terrain (Caplan 1994; Massey 1994). The sale and consumption of prepared food in the city's ubiquitous "food shops" (*raan ahaan*), or general restaurants, illustrates wider social processes.[1] I begin by discussing the cross-cultural differences in gendered use of public space and associated ideologies of femininity and masculinity. Following this a conceptual framework for the study of gender, food habits, and place is advanced by developing the foodscape concept. Finally, I outline the theoretical foundations of my research by advancing Michel de Certeau and Dorothy Smith's approach to social research and critically assessing the literature on private/public sphere models.

Gender and Public Space in Cross-cultural Comparison

The wives of the people managing all the trade do enjoy a perfect liberty. Those of the nobles are very reserved, and stir not abroad but seldom, either upon some family visit or to go to the pagodas. But when they go out, they go with their face uncovered, even when they go on foot; and sometimes it is hard to distinguish them from the women-slaves, which accompany them.

Simon de la Loubère, *The Kingdom of Siam* (1693)

It is often stated that Southeast Asia is a crossroads where South and East Asian influences mix with indigenous cultural traditions. In terms of gender ideologies and practices, a "bedrock" of typically Southeast Asian femininity persists in many rural areas today and is characterized for the most part by matrilineal descent systems, bilateral inheritance, and the importance of pre-Buddhist and pre-Islamic feminine deities/spirits (Tambiah 1970; Potter 1976; Reid 1988; Sharp and Hanks 1978). Women in this region traditionally have access to money and land and do not lose kinship ties after marriage. Whereas on a regional scale of comparison it is true that women in Southeast Asia tend to follow the patterns described above, it is important to note the high degree of intra-regional variation. For example, Vietnam continuously stands out due to its Chinese heritage whereby patrilineal descent and patrilocal residence after marriage are the norm. Yet women there continue to dominate as food vendors in public places and are often exclusive custodians of food knowledge (Drummond 1993; Nguyen 1993). Similarly, Islamized societies, such as Malaysia and Indonesia, have customarily placed greater restrictions on women.[2] An added complexity is Chinese influence in the region, pervasive and highly diverse as well as with upland/lowland distinctions (see McKay 1994 and 1995 for the upland Philippines).

Keyes (1996) argues that the roles of women in Theravada Buddhist societies has been much more varied historically than in areas influenced by Islam or China (such as Vietnam). Perhaps this is because lowland island Southeast Asia, except for parts of The Philippines, and was more thoroughly Hinduized prior to Islamicization. Within the geographical space today known as Thailand there is also considerable variation in gender ideology and practice according to region, class, urban/rural residence, and so on. Although the Tai (or T'ai)[3] peoples who share a common linguistic heritage are difficult to characterize given this high degree of regional and historical difference, Wyatt has attempted to do so showing the regional distinctiveness of traditional gender relations:

> They lived as nuclear families in small villages, among which there was regular communication and some trade in such items as metal tools, pottery and salt. Because the region was under populated, manpower was highly valued and women enjoyed a relatively high social status, certainly by contrast with the low social and economic status of Chinese and Indian women . . . Women frequently were believed to have a special power to mediate between mankind (sic) and the spirit world, and were called upon to heal the sick or change unfavourable weather . . . Young people customarily were allowed free choice of marriage partners and were given wide sexual license in an annual spring festival. (1984: 4–5)

This partly explains why women in the region have traditionally been active in the public sphere where they play key roles in local politics and commerce in addition to the household (Atkinson and Errington 1990; Manderson 1983; Potter 1977; Van Esterik 1982). An addition factor was the regular recruitment of men in *corvée* labor for various projects under royal patronage leaving women behind to "keep the home fires burning."

The contemporary cosmopolitan society of Bangkok exhibits a far more complex system of gender relations than those summarized for "traditional" Tai ethno-cultural groups. First, the nobility has adopted Brahminic traditions to a far greater extent than commoners in the provinces. Secondly, Chinese immigrants to the kingdom—themselves a mixed group—have mostly settled in Bangkok as well as other Thai cites and influenced the local culture. Both Brahminic and Chinese traditions, for the most part, are detrimental to women's equality. The Chinese generally practice patrilocal residence, passing on property to sons and restricting the movement of women and girls.[4] The same can be said for most of South Asia. Brahminic influences originating from India, like Theravada Buddhism, which made a circuitous route through Sri Lanka, have had profound influences on Thai society influencing rituals, mythology, and other aspects of life.

Patriarchal notions imported from India and China are partially responsible for the erosion, among some elites and members of the middle-classes, of relative gender symmetry in Southeast Asia in terms of granting women access to the public sphere (Bencha 1992). These traditions associate the proper conduct of women with being spatially bound to the home sphere. Aspects of these influences can be detected in contemporary Bangkok although one cannot identify a simple straightforward pattern. Migrant women from rural areas may be found boldly selling food on the streets but may be subordinated to their socio-economic superiors. Educated middle-class women might be homebound but more comfortable than vendors among government officials.

Gender in East and South Asia: Implications for Thailand

The gender ideologies borrowed from China and India resemble one another by striving to seclude women. The ideas behind seclusion pertain to the appropriateness of spatially secluding women to a greater extent than men to "protect" them and preserve family "honor." The core of these practices find their rationale in patrilineal descent and inheritance systems where the identity of the father is a crucial factor in order to pass property from father to son. Traditionally, female and male children both inherit property in most of Southeast Asia except among the unassimilated Chinese minorities and in Vietnam. The form that this inheritance takes, though, is varied. In Lao-speaking areas and in Northern Thailand, the youngest daughter usually inherits the family home and is expected to care for ageing parents in return (Keyes 1996; Potter 1977).

Confucian ideas of femininity, for example, revolve around the concept of the "three obediences" whereby a girl first obeys her father until marriage. After marriage, she must obey her husband and, in the case of widowhood, obeys her son (Salaff 1984; Wei 1989).[5] More specifically, in terms of access to the public sphere the idealized spatial segregation of women in old China is summarized by the proverb *pau to lo min*[6] — or "to uncover your head and show your face" in public –behavior considered shameful for a woman. To step outside the family compound and interact with strangers is considered an unrespectable and dangerous activity (Lin 1995; Smart 1989).

Similarly, *purdah*, a concept borrowed from Persia and prevalent in North India and Pakistan, comprises a whole set of activities that aim to segregate women from the public as well as within the domestic sphere (Papanek and Minault 1982; Ward 1963). The essence of *purdah* is to impede the social and spatial proximity of women to men who are not their fathers, husbands, brothers, or sons. Women are further segregated within the home from men when the "need" arises, for example, when male guests enter the home (Reddy 1994). Women and men consequently inhabit highly different social and spatial spheres. As Johanna Lessinger explained in great detail, these ideologies seriously hamper women's abilities to independently operate small enterprises in urban public space:[7] "This marginality of women vendors is particularly striking in comparison to Latin America, the Caribbean, West Africa and South-East Asia, where petty trading, and particularly the retailing of food, are viewed as an almost exclusively female preserve, as 'women's work'" (1989: 104).

The imported ideology of seclusion explains why Thai noblewomen, who as part of the elite were more highly affected by Brahminic ways, were usually confined to the palace and sheltered within a sedan with a retinue of handmaids and eunuchs when venturing into public (de la Loubère 1693; rpt. 1986).[8] This is echoed in the contemporary middle-class role of housewife in urban Thailand:

> Urban women who remain in domestic roles often find themselves more estranged from their husbands than do rural women. Not only is an urban housewife cut off from her husband's workplace, unlike in villages where men and women work in the fields together,

but she rarely sees her husband in the latter's *public roles*, again unlike in the villages where women witness much of what the men do in their meetings or ritual activities. (Keyes 1987: 124; emphasis added)

Exceptions can still be found in East and South Asian societies, which contradict the model sketched above. Keyes (1996) notes that Taiwanese women still play an important role as vendors in the informal sector. I was also surprised to see so many Korean women selling goods, including prepared food, in the markets of Seoul in 1993. Though not a Sinitic society, Koreans have certainly been highly influenced by Confucianism and other Chinese traditions. As Smart (1989) explains for Hong Kong, women vendors in Chinese societies are looked down upon because they are forced by economic circumstances to earn their living in public space, thereby transgressing gender ideology.

But perhaps it is important to resist essentializing cultural factors and turn toward a more materialist explanation of the spatial segregation of women. Creation of the "housewife" role is not solely an imposition from neighboring India and China, but, as in the West, a product of later industrial capitalism (Mies 1986). "Housewifization" nevertheless draws on antecedent gender ideologies. Traditional Chinese and Indian ideas and practices are similar to the "honor/shame" complexes in Mediterranean societies and in Victorian England that gave rise to the concept of feminine domesticity and the housewife role (Hayden 1984; Sennett 1974):

The limitation of women's mobility, in terms both of identity and space, has been in some cultural contexts a crucial means of subordination . . . spatial control, whether enforced through the power of convention or symbolism, or through the straight-forward threat of violence, can be a fundamental element in the constitution of gender in its (highly varied) forms. (Massey 1994: 180)

Although Thailand has been influenced by its neighbors, it has never adopted the idea(l) of spatial segregation of the sexes *in toto*. Even elite women were known to have more spatial freedom than their counterparts in neighboring regions and went about with their heads and faces uncovered. Foot-binding or complete seclusion were never adopted to hamper feminine mobility, except among ethnic minorities. This does not mean that Thai women are equal to men in theory or practice. Thai-style sexism and machismo are still present and part of women and men's lived realities. Spatial mobility and the visibility of women in public is no indication of equality or that women have roughly equal control of the "public sphere."

There are many debates in Thai studies about the status of women as either traditionally subordinated (Kirsch 1982; Khin 1980), or part of a complementary system (Atkinson and Errington 1990; Ong 1989). Despite generalized access to public space, women are presently excluded from the upper echelons of power and are involved in struggles to change their social, economic and legal positions (see Darunee and Pandey 1991; Decade 1992). These realms are also part of what is usually thought of as the "public sphere." Even in terms of spatial access, "good" women, do not frequent certain insalubrious institutions such as private member clubs, "cafés," and bars (Mills 1990). Women's spatial mobility is conditioned by class, age, ethnic, and educational factors.

Symbolically, many argue that Thai women and femininity are subordinated to men and masculinity within an ascetic Theravada Buddhist value system and its characteristic *contemptus mundi* (Khin 1980; Kirsch 1992). This point, however, is debated (Keyes 1984; Kirsch 1985). For example, Thai Muslim women, ethnically Malay for the most part, occupy similar positions in small business, notably as market women (Chavivun 1985). The same holds true for parts of Malaysia, Indonesia, and The Philippines, which do not profess Theravada Buddhism. The public presence of women, as suggested, is a wider Southeast-Asian cultural phenomenon although Thailand appears to present the observer with the starkest example.

Thai Femininity and the Image of Motherhood

Maternal images have an important place in Thai iconography and point to the strong symbolic association between femininity and the giving of life and sustenance. Some argue that this points to the strong position afforded to femininity in the pre-Buddhist heritage. Feminist explorations of the study of emotionally charged concepts of home and motherhood are of direct relevance here because of the relationship between the constructions of femininity that are "built-in" to wider social processes. Doreen Massey describes one regionalization of British femininity, circa 1950, and its ideological spatialization: "The occasional idealizations of home by the working-class lads . . . often constructed that view around "Mum," not as herself a living person engaged in the toils and troubles and pleasures of life, not actively engaged in her own and others' history, but *a stable symbolic centre*—functioning as an anchor for others" (1994: 180).

Thai society, too, has its idealizations of femininity that revolve around a central symbolic mother image (Keyes 1984). There is a sacred dimension to this association of all things nourishing and fertile, most notably food, with women. Linguistically, the mother prefix, or *mae* is used to refer to rivers (*mae nam* or "mother of waters") as well as women-dominated occupations, such as food vending (*mae kha*, literally, "mother vendor").[9] Femininity is symbolically and practically aligned with nurturing activities ranging from tending rice-fields to selling rice and curry in a food stall. This does not preclude men and boys from participating in similar activities. Chapter 4 explores the linkages between the ideology and practice of nurturing as it relates to the Thai food-system in general and urban public eating in particular.

Thai gender relations are complex, and one cannot argue firmly one way or another that women and men are considered "equal" or contrastingly, that femininity is subordinated outright to masculinity. Rather, women and men occupy contradictory positions depending on the circumstances. From this point of departure, one that views Thai gender relations as a paradox, I engage Bangkok's foodscape. What is unique about gender relations in Thailand compared to most other parts of the world is the relative spatial freedom women enjoy. Women and girls walk the streets unchaperoned by men, work in services as well as construction, and are involved in entrepreneurialism that takes them outside the home: for example, as restaurant and food-stall owners. There are, however, more spatial restrictions placed on women relative to men due to the Thai sexual double standard. "Virtuous" women do not consume alcohol nor frequent places where there might be prostitutes. The infamous commercial sex industry in Bangkok further complicates discussions of Thai women "in public."

Gender, Food, and Place: "You are *where* you eat"[10]

Although the literature contains disparate references to the interweaving of place and food (see Konvitz 1987; Zukin 1991) as well as gender and food (Bowlby 1988; Charles and Kerr 1988; Curtin and Heldke 1992; Goodman and Redclift 1991; Klopfer 1993), a concise articulation of the conceptual and theoretical relevance of studying gender, food, and place together has yet to be stated clearly. French-speaking geographers have addressed food issues but not specifically in relation to sex/gender systems (Peltre and Thouvenot 1989). Feminist geographers and others sensitive to these issues have only begun to formulate a discourse around the spatialization of foodways with respect to gender. Bowlby (1988) for instance, has discussed the importance of women in food retailing in Britain. Cook (1995) pays explicit attention to the entanglement of gender, class, and ethnicity in discussions of foodways and place. The lack of concise attention to food is astounding given the enthusiasm with which feminists in the environmental disciplines have studied gender issues surrounding housing and urban design (see Keller 1981; Klodawsky and Spector 1988; Peake and Moser 1987; Wekerle et al. 1980; Wekerle 1988).

We spend much of our lives growing food or "winning our bread" (or rice) through labor and subsequently spend large amounts of time and energy shopping for, storing, preparing, serving, and disposing of food. All these activities occur in space and recursively help constitute the places in which we live and work.

Eateries, Economics, Women and Men

In Switzerdeutsch and certain southern German dialects, the word *Wirtschaft* has two separate meanings. The more widely known and standard German definition is that of "economics." A second connotation limited to the aforementioned dialects is an archaic usage meaning a pub or small restaurant. This is certainly not a coincidence. Inns and small eating establishments have been primary economic institutions since ancient times. The local innkeeper often acted as community banker, employer, and local leader. The London Stock Exchange is said to have begun in a coffee-house (Kelly 1995).

Inns and taverns have historically been important commercial institutions throughout human history catering to the needs of merchants, travelers, and adventurers by providing a meal, drink, and a place to sleep. As places for social interaction, restaurants and other eating or drinking establishments contribute to the edification of certain types of human relations be they related to gender, ethnicity, or other aspects of group identity (Bell and Valentine 1997).

Important social and economic roles are played by cafés and bistros in Parisian society where drinks, light meals, and socializing can occur, the preferred haunt of the *flâneur* (Sennett 1974). Feminist critiques of the masculinist experience of the *flâneur*, especially as represented in literature, abound (Pollock 1988; Wolf 1990). Statistics point to a swift transition in the French food-place matrix: "Before the First World War, cafés numbered more than half a million. But by 1980, there were just 80,000; and today there are fewer than 50,000 left, including 10,000 in Paris. In 1994, more than 1,500 cafés closed in Paris alone" (*Weekend Sun* 1995).[11]

These neighborhood institutions, like the British pub, are in swift decline demographically as larger-scale international capital comes to dominate the food-system to the detriment of local entrepreneurs (*The Economist* 1994). Ironically, pubs, cafés, and diners are important social and economic institutions for the urban working-class in the early days of industrialization but lose their foothold with further economic "development" (Walton 1989).

Gendered identities are constructed and practised through and in specific places designed for the manifest purpose of consuming food and drink. Alcohol or other intoxicants seem to have a privileged cross-cultural relationship to institutions catering to men and include the business of prostitution. Urban Thai society houses plenty of such institutions—"cafés," hostess bars, and the newer "private member clubs"—where women employees are available for entertainment, conversation, and "extra services" to a predominantly male clientele. Even seemingly innocent food shops are sometimes fronts for brothels and "freelance" prostitution.[12] The Thai case provides further evidence of the long-standing relationship between food places, such as restaurants, and the evolution of culturally specific sex-gender systems and the power relations imbricated within such aspects of social organization.[13] (For detailed comment, see Chapter 4).

"Eating and working are questions of survival, not taste" wrote Ginny Berson in "Slumming it in the middle-class" (1974). For those with more disposable income, however, matters of taste, as the late Pierre Bourdieu well explained, are central (Walker 1991). Contracts worth millions are often negotiated around sharing a meal; the choice of the restaurant, food, and knowledge of table etiquette are all significant in the process (Visser 1991; Finkelstein 1989). Chinese business protocol requires one to partake in a meal with potential partners: "It is here business begins and business is done. It is here silent language is read and a code of conduct is followed" (Wong 1995). Economic survival, by contrast, is the primary concern for the poorest strata of the population in matters of food provisioning and employment. Food-gathering and preparation for household subsistence has almost universally been defined as "women's work," which points to the sexual division of labor, the gendering of knowledge, of spaces, and places. Foodways of all types are simultaneously "placed" and "gendered."

As we have seen, women dominate the retailing of foodstuffs in Southeast Asia as a whole. There are significant distinctions, however, between the patterns of gendered micro-entrepreneurialism in the food sector in different regions and societies. The operation of a *warung* or *warteg* in Jakarta sharply contrasts with managing a *paeng lo*y in Bangkok. Both are types of food stalls but encompass different spaces and gender relations. Men are involved in these businesses as owners/workers or customers and sometimes dominate certain types of enterprises, albeit in varying ways. This is an outcome of the ways in which femininity and masculinity are constructed in each local context.

Gisèle Yasmeen

Food-systems and Foodscapes

The concept of food-system is a well-established research tool. A food-system is a heuristic device used to grapple with the complex sets of activities interrelated in the human quest for nourishment: "A *food-system* is a dynamic and complex unity consisting of all the purposive, patterned (institutionalized), and interdependent symbolic and instrumental activities carried out by people in order to procure, process, distribute, store, prepare, consume, metabolize, and waste food" (La Bianca 1991: 222).[14] Like any "system" concept, a food-system is a type of representation that has definite cybernetic implications. By looking at inputs, agriculture produce, human labor, and capital, for example, one can better understand processes at work that conclude with outputs of the food-system: that is, prepared meals, disposed food matter, proper nutrition, and so on.

The traditional concept of "landscape" in geography has been questioned and reworked in light of theoretical developments in the social sciences (Duncan and Ley 1993). I propose the term "foodscape" to describe a complementary representation of foodways and place.[15] It is also intended to be used as a heuristic device, one that implies spectacle—a "show" and also an "aid to vision," like landscape (see Daniels and Cosgrove 1993). "Viewing" and visuality should be referred to with caution as they have played a key role in marginalizing women and persons subjected to colonial rule and thus at times acted as a rather violent "scopic regime" (Escobar 1995: 191). "Scopophilia" has been criticized by feminists and post-colonial think-ers (Haraway 1988; Jay 1992; Mohanty 1991; Trinh 1989). The attempt here to represent Bangkok's foodscape tries to remain aware of the non-visual, particularly by citing at length the informants interviewed and refusing to see them as victims without agency.

"Scape" words have become popular, no doubt because of the recognition of the cruciality of space and place in social theory and have an element of visual display, or way of seeing connoting a text to be read (Lyotard 1989; Porteous 1990).[16] Appadurai (1990), for example, proposes a framework of ethno-scapes, media-scapes, and other "scapes" to convey the disjunctures in the flows of people, objects, capital, and ideas in the contemporary global cultural economy:

> I use terms with the common suffix scape to indicate first of all that these are not objec-tively given relations which look the same from every angle of vision, but rather that they are deeply *perspectival* constructs, inflected very much by the historical, linguistic and political situatedness of different sorts of actors. (296; emphasis added)

28

To use "scape" is to imply that, like all abstraction, interpretation is a subjective process that necessarily comes from the viewer's or author's perspective.[17] The neologism "foodscape" is used to refer to a process of selective viewing of spatial and spatializing phenomena—a lens through which to view and understand place. Like landscape, a foodscape is a representation created by the viewer. Geographers have examined the creation of the landscape concept and its relation to the emergence of Archimedean perspective in the visual arts (Cosgrove 1986). Too often we tend to reify landscape without fully realizing that it is the product of a certain era of geographical thought. Unlike traditional views of landscape, however, the discussion here focuses specifically on the social relations contained within and helping to (re)create the built environment rather than present a dehumanized portrait of a place (Cosgrove 1986). The "social relations implicated in the creation of spatial forms have not been included in the research agenda" Ley explains in his discussion of the "moral landscape" of cooperative housing regarding mainstream studies of landscape (1993: 128–29). By appealing to the techniques built into complimentary food-systems and foodscape concepts, the reader should obtain a coherent description, analysis, and synthesis of public eating in Bangkok. This ties in with discussions of "public culture" by Breckenridge, Appadurai, and their colleagues.[18]

The representation constructed in this study borrows from other people's views and voices. Indeed, it is my position that all knowledge is necessarily representational and that recent work that criticizes the subject position and the ostensible death of "authority" should be taken as a cue to improve the ways in which we *choose* to represent other people, places, times and, of course, ourselves (see Spivak 1988). These critiques also pertain to the ways in which our academic canons are formed and refute the use of an "objective" authoritative voice by the researcher/writer. Non-representation is an ontological impossibility. This point, unfortunately, has been grossly misunderstood by those who, with the best intentions, wish to "let the subaltern speak for themselves."[19] The ways in which this book experiments with feminist/post-colonial ethnographic practices is outlined below. First, however, a brief overview is given of the concept of public and private spheres, a highly debated model within social theory.

Ways of Doing and the Public-Private Continuum

The theoretical orientation of this book draws from developments in cultural and social geography. Theory should not be divorced from practice and the dichotomy

Gisèle Yasmeen

between the conceptual and the empirical is a spurious one. It appears as though higher levels of abstraction are given precedence over what Geertz describes as "thick description" although even detailed description rooted in space and time is an abstraction. I want to move between ideas that are close to "the ground" and those that may shed light on larger scale processes.

I find Dorothy Smith and Michel de Certeau's approaches to be the most engaging positions encountered (de Certeau 1990; Smith 1987). Smith's feminist position is the more radical but resembles de Certeau's body and space-centered approach to social theory. In *L'Invention du quotidien: Tome 1: Arts de faire*,[20] de Certeau explains the point of departure of his research: "The research concerned itself primarily with spatial practices, the ways in which places are inhabited, on the complex process of the culinary arts" [translation mine].[21] De Certeau does not see human beings as "dupes" but as creative agents who make the best with what they have and employ various strategies, or ruses, to resist the forces of "the system." He deliberately rejects the "objective" stance of the Archimedean perspective, as do Smith and many feminist thinkers, preferring to stay close to the ground where the optical illusion of the panopticon is less evident and the deeper meanings of action can be excavated:

> If it is true that the grid of "surveillance" is spread and articulated everywhere, *it is even* more important to discern how an entire society does not submit to it. . . These "ways of doing" constitute the thousand practices whereby the agents re-appropriate the space organized by the techniques of socio-cultural production for themselves. . . These procedures and consumers' ruses create, in the end, a network of anti-discipline (de Certeau 1990, xxxix–xl; translation mine; emphasis added).[22]

Here, the author is clearly making reference to the work of Michel Foucault and intends to balance his contemporary's project by focussing on human resistance to social control. De Certeau and Foucault are often contrasted with one another offering complementary positions (Dubuis 1995). De Certeau, drawing from Lefebvre, employs a very geographical perspective by valorizing the small victories created by everyday activities and the diverse ways individuals appropriate space for their own ends (Lefebvre 1991).

Smith, from an explicitly feminist position, points to the importance of paying attention to the mundane exigencies of daily life: cooking, shopping, and cleaning, tasks often performed by women and taken for granted by traditional male scholars: "The everyday world is that world we experience directly. It is the world in which we

30

are located physically and socially" (1987: 89). Our lived realities are necessarily local and historical, argues Smith. By extension, our lives are geographical; however, "it is essential that the everyday world be seen as organized by social relations *not observable within it*" (Smith 1987: 89; emphasis added).[23] This is why a proper analysis of context and events not directly part of the research topic needs to be undertaken.

Smith's position challenges the oppressive nature of the "relations of ruling." These relations, in many societies, relegate women to the ranks of those who perform bodily maintenance and routine tasks such as cooking, childcare, and office tasks. Not only are these activities taken for granted, ill paid, and undervalorized, but their performance is necessary for those in ruling positions to maintain their discursive and material privilege (Smith 1987: 81–83). I identify a few of the ruling relations, some related to gender, that frame the daily lives of cooked-food sellers in Bangkok.

Through the use of "blurred genres" this study conveys the nature of my everyday interaction with various "informants" and pieces together a puzzle explaining one aspect of the Thai urban food-system. I refer to a vast array of source materials ranging from direct citations, paraphrasing, quotations from field notes, and references to other sources. The "ways of doing" employed by food shopowners and employees, their everyday activities, and uses/appropriations of space are summarized and interpreted in this portrait of Bangkok's foodscape.

Following Smith and de Certeau, the following pages are deliberately embodied, that is, firmly contextualized at the site of social interaction (or "data" collection). To stand "outside" the world of which I am writing risks the unwitting reproduction of oppressive representations (Smith 1987: 221). This study's conclusion identifies the ideological and practical relations of ruling inherent in the gendering of public eating in Bangkok.

Private/Public Sphere Models

> The often-discussed problem of "the invisibility of women" has to be viewed in conjunction with the kind of visibility that they have. Women are often literally invisible—absent or unseen—on certain occasions, or in particular places, in many societies. . . But elsewhere, and at special times, the visibility of women may be very marked.
>
> Shirley Ardener, "The Representation of Women in Academic Models" (1993)

The classification of urban space into the realms of "public" and "private" is by now a classic element of much social theory.[24] Constructs of private and public spheres that model the nature of social life are attributed to the work of a host of theorists (Elshtain 1981; Habermas 1989; Sennett 1974).[25] Feminist conceptualizations of public and private are often drawn from the more general social theorists who have dealt with the subject, particularly Habermas as advanced in *The Structural Transformation of the Public Sphere* (1989).[26] However, as critics have remarked, Habermas' mediatized view of public and private may not be as useful as Arendt's more geographical depiction of private and public spaces (Benhabib 1992; Howell 1993).

Arendt (1957; 1960) and others (Gregory 1994; Rose 1990) see the ideological construction of separate spheres as a longer standing phenomenon—one going back to the ancient Greeks and present in many non-European civilizations. Here the public is the province of the *polis* and the "private" represents the deprived and secluded realm of women and slaves. The meaning and specific formulations of public/private distinctions, however, is historically and geographically differentiated and it is with caution that I refer to its use in Western historical scholarship.

Only with the sustained feminist critique of this formulation does a more spatialized definition of public/private sphere models introduced, first by Michelle Rosaldo and Louise Lamphère in *Woman, Culture and Society* (1974) and expanded by others (Davidoff 1995; Elshtain 1981) including geographers (Rose 1993). "Rosaldo, a cultural anthropologist, argued that women's status is lowest where women are most separated from public life" (Hayden 1984: 50). These initial feminist formulations have been refined, and subsequent work discards a fixed, empirical, and dichotomous vision of private and public realms bearing in mind the culturally and class specific experience on which these models are based. Scholars also interrogate how we define and mark "status," highlighting the dangers of applying foreign criteria that may not be appropriate to other regions, such as Southeast Asia (Atkinson and Errington 1990).

The public sphere has habitually been used to refer to the world of paid employment in the city's factories, offices, and streets whereas the private realm was that of the home, family compound, or neighborhood. This model suggests that, traditionally but especially subsequent to industrialization, men were associated with and had greater access to the public sphere whereas women inhabited the private sphere, performing unpaid "reproductive" work in the confines of domesticity.

The public and private model of gendered urban space has been the subject of considerable debate with feminist revisionist historians offering plenty of examples of women's involvement in activities outside the home (Davidoff 1995; Hayden 1981; Ryan 1990). Other critiques emanating from a post-colonialist perspective assert that notions of public and private are based largely on the historical experiences of white, Western, middle-class society and the ideals that conditioned this experience (hooks 1984, 1990; Mohanty et al. 1991). We need to distinguish between activities classified as either "public" or "private" and the spaces uncritically associated with these activities. Political organizing, for example, has often taken place in "private" kitchens, and nurturing activities, such as child-rearing, are often conducted in what are thought of as very public places (Staeheli 1996).

Further weaknesses in this model have been identified because of the experiences of gentrification and economic restructuring whereby the resurgence of cottage industries, home-working, and sweatshops results in the blurring of putative "private" and "public" spaces (Mills 1989). Many authors have summarily dismissed the concept as a product of spurious dualistic thinking of little, if any, utility. "Post-modern" and "post-structuralist" positions question the validity of all binary models and suggest that we ought to find conceptual replacements for these and other enlightenment categorizations, a laudable and challenging goal (see Davidoff 1995; Nicholson 1990). Aspects of such binary models may, however, still be useful.

Public/private sphere models, as well as the productive/reproductive schisms need to be rejected *empirically* but not necessarily metaphorically (Moore-Milroy and Wismer 1994). In my opinion, as well as others, these dualisms need to be re-worked as ideological constructs of allegorical utility rather than categories of existence (Demerritt 1995). They are therefore, models literally-speaking. Public and private will be used in this sense to help categorize types of spaces encountered in Bangkok's foodscape: "Feminist geographers have long argued that associations between women/the home/consumption/the private sphere on the one hand, and between men/work/production/the public sphere on the other hand, are *ideological constructs rather than empirical descriptions*" (Bondi 1992: 99; emphasis added). Bondi describes how feminist geographers have sought to critique these stereotypes by describing the complexity of women and men's lives. She concludes by indicating that other positions have examined and challenged the usefulness of these dichotomies "thereby disclosing more fully how our material and intellectual environments are gendered" (1992: 99).

What is interesting about the case of Southeast Asia in general and Thailand in particular is the historical importance of women in what outsiders have defined as the public sphere. The stumbling block for foreigners has perhaps been the fact that gender markers and status indicators are ascribed differently in Southeast Asia than in most Indo-European and East Asian societies (Atkinson and Errington 1990).

Gisèle Yasmeen

Many have noticed the apparently more egalitarian relations between women and men in the putative "domestic" sphere. Certainly, it has been my experience that Thai men are very capable childrearers and sometimes play a househusband role while their wives mind a business such as a hairdressing salon or food shop.

It appears clear that Thai non-elite women occupy significant positions of power within their own socio-economic group (or class) due to their access to and use of material resources (i.e., money, land, labor). However, these same women are often subordinated in the symbolic realm of Thai Buddhism and avenues to upward mobility are blocked. Women, as previously explained, are excluded from certain important positions of power that are mostly occupied by men in the bureaucratic, military, and religious spheres.[27] These too are crucial aspects of the public sphere.

From the point of view of urban feminist geography, however, Thai men and women as producers and consumers of prepared food appear to have largely equal access to the streets and lanes of the city moderated somewhat, however, by neighborhood, time of day, and the socio-economic background of the person in question. Indeed, women dominate the retailing of all types of food, raw and cooked. Selling cooked food is a profitable occupation, but it is also a refuge for those lacking credentials to work in more formal employment. It is often an occupation used to supplement household income. These issues are addressed throughout this book while reference is made to the debates in Thai studies surrounding the question of nurturing (*liang*) as a gendered activity and larger questions of gender equality in the region.

What was considered innovative and liberatory feminist research in the 1970s and 1980s has been criticized as ethnocentric and suffering from middle-class bias. It is standard academic practice now to question the ontological and epistemological foundations of our endeavours as social scientists, and we are encouraged to experiment with new forms of representation that do more justice to the subjects/objects of our scrutiny and engage in a self-reflexive stance. These basic issues are not addressed here, having been more adequately discussed elsewhere (see Clifford 1988; Haraway 1991; Harding 1986). Instead, the specific conceptual bases of my enquiry are outlined. These revolve around the defined notion of foodscape and interrogate private and public-sphere models.

Chapter 3

Feminist Ethnography and Field Research

This chapter introduces the ethnographic approach that has been the object of considerable scrutiny (Appadurai 1991; Marcus and Clifford 1986; Visweswaran 1994). It begins by interrogating the nature of "feminist ethnography" and the ways in which operationalizing such a methodology have been attempted. The following section describes the ways in which the fieldwork was organized and information gathered. Specific attention is paid to my fieldwork diary, interviews, and transcripts, sketch maps and the quantitative survey. Finally, a justification of the case study site, the Victory Monument Area, forms the final part of this chapter.

It is difficult to ascertain exactly when research begins on a project such as this. Is travel to the place of interest the only valid way of gathering information? I became interested in this topic in 1990 when I initially proposed the research. My ideas at the time were based on experiences I had in Thailand while on a study tour in 1985. Through library research, coursework, and discussions with colleagues, some Thai, I slowly began to refine my crude perceptions of life in Bangkok. Further opportunity was presented in summer 1992 when I studied Thai as well as a course on Thai society at the Southeast Asian Studies Summer Institute at the University of Washington. This was a precursor to formal fieldwork but was part of the same process as it enabled me to strategize on how best to glean information once in Southeast Asia. The organizational techniques were developed through discussions with mentors and more experienced colleagues.

Methodology

A general ethnographic approach was deemed to be the most appropriate way to delve into the world of Thai urban "public" eating. During my two principal periods of fieldwork, I met and spoke with hundreds of people, some more or less formally than others.[1] Everyday life experiences formed the basis of the study and were recorded in detail in diaries. This, combined with library research, reading of local publications and collection of statistics, gave the needed background information to continue with phase two of the project.

In 1994, I returned to conduct tape-recorded in-depth interviews with cooked-food sellers and restaurant owners in the Victory Monument Area of Bangkok and supplemented this qualitative data with a quantitative survey of most cooked-food sellers in the district, mapping of eating establishments and interviews with government officials and consumers as well as general participant-observation. I also visited other Southeast Asian cities to compare foodscapes, particularly Singapore where I conducted interviews and examined theses/research reports on the emergence of the food centers that now dominate quotidian "public" eating. I also kept a detailed research diary of my observations and conversations with people during the second phase of fieldwork.

My role as a researcher principally revolved around the recording of details that others, including Thais, take for granted. Interpretations reflected in this study contribute to more abstract debates on urbanization, food-systems, and gender relations in Southeast Asia and other parts of the world. By extension, policy can perhaps be influenced in the long run.

Feminist Ethnography

Several authors have asked whether feminist ethnography is indeed possible (Visweswaran 1994). It appears that many of these queries and, by extension, critiques of "traditional" academic enquiry including ethnography echo earlier attempts by feminists and others to reformulate the social sciences (Haraway 1991; Harding 1986; hooks 1984, 1990; Smith 1987).

There are three main points to be made regarding the vast body of literature. First, impartiality is an ontological impossibility and we should therefore, as much as possible, put our own views forward while aiming to be fair in our portrayal of others. Secondly, we need to revise our understanding of experience and sub-categories such as work to include the types of activities performed by women. Much of the work historically performed by subordinated social groups has been either ignored or devalorized. This has distorted the ethnographic record. Many of these omissions concern the care of the body, including cooking, work that constitutes the everyday lives of many women (Smith 1987). The third, and perhaps most important, point relates to ways in which we perceive ourselves and our informants. Feminists have been guilty of making inappropriate generalizations about "sexist oppression" worldwide and have reified the category "woman" while leaving the important differences among women in the background. We need to situate ourselves better in the research context and more concisely articulate the variegated relations of power, with respect to gender, age, ethnicity, or "class" at play in any social setting. Escobar reminds us that "the concept of woman as the subject of liberal humanism may not be appropriate to many Third World contexts, and the refusal to separate women and men in some Third World feminisms needs to be entertained" (1995: 189).[2]

In the case of Thailand, many women appear to see themselves as nodes in a set of social relations rather than as "individuals" in the Western sense. This, however, has never been an obstacle for having discussions with Thais of various social "classes" about the "status of women." I spent many evenings in food shops discussing the cross-cultural gender relations with women from Isaan, Thailand's poorest region, who were from farming backgrounds and typically had no formal education past the age of twelve or thirteen. The ethnographic encounter, especially in an obviously cross-cultural setting, has more often than not been framed within a set of neo-colonial economic relationships and delicate sensitivities to issues of power. This requires the ethnographer to probe deeply personal motivations, ideologies, and perceptions.

My approach to feminist research combines a post-colonialist sensitivity to and critique of ethnocentrism and searches for empirical examples that challenge traditional Western conceptualization of foodways, gender, and urban life. Theoretically, the research has a heuristic purpose: to propose a new model for the study of urban social life and gender relations by looking at the "public culture" associated with cooked-food retailing. Though the approach is primarily materialist, I am aware of the post-structuralist[3] problematization of "experience" and sensitivity to questions of subjectivity, language, and power and try to incorporate some of these concerns into my work (Butler 1990; Weedon 1987). The writers I tend to look toward for inspiration, however, desire to communicate to an audience beyond the academy and therefore keep their texts focused on questions of survival as well as identity and discourse (see Afshar and Agarwal 1989; hooks 1984, 1990; Mohanty 1991; Trinh 1989). The newer approaches to social theory sometimes lose sight of this. As bell hooks summarizes on the "new" feminism and ethnography: "Words like other and difference are replacing less fashionable terms such as oppression, exploitation and domination" (1990: 51).

My feminist approach attempts to be "grounded" and stems from a desire to understand how everyday life is organized and experienced by individuals and groups of women and men. The feminist approach advocated in this study is one of understanding the foundations of everyday food habits in Bangkok including the subjectivities of those who play key roles in the system, that is, the cooked-food producers themselves.

Field Notes, Maps, and Transcipts

What is known as the ethnographic method is actually a diverse set of data-gathering techniques that pay attention to what is often taken for granted (Eyles 1988; Hammersley and Atkinson 1983; Smith 1988). There is debate, however, as to what aspect of and how everyday life should be paid attention to, recorded, and finally presented in finished form:

> There is disagreement as to whether ethnography's distinctive feature is the elicitation of cultural knowledge (Spradley 1980), the detailed investigation of patterns of social interaction (Gumperz 1981), or holistic analysis of societies. Sometimes ethnography is portrayed as essentially descriptive, or perhaps as a form of story-telling (Walker 1981); occasionally, by contrast, great emphasis is laid on the development and testing of theory. (Glaser and Strauss 1967; Denzin 1978) (Hammersly and Atkinson 1983: 1)

Critics of ethnographic methodology and other interpretative approaches in the social sciences dismiss qualitative and "soft" data-gathering techniques as unrepresentative of the population as a whole and, rather, idiosyncratic to the case under study. To this, advocates of interpretative paradigms critique positivist conception of knowledge and instead promote the development of grounded theory "generated by a grounding in the data collected instead of arising from *a priori* constructs, and refined in the ongoing interaction of data and theory" (Smith 1988, 264). Smith calls for theory-informed case studies. Smith's position resembles Haraway's now widely cited call for situated knowledge, previously articulated by other prominent scholars (Geertz 1983; Haraway 1991; Ley and Samuels 1978; Smith 1987).

Ethnography involves observing what is around us (participant-observation), talking with people, and asking them questions in formal or informal ways (interviewing) as well as more standard social science methods such as surveys and consulting secondary sources like reports, maps, and statistics. All these techniques were used in addition to drawing sketch maps of the study site.

While conducting my two principal field visits, I kept a research diary. This entailed detailing everyday experiences by listing the names and affiliations of the people met, summaries of our discussions and general observations made about the people, places, and things encountered. In the first few months, my life was completely research oriented, and the diary reflected this. Gradually, it became difficult to separate my research proper from general everyday life and entries began to cover a range of topics encompassing my forays and foibles into Thai society at large. This led me to revise my strategy for the second installment of fieldwork by including only reports on topics of direct relevance to the book or future work.

The Diary as Research Tool

The recording of my everyday life, impressions, and interpretations was a first and crucial step in the research. Particularly during the first phase of fieldwork, I was a neophyte and took very little for granted. I recorded the way the food-system appeared to work and, with time, was able to refine initial and crude observations. Often, however, my interpretations were completely inaccurate, only with later interviews could I sort out key issues. This is obviously related to the fact that I was an outsider in Bangkok, a foreigner gradually trying to work her way "in." As has been said: "The need to learn the culture of those we are studying is most obvious in the case of societies other than our own. Here, not only may we not know *why* people do what they do, often we do not even know *what* they are doing" (Hammersly and Atkinson 1983: 7).

My being foreign was not a complete impediment. In fact, when explaining to Thais my choice of research topic the most common response was "That's fascinating. I would have never thought of that!" As an outsider, I did not take certain things, like the food-system, for granted whereas many natives of Bangkok, particularly the younger generation, are completely accustomed to public eating and do not find it at all unusual. Nevertheless, it would take a lifetime to achieve the complete knowledge of Thai foodways of average Thai people. This is where reliance on Thai colleagues and long-time scholars became indispensable.

Since I did not appear as a typical *farang* or "Westerner" but rather a *khaek* (a person of Middle Eastern or South Asian descent), my experience as a Western researcher was somewhat different than many other researchers from North America.[4] First, nearly every day I was thought to be a native Bangkok resident. I was routinely addressed in Thai, and my foreign accent confused my interlocutors. Some thought I was *luuk kreung* or half-Thai and/or else one of the many Thai citizens who trace their origins from South Asia or Iran. This afforded me certain privileges as well as a number of disadvantages. When I dressed in a way typical of a Thai woman of my age, class, and educational level I was able to blend in like an "insider." This disguise was illusory because of my lack of knowledge and experience in Thai society, a discrepancy that sometimes caused me problems due to the expectations of Thais encountered.

I was also looked upon with a certain fascination by Thais who were very flattered and keen to participate in the study. Some people confided in me, knowing that I was not "really" a member of the neighborhood and therefore a safe confidante. I established friendships with some informants that lead to difficult situations such as jealousy when eating at another food shop or on the owner's insisting that I not pay for my meal. An informant to whom I had become quite close to after nearly two years,[5] Daeng, even accompanied me on a trip outside the city.

Field Notes 3.1: Out-of-town Trip with Daeng

Thursday, 22 September 1994: Went on trip with Daeng. Noticed that she is very timid and unused to dealing with making arrangements for transportation, etc. perhaps this is because she knew I was paying. It was awkward at times. She also was unable to put up with heat as much as me, which I found strange since I'm the one who lives in air-conditioning. I was described as *jai ron* at one point.[6] We went to the floating market in Damnoen Saduak first.[7] Daeng was quite talkative with the woman who rowed the boat. . . someone who makes less money than she and of lower status. . . I assume this is why she felt comfortable talking. It seems as though at other times she was feeling displaced. She doesn't get out much and is not used to acting as that "consumer-boss."

This was the only experience I had interacting with an informant while not on her "turf." It was only when Daeng was displaced from her usual context that I was able to observe certain elements of behavior not evident before. It made an immense difference to our interactions and what I observed between Daeng and others. I was required to re-evaluate my usual interpretation of Thai women as mobile, forthright, and confident, a trait I had perhaps wrongly associated with small food-shop owners who are most often at the bottom of the Thai social hierarchy.

My emotional responses to fieldwork have also helped me re-evaluate my own position on the Bangkok food-system. For example, my position was influenced by a certain romanticism that depicts the foodscape as convenient and inexpensive as well as a source of employment for women.

Field Notes 3.2: The Inconvenience of Public Eating

Saturday, 3 September 1994: Unless one has a rice-cooker in one's room so that noodles and simple cooking can be done, this Bangkok food-system is a bit of a pain I've decided. Most people have rice-cookers in their rooms and therefore have the option of staying home when it rains, for example. I don't, and it's getting on my nerves. Also, when I was at Tara Apartment there was a food shop as part of the complex and one could phone down and get food delivered. Much more practical a situation than what I have now. Perhaps I'll get a rice-cooker. The family said that I can use their "pantry"[8] If I want to cook so maybe I'll get some packaged instant noodles. I believe this is the practice in these types of places . . . or here.

Public eating has its disadvantages and inconveniences such as those described above. Kitchenless housing makes the occasional desire for simple home-cooked meals very difficult without at least a rice cooker. Eating on the street can also lead to serious cases of food poisoning. Studies have been devoted to the health risks associated with Thai street foods (Sunanthana and Sriparat 1993; Charinya 1994). I also had the habit of downplaying the extent to which cooking is still done at home in many suburban parts of the city; particularly where households are composed of extended families.

Field Notes 3.3: Dinner at Angkhana's House

Tuesday, 6 September 1994: Khun Angkhana, a research assistant in the office, invited me to her house in Ladprao. We took a special bus from Chula to get there. . . it wasn't air-conditioned and had a television. The trip took about an hour and a half and then we walked. She lives on Ladprao *soi* 56. . . you follow a very narrow pedestrian path and reach a residential neighborhood full of private, single-family houses with gates and broken glass on the tops of the surrounding walls. We had dinner there. Her sister had made it. Hard-boiled eggs in a sweet sauce, Angkana stir-fried some green veggies in oyster sauce and garlic. *Tom Yum Plaa* and rice. It was very good . . . very different than restaurant food.

Food shop fare can become tiresome in addition to the attendant health risks. Although some of the best quality food can be found in the humblest eating establishments in the city. As the *Shell Chuan Chim*[9] guide to eating out indicates, many people agree that home-cooking by a family member or a hired employee is considered by many to be the best quality.

Quotations from my research diary illustrate the concrete sites of knowledge acquisition and present my vision of events and contributions of others to my understanding of Thai society. It is impossible for me as a researcher to be invisible to the reader and to speak from a distanced, disembodied perspective. Field notes were sifted through, indexed, used as a basis for further work, and later re-evaluated in light of more formal research findings.

Maps and Sketch Maps

When I established a case study area, my first priority was to obtain existing maps to glean useful information. The most relevant were those produced by the Bangkok Metropolitan Administration at the scale of 1:1000. These were initially traced and then my personal blueprints were obtained in order to design a map of the neighborhood (Fig. 3.1). Despite being slightly outdated, since maps were

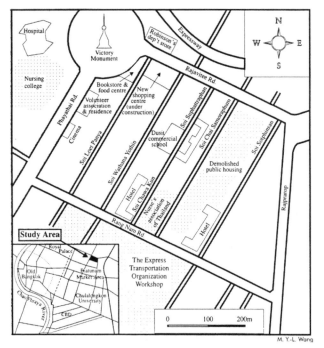

M. Y.-L. Wang

Figure 3.1 Victory Monument Area, Bangkok

based on site surveys in the mid-1980s, these provided a foundation for my own sketch-mapping of stalls and restaurant agglomerations (see Fig. 3.2).

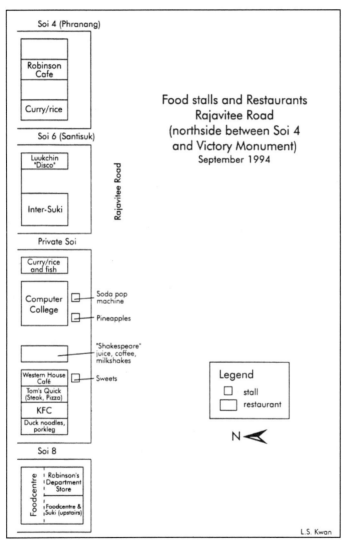

Figure 3.2 Food Stalls and Restaurants, Rajavitee Road

I ventured to the Victory Monument Area to map out the location of various types of food establishments, often with an assistant but sometimes solo.[10] This was done at different points of the morning and afternoon due to the fact that mobile vendors and those without a fixed-pitch often work different shifts. The "night time" foodscape was not systematically surveyed, principally because this would be a volume in itself because it includes many establishments connected to the sex industry. This reputation also made at least one of my potential assistants refuse to continue with employment. The data gathered are therefore relevant principally for daytime eating patterns.

Nevertheless, I was able to keep track of the different "nightscape" of the site through my own personal meandering, with the help of friends, colleagues, and research assistants, or as part of a group of acquaintances on an outing. A total of 71 food-establishment owners or employees were formally interviewed in 1994. These informants were divided into two groups: those questioned as part of a quantitative survey numbering 58 individuals, and thirteen interviewed in-depth. Members of the former group were generally unknown to me prior to the interview except occasionally through casual contact, whereas the latter group was established based on networks in the neighborhood and the building of trust.

The Quantitative Survey

Within the Victory Monument Area a set of qualitative semi-directed interviews were conducted with a sample of cooked-food vendors, restaurant owners, and food center operators. A quantitative survey was conducted during the day with all types of cooked-food vendors in the area with the help of five assistants. Given the fact that most small food-shop owners work by themselves and have very little time, the survey form was kept short and required ten or fifteen minutes. My role was that of supervisor, and I rotated between the assistants to be certain that sections were not being skipped. Indeed, quality control was a problem, and some assistants omitted important parts of the questionnaire when I was not present.

The 58 informants formally questioned as part of the quantitative survey provide basic socio-economic information related to age, place of birth, type of food sold, customer flows, and data on assistants/employees.[11] Twenty-three questions were asked on a variety of general subjects concerning the nature of activities in the shop (see Appendix 4).

Some potential informants, often the busiest "one-woman shops," refused to be questioned due to lack of time or suspicion, and others declined answering certain parts of the survey. The results are therefore skewed by excluding the smallest micro-enterprises. The qualitative interviews described below were designed to fill these gaps and provide detailed information on the day-to-day lives of a range of food-shop owners.

The results of the quantitative survey were coded and entered into a data base with the help of my assistant Kamolrat Sa-Ngeam. The data base was uploaded into SPSSx after returning to Canada, and I was able to perform calculations and generate statistical tables and diagrams. The original questionnaire forms sometimes had to be double checked to clarify answers. The results of the survey are presented and interpreted in Chapter 5.

Qualitative Interviews

In addition to the 58 informants formally interviewed as part of the quantitative survey, thirteen in-depth qualitative interviews were conducted with individuals from nine food shops.[12] The manager of a large food center was briefly interviewed but refused to let us question shopkeepers in the center. I have included some information on this food center. For the qualitative interviews, I chose to engage the help of an assistant to help clarify meaning, mine and that of the respondents. We spent at least an hour with each informant collecting life trajectories, documenting the history of the food shop, asking detailed questions about budgets (except for the larger businesses, which were reticent to share this information), and inquired about employees, customers, and relations with authorities. Particular attention was paid to how the selling space had been secured and what the future held for the area in terms of potential real estate development (and displacement) or changing state policies affecting the business.

The interview guide (Appendix 2) varied slightly from interview to interview. Responses ranged from simple "Yes," "No," or "I don't know" to long beautifully detailed treatises.

Field Notes 3.4: Luung's Interview

Tuesday, 4 October 1996: Went back to the *kwayteow phet* place and interviewed the owner who ended up interviewing us. He started making a speech about how lazy Thai people are before I could turn on the tape recorder. A customer was there the whole time at another table and put in his two cents' worth.

I decided to tape-record interview sessions, despite warnings by two anthropologists stating that "Thais don't like to be tape-recorded." I never had any problems and always explained that, as a foreigner who did not understand Thai like a native speaker, I needed to record the words of interviewees precisely. After each interview, my assistant and I would listen to the cassettes and simultaneously translate the responses of informants directly into either English or French. As much as possible, translation was word for word with Thai phrases sometimes transliterated into the text.[13] I chose to deal with transcription in this manner rather than hire a local secretary or assistant to transcribe the cassettes into English or French and then work from those documents. I did not trust another individual fully and accurately to transcribe the words of informants and since I read Thai very slowly and with some difficulty, I preferred to listen to the cassettes with an assistant. Through this process I was able to gain much supplementary information from my assistants about why an informant had chosen one mode of expression rather than another. Translation and transcription was an enriching socio-cultural learning process.

After returning to Canada, I formatted the interview transcripts to be used with a software program called "The Ethnograph," which allows the organization of qualitative textual information by way of assigning rubrics, or coding schemes, to the text. I found this immensely useful. This process forced me to pay close attention to each part of the 201 pages of text and decide what types of themes and sub-themes best fit the data rather than *vice versa*.

While interviewing and conducting the survey I was asked many questions in return and exchanged information with those informants who were interested in my research. All identifying characteristics of respondents were changed. Others did not appreciate me meddling into their affairs, or asked me very pertinent questions such as "How will this information help us in Thailand?" The answer to this query is more difficult and will be dealt with at the end of this book.

The Victory Monument Area

The Victory Monument Area (VMA) of Bangkok accentuates public eating and was selected for in-depth study using the above data-gathering techniques. Many other parts of the city were visited regularly, initially to decide which neighborhood to select and, later, to supplement information from the VMA. The site includes a range of eating establishments and is a mixed income area with a variety of land uses: commercial, residential, and institutional (schools, hospitals, government offices). The VMA is a microcosm of the city as it includes nearly every type of commercial environment found in Bangkok. It is known for its abundance of stalls, restaurants, and food centers due to a diversified population including many young people and migrant workers. The field site highlights many of the phenomena of interest.

I decided to live in the VMA to facilitate research as the location is very central and, in some ways, a microcosm of Bangkok. Living there enabled me to experience the VMA's day-to-day rhythms. My transportation requirements were minimized as a result, an absolute necessity in a traffic-jammed city (Robinson 1992). Having been a resident of the neighborhood for both periods of fieldwork, I know the site very well and have built trust with many food-shop owners. Building these relationships enhanced the quality of the interview results. I was able to trace developments in the neighborhood over a two-year period and capture the texture of some informants' lives.

Historical Geographical Description

Although the VMA is quite central in relation to the expanse of contemporary Bangkok, thirty years ago it was an undeveloped suburb. In the 1930s, the area was largely agricultural with rice paddies and guava orchards. The niece of the founders of one of the oldest Chinese restaurants in the city located in this area provides a description: "There were gardens . . . guava orchards . . . and rice paddies, small streets, only one main road, very small. Sometimes, a vehicle passed by. There were bicycles, and samlors. So, to go and buy food we had to go to *Sampeng* (Chinatown) by samlor."

Some families in the VMA have owned their parcels of land for a long time and have become quite wealthy as landlords of shophouses, and now apartment tenants. One informant, Wira, is a wealthy man, who with his wife, Goy, manages family property containing shophouses, an apartment, and a food center. The land is in fact owned by Wira's mother. "My mother is the proprietor. We're the landowners in this neighborhood. . . It's been our land for a long time," he explained. The family had purchased the land 34 years before.[14]

The Victory Monument Area in the mid-1990s

Today, the VMA is a hub of the city (Fig. 3.3). A mixed-income area, with mostly residential and commercial uses, it is an important transfer point for many bus routes. The district is busy both day and night, and there are several night markets in operation near the bus stops and along Rajavitee Road. These markets become quite crowded in the evening with people on the way home from work stopping to buy clothing, take-out food, or stop by with friends to eat in a street restaurant.

The new above-ground rapid-transit on the Phaholyothin-Phayathai Road axis cuts through the VMA. The area is simultaneously under massive real estate re-development as shophouses are razed to make way for higher density housing in the form of rental apartments and condominiums. As evident in Figure 3.4, which depicts two photographs of the same street corner taken at a year-and-a-half year interval, the VMA is in a rapid state of spatial flux.

A major part of the study site was under the process of re-development during the 1990s. The land, owned by the Bangkok Metropolitan Administration (BMA), contained demolished public row-housing where people continued to live and conduct business at the time this research was conducted. Three food stall owners who operated their businesses on nearby streets lived in the torn-down shophouses that included one food shop. The site was meant to be transformed into a public park ten years before it was finally opened in the late 1990s.

Figure 3.3 Bird's eye view of the Victory Monument Area, 1994

Figure 3.4 The Victory Monument Area's southeast corner, 1992 and 1994.

Gisèle Yasmeen

Omissions

The quantitative data omit the activities of many late night food-stalls and bars-cum-restaurants that are important food and drink establishments in the area and all over the city. The omission is justified for three reasons. First, night stalls play a primarily recreational function in Thai society rather than service the core dietary needs of urbanites. Night-time eating is a world of its own in Southeast Asia and would require separate study. Secondly, some night-time eating establishments are explicitly related to the commercial sex industry that is not the main focus of this study.[15] Thirdly, my mostly young women research assistants resisted the idea of conducting interviews at night in locations that sell alcohol and are associated with prostitution.

Field Notes 3.5: Prostitution on Rangnam Road

> When I mentioned to Gei that I wanted to research *soi* Rangnam, she immediately men-tioned that here are many prostitutes there and that it's a "dirty" street. . . Gei expressed concern about walking around Rangnam at night. . . she said it can be dangerous if we look like we're doing research. She said "dangerous for a woman like me." Rangnam is well known for its bars, cafés, and private members clubs. (Monday, 5 September 1994)

A study of the foodscape at night would require different research methods. An effort would have to be made to be less conspicuous. This methodological issue is an indication of spatial perceptions and gendered barriers surrounding urban space.

Chapter 4

Thai and Southeast Asian Food-systems

Villagers in Thailand, as well as parts of Burma, Malaysia, Bali, and Vietnam, see themselves as physically and psychically made up of rice. The Christian God made man and woman in His own image; Southeast Asians think in the same general way, but their self-image is one of rice. For them, rice is literally "the bones of the people."

Jeremy MacClancy, *Consuming Culture* (1992)

This chapter begins by explaining the historical foundations of Thai and Southeast Asian food-systems and ends with a prospectus on the future of public eating. First, the discussion focuses on the Thai diet and eating habits including the symbolic significance of food. Following this, how the food-system has been modified following the penetration of local and international capital into agricultural production and food-processing is outlined. Attention is paid to patterns of food retailing in Bangkok, including the system of public markets, and the changes that have taken place in food distribution over the past twenty years. I also discuss the health and environmental consequences of changes in the food-system. The various reasons for the emergence of public eating in Bangkok are identified. Subsequently, I look at household budget data, secondary sources, and informants' reports to build a compendium of "everyday" food strategies and contrast these patterns with a detailed description of the city's elite foodscape. The chapter concludes with thoughts on the future of street foods in urban Thailand and the recent trend to "museumify" public eating in larger-scale developments.

Rice, Fish, and the Foundations of Southeast Asian Eating

One of the defining characteristics of Southeast Asia as a region is the fact that its diverse societies share a few basic characteristics related to diet. The primary factor is dependence on rice as a staple. Most Southeast Asian languages equate the word for rice with food and or eating.[1] Indeed, the region is considered home to the domestication of rice, and its wet-rice agricultural system has been looked on with fascination because of its efficiency (Bray 1986), complex irrigation systems (Lansing 1991), and the ability to support high population densities (Geertz 1963). Historically, there were hundreds of varieties of rice in Southeast Asia but much of that diversity has been lost in the past hundred years, likely due to "modernization" and the standardization of production (McGee 1992). Several varieties of glutinous rice (white, red, and black) are still cultivated and used extensively in Northeastern food and in sweets. In general, upland rice tends to be more diverse both in variety and cultivation methods (McGee 1995).

The Thai Diet

Rice is so important to Southeast Asians that it is an almost sacred substance associated with life essence (Thai = *khwan*). As explained by Jane Hanks, femininity — specifically women's bodies — is associated with rice and with this essence (Hanks 1960: 299):

> Thus the *khwan* is sustained by, and its incarnation grows from, the physical nourishment of a woman's body. What is to sustain it after a woman's milk gives out? Rice, because rice, too, is nourishment from a maternal figure. "Every grain is part of the body of Mother Rice (*Mae Posop*) and contains a bit of her *khwan*." When weaning is to rice, there is no break in female nurture for body and *khwan*.

Indeed, residual pre-Buddhist fertility rituals persist in the Thai countryside and principally involve women during rice-planting. Based on research in Central Thailand in the 1950s, Sharp and Hanks write: "In November, as the padi kernels begin to form, a woman goes into the fields with offerings for the Rice Mother. This deity is so beautiful in her pregnancy that a man, carried away by her charm, would frighten her with his advances. Consequently it must be a woman who brings the sour-tasting fruits that pregnant women prefer and invokes her" (Sharp and Hanks 1978: 132). Aspects of these rituals are shared with neighboring societies. Keyes has thus characterized the Southeast Asian region as subscribing to the cult of "women, earth and rice" (Keyes 1977: 132).[2]

Fish is also a substantial element in the Southeast Asian diet and a distinguishing characteristic of the region is the preparation of spicy fermented fish paste, served as a condiment (Thai = *nam phrik*).[3] The Thai dependence on fish and rice is represented in the often quoted "In the fields there is rice; in the water, fish," a stone inscription in Sukhothai attributed to the fourteenth-century monarch, King Ramkamhaeng (Van Esterik 1992; Walker 1991). Keyes has also observed: "In addition to rice and fish in some form, the villagers of the region also eat a variety of vegetables, including cucumbers, squashes, certain types of aquatic plants, cabbages, cauliflower, beans, and some root vegetables such as yams (1977: 127).

Thai cuisine also includes a great variety of vegetables, a number introduced by the Chinese, and characteristic fragrant herbs and pungent spices. The familiar combination of fish sauce (a Chinese invention), garlic, lime juice, and chillies introduced by the Portuguese in the sixteenth century is considered the essence of Thai flavour although tamarind (sweet and sour varieties), palm sugar, lemongrass, and galangal also play a prominent role. Insects are not overlooked as sources of food, especially in the impoverished northeast (Isaan) but also in Central Thailand although this is in decline (Desai and Prapimporn 1995). Middle-class Thai find eating insects aesthetically repugnant and prefer to use the bottled essence of water-beetle (*maeng da*) to flavour some dishes. This replaces the necessity of pounding the large pregnant female bug in a mortar and pestle (Walker 1991). Fastidious Thai cooks prefer the authentic method of preparation.

Traditional Retailing

Prior to the introduction of the automobile and other forms of land-based transport in Central Thailand, food retailing most often took place on canals both for intra-urban distribution of food and to bring food from rural areas to the city (Chira 1986, 9; McGee 1995). Upcountry markets were usually conducted on land (Keyes 1996). Floating markets (*talad nam*) were the dominant type of food market in the central plain and continue to operate today in parts of Thonburi and the more well-known Damnoen Saduak in Ratchaburi Province, catering mostly to tourists. Land-based markets (*talad din*) selling fresh produce, meat, and fish have replaced the quintessential Central Thai form of retailing (Chira 1986: 9). Land-based markets are considered by many to be originally a Chinese commercial form; "in those days the Chinese were the pioneers of street-living hence the *talad* or food markets usually resembled the fresh food market pattern in China (Chira 1986: 9, citing Crawfurd). Skinner (1957), however, details the involvements of Chinese merchants from water-based living and selling places to the eventual preponderance of land-based shophouses.

Margaret Crawfurd identified and studied 203 fresh food (or "wet") markets in Bangkok-Thonburi in the period 1969–70 (Crawfurd 1977a and b).[4] At the time, 160 of these were registered with the municipal government while some of the remainder were pending registration. Most vendors sold fresh vegetables, groceries, fish, and meat (see Table 4.1). Crawfurd demonstrated that three-quarters of the markets were used directly by households to provide the family with daily food as opposed to restaurants and other food businesses. Two-thirds of the markets had fewer than a hundred sellers and served a local clientele. Her work criticized the envisioned planning at the time, which favoured developing automobile-oriented shopping centers as opposed to the existing efficient pedestrian neighborhood markets (1977a, 61). In the late 1950s, an American consulting firm designed the 1960 plan, which proposed US-style decentralized integrated shopping complexes. These recommendations were adopted by the Bangkok-Thonburi administration of the time.

Table 4.1 Distribution of Goods Sold in Food Markets

Type of food sold	Percentage
Fresh vegetables	39
Groceries (dry goods)	23
Fresh Fruit	13
Fish	11
Pork	8
Poultry	4
Beef	3

Source: Crawfurd 1977a: 25. These data only pertain to sellers on *paeng* (selling platforms) and do not include those selling unofficially adjacent to markets.[5]

Twenty years later, Chira (1986) counted 218 public retail markets in Bangkok but apparently did not consider unregistered markets. Of these registered markets, 204 were privately owned and managed while fifteen were run under the Bangkok Metropolitan Administration. As Chira and Crawfurd before him clearly explained, the local government is involved in the sanitary practices and design of privately-owned markets. Inspections are conducted regularly. Again, most of the markets were located at the neighborhood level, and the author stated that at the time of data collection in 1982, "new supermarkets in the new department stores were not yet established" (Chira 1986: 27). The number and diversity of food markets between 1969 and 1982 had proliferated due to Bangkok's rapidly growing population. Chira and his team identified the role of the private sector as crucial in providing Bangkok residents with locally produced, inexpensive food. They also provide detailed socio-economic characteristics of market-sellers.

Today, Bangkok continues to have the same basic system of public markets but elite shopping practices now include regular trips to North American-style supermarkets. Walker's Food Consumption Survey (FCS 1990) indicated that 88% of Bangkok residents had shopped at supermarkets, with 80% and 82% stating that they had frequented local markets and stores, respectively. The city has one large wholesale market (*pakklong talad*) that supplies many of the smaller neighborhood *talad* with fresh fruit, vegetables, and flowers (Warren and Lloyd 1989: 48–49). Fish and meat are obtained from government controlled marketing boards, whereas poultry is less regulated by the state, creating a window of opportunity for agri-business conglomerates to supply chickens and ducks.

The following vignette of one of my experiences in a neighborhood market describes the rhythm of transactions. I joined my informant, Daeng, who goes every morning to obtain supplies for the food shop she operates with her aunt and adopted mother, Ying.

Field Notes 4.1: Early Morning at Say Yut Market

Sunday, 11 September 1994: Woke up at 4 a.m. Everything was dark, and I was exhausted. The street-stall near my place still had customers at a few tables. Mostly men drinking whiskey with their food but also a few women. Made it to Daeng's shop at 5 a.m. sharp. Her mother was already up and had prepared a shopping list, which I obtained when we were through. There were a couple of men hanging around whom Daeng evidently knew. I asked about them and apparently they work as security guards in the apartment across the street. They help lift heavy loads and keep an eye on the shop at night.

The two of us walked with her blue shopping basket and when we arrived at the small market area many of the vendors had not come yet. We went to a vegetable stand Daeng usually shops at, and I took a picture. I asked the woman where she gets the veggies, and she answered "Rangsit." . . . she also lives there. I asked her what time she wakes up in the morning — 1 a.m. was the answer! She asked if I'd ever been to Rangsit and was very friendly. I bought some small bananas from her. We then went and left Daeng's basket behind another stall . . . she leaves it there even when it's full of purchases. . . she says nobody will take anything. Daeng knows most of the vendors since she's been going there every morning for five years. We went to all her regular shops. For example, a husband and wife chicken-vending team (man looks Chinese and woman looks like *Khon Isaan*), a curry paste and coconut milk stall in a covered part of the market (two men), various fish places, and another veggie stand. Also, a special stall that sells spices, etc. I took about four pictures and felt ridiculous but always asked people's permission, and they smiled and seemed amused. I promised to give them pictures. The monks started making their rounds around 6 am . . . usually interspersed, many with assistants who put the food in buckets. I wanted to take a picture but wasn't sure if it was proper. Daeng said "No problem" and offered to make an offering so I could take a picture more confidently. We both ended up making merit and a vendor took the picture. This specialized food vending woman sells "kits" that cost 15 Bt containing one lotus flower, one package of incense, a curry and a soup (in plastic bags), and a little cup of rice that one empties into the rice bowl . . . as well as a mini-bottle of drinking water. Quite an experience.

I was amazed at the number of men working in the market. I also noticed a lot of semi-prepared items such as curry pastes, which I figured people like Daeng make themselves. Daeng buys *khao tom* at the market every day for her niece's breakfast.

That morning, Ying had asked Daeng to purchase the following supplies:

Shopping List[6]

1 *maeng da* (giant water beetle)	Frying chicken
3 kgs of fish for frying	10 pomfret (a small round fish)
10 Bt worth of spices to make *gaeng som*	2 kgs ready-to-eat fish (*pla ré*)
10 Bt worth of small green eggplants	Vegetables to boil and make *nam phrik*
Pork for *nam tok*	Sliced pork
Pork ribs	1.5 kg lotus stems
1.5 kgs of coconut	plastic bags, 6 x 11cm and 6 x 14cm
small bags for sauce	1kg cauliflower
3 blocks of tofu	2 packages cinnamon
1 kg oil	

Daeng spent more than 1,000 Bt, not including the price of the hired tuk-tuk. Small food shops operate on a cost-recovery basis; most daily earnings go toward purchasing raw materials and supporting family members. Food and the education of younger siblings are expensive. Daily incomes are therefore quite high but do not necessarily result in the producers accumulating wealth. This corresponds to Tinker's findings (1987). Detailed monthly budgets for Daeng and other food sellers are included in Chapter 6 and Appendix 6.

The above vignette clearly illustrates that neighborhood markets involve both male and female entrepreneurs who work in the middle of the night to get food ready for dawn. Relations between market vendors and customers are based on regular purchases and trust. The markets sell semi-prepared items such as curry pastes and coconut milk, labor-saving devices for housewives and food-shop owners. As the reference to the monks indicates, even making religious offerings has been commodified so that local residents can easily purchase "kits" to give alms and make merit. The creativity of Thai food micro-entrepreneurs incorporates traditional beliefs and religious practices.

Supply Linkages: Where the Food Comes From

Crawfurd paid considerable attention to the ways in which Bangkok food markets obtained their supplies and the sources of this food. She remarked on the decline of water-based transport in favour of trucking (1977b: 108). There were great divergences in the patterns of supply depending on the commodity being studied. Fish, for example, must be delivered quickly from ports on the eastern seaboard in order to maintain its freshness. Fruit came from points all over the country and was highly dependent on seasonality. Market gardening of vegetables on the urban periphery was also supplemented by produce grown in more distant parts of the country. This has taken on even greater importance as agricultural land is rapidly swallowed up by land developers (Greenberg 1994).

In the 1980s, Korff described the supply linkages for Khlong Toey Market in the city's largest slum district near the port. The market is known for its cheap goods. Table 4.2 chronologically summarizes activities of this large market.

Many of the traders studied by Korff go to the central wholesale market (*pak-klong talad*) between 2–3 a.m. to get fresh fruit and vegetables. They then sell these goods in the types of neighborhood markets described in the previous section. Other suppliers make their deliveries by truck in the late evening after 9 p.m. The peak selling periods in this neighborhood market, like most others in the city, is between 4 and 7 am, and then late afternoon between 3 and 6pm. The city's poor tend to shop for their families in the afternoon because supplies are less expensive then.

Table 4.2 Twenty-Four Hours at Khlong Toey Market

Time	Activity
01:00	Transportation
02:00	Wholesale market
04:00	Retail market peak begins
07:00	Retail market peak ends
15:00	Retail market peak begins
18:00	Retail market peak ends
20:00	Night food stalls begin sales
21:00	Trucks arrive with food
22:00	Unloading of truck contents

Source: Korff (1989: 66–67)

This is a generalized pattern. Korff adds that many vendors from Khlong Toey also go directly to the provinces (such as Nakorn Pathom) in the middle of the night to obtain supplies (Korff 1989: 68). This is cheaper than going to the wholesale market because a system of intermediaries is bypassed.

The (Post-) Industrial Palate

The term "industrial palate" refers to the growing share of value-added (often mass-produced) food products in the diet of the average consumer (Salih et al. 1988: 4). Urbanites figure prominently in this shift from family-based food production to the commodification of "people's most basic requirement—food—from a part of their place to a placeless industrial commodity" (MacLeod 1989: 4).

Following Goody (1982), it is clear that as a society industrializes and urbanizes it becomes uprooted from its agricultural way of life, and food becomes a commodity purchased from the market. With the involvement of both women and men in the paid labor force, an opportunity for the sale of value-added (i.e., processed) food arises. This demand can be fulfilled in several ways—for example, through neighborhood catering networks or the hiring of a cook. However, it is in the interests of large-scale business to direct consumer spending to a standardized range of value-added goods, usually those manufactured and packaged in order to extend shelf life. The classic theatre for the sale of such goods is the supermarket where highly processed foods are the most vigorously promoted because of their profitability.

Social and Environmental Costs

The shift in the composition of the consumer's shopping basket is closely integrated with the emergence of capital-intensive agriculture, agri-business, and the edging out of the small farmer, which results in lower overall production costs. It is said this also results in a decline in the quality of agricultural output, loss of species diversity and severe environmental damage (see Sanitsuda 1990).

To increase yields, for example, farmers in the provinces have been using massive quantities of pesticides and herbicides on their horticultural produce, with detrimental consequences on human health and the environment (Sanitsuda 1990). Suntaree Komin explains: "Testing of pesticide residue in food has shown that in the vegetable samples tested, 40–90% of the sample contained detectable levels of pesticide" (1989: 113).

Vegetable farmers in the north have been experiencing severe health problems due to the excessive use of a plethora of chemical pesticides (Sanitsuda 1993). The insidious aspect of this is that most consumers of these vegetables and fruit are unaware of the health risks involved. Testing has revealed that a high percentage contain more than maximum recommended levels of chemicals (Shankar 1992). However, a small group of informed consumers have begun to protest by demanding organically grown produce. The *raison d'être* of *Tamada*, an organic food store in Chiang Mai is an example: "[M]ost customers are middle-class and well-educated people who are also concerned about the environment. They are willing to buy products that are a bit more expensive than those commonly sold in the market" (Chanyaporn 1992). The managers of the cooperatively owned *Tamada* predict that prices will drop below those of non-organic produce in the long run if the food is mass produced. This is due to the fact that pesticides are not used. Instead, nets are used to keep vermin at bay.

A more difficult problem to be dealt with concerns the issue of lead contamination of food due to exhaust fumes. Toxic emissions from vehicles in Bangkok make their way into the food chain. Babies in Bangkok are born with dangerously high levels of lead in their blood (Suntaree 1989: 108–09). This problem will not be resolved in the near future as Bangkok's development continues to be highly automobile-oriented. Local newspapers reported a few years ago that at least 900 new vehicles per day found their way onto Bangkok's roadways (Vespry 1993).

Profitable Palates: New Food Retailing

Due to its spectacular levels of economic and demographic growth, "the Asian food market could be worth over $450 billion a year by the end of the century" (*The*

Economist 1993: 15). "Asians" are also seen as a profitable target population by large food multi-nationals because of their brand consciousness: "At the luxury end of the market, especially, Asian consumers seem to be more conscious of the snob value of brands than their Western counterparts."(*The Economist* 1993: 16).

The appearance and diffusion of supermarkets, related retail outlets such as convenience stores and the newest addition, the mega-wholesale outlet (e.g., Costco, Makro, and/or Wal-Mart) is a burgeoning feature of the Asian urban landscape:

> In Taiwan the number of convenience stores, supermarkets and hypermarkets rose from 2,000 in 1986 to over 3,000 in 1991 as thousands of mom-and-pop noodle shops disappeared. Supermarkets are setting up in China too. Hong Kong's Dah Chong Hong has recently opened stores in southern China, as has Dairy Farm's Wellcome. As retailing is still in its infancy in much of Asia, space on many supermarket shelves is up for grabs. The food groups that capture it can flaunt their brands (*The Economist* 1993: 16).

The above remarks hold true for urban Thailand where convenience stores such as "7–11" have made impressive inroads in the past 14 years. It would be spurious, however, to associate these changes simply to the "convergence"[7] of consumption habits or the infiltration of "Third World" economies by foreign, especially Western and Japanese, capital. More precisely in the case of Thailand, locally owned conglomerates seem to control the largest share of the domestic industrial palate and have expanded their operations to China and other parts of Southeast Asia. The domination of local conglomerates is a general feature of the food industry in Asia (*Korea Newsreview* 1996; McGee 1995):

> Take Thailand's Charoen Pokphand, Asia's biggest animal-feed supplier and the country's largest conglomerate, with sales of about $5 billion. Boasting that "from the farmyard to the dinner table it's Charoen Pokphand all the way," the company, which was set up by Chinese emigrants, produces feed for and then raises and processes broiler chickens. It also handles prawns and pigs. One of its greatest assets is a network of feed mills and poultry-processing plants sprinkled across China. These and Charoen Pokphand's fast-food joint ventures with America's Kentucky Fried Chicken should allow it to cash in on the country's culinary revolution. (*The Economist* 1993: 17)

Charoen Pokphand not only owns the rights to most of the KFC's in Thailand, but it also controls the "7–11s," numerous motorcycle, and automobile manufacturing operations and is the major shareholder of Telecom Asia. CP is one of the biggest foreign investors in China, and is now apparently the biggest Asian multinational (Keyes 1996). Interestingly, however, it continues to supply small cooked-food vendors with ducks and chickens (see Chapter 6).

Convenience stores are new institutions that have multiplied rapidly in the last ten years. They are generally open round the clock and sell household products, Western and Thai fast-food, and fountain drinks. Customers include school children, the increasing number of people working late, and commuters (*The Nation* 1992: B1–3). The near grid-lock traffic situation in Bangkok has been identified as contributing to the success of convenience stores located on major routes. Managers of some of these stores (such as "7–11" and Central Mini-Mart) claim that their *clientele* includes lower income groups as well as wealthier urbanites.[8]

The expansion of the wealthier classes and accompanying automobile culture has resulted in the proliferation of scores of large shopping centers throughout the Bangkok Metropolitan Region:

> Last year, shopping centers posted Bt78 billion in revenue, representing about 30% of the entire Bt 264 billion retail industry. Of the Bt 78 billion, department stores and supermarkets dominated and accounted for Bt 50 million, while small retail stores took Bt 20 billion and fast-food outlets and restaurants about Bt 8 billion. (*The Nation* 1993: B16)

These new cathedrals of commerce are expected to erode traditional retailing businesses and ultimately carve out 50% of market share according to a Siam Retail Development executive quoted in the above article. Table 4.3 lists the principal shopping plazas of Bangkok in the 1980s. Since that time, many mega-malls have appeared, especially on the urban periphery (*Asia Magazine* 1992).

Field Notes 4.2 The Mall, Nonthaburi

Sunday, 18 October 1992: Went to "the mall" shopping center in Nonthaburi to see the FAO Expo, which was so thoroughly advertised on Radio Thailand. Got there after two buses and much walking and was quite disappointed. There were kiosk-type displays, all in Thai, but seemingly no representatives from FAO—pathetic.

I walked through this gigantic mall (six or seven stories). There is a huge amusement park for children on the very top floor. There is also a waterslide park and swimming pool on the top floor.

Table 4.3 Shopping Centers and Department Stores

Name of shopping centre/ department store	Founded (year)	Size (m²)	Department store / other main enterprise
Pathumwan			
Amarin Plaza	1984	14,300	Sogo
Big Bell	1984	8,540	Big Bell
Central Chidlom	1974	13,650	Central
Galeries Lafayette	1985		Peninsula Hotel
Mahboonkrong	1986	100,000	Tokyu
Peninsula Plaza	1986		Peninsula Hotel
Ploenchit Arcade	1970		Foodland
Robinson Radamri	1981	10,800	Robinson
Siam Center	1972	28,000	
The Mall Radamri	1981	18,888	The Mall
Radamri Arcade	1972	28,785	Thai Daimaru
Phranakorn			
Bangkok Co-op			
Banglamphu Center	1981	2,677	Central
Central Burapha			
Danh Hua Saeng			
Garufa Plaza	1979	4,876	Merry Kings
Merry Kings	1984	20,000	New World
Nightingale			
Ratprasong Center			
Phyathai	1984	16,372	World
City Plaza	1991		Pata
Hollywood Mall	1969	18,900	Indra Hotel
Indra	1980	8,000	Merry Kings
Merry Kings	1984	1,823	Excel
Panthip Plaza	1985		Robinson
Robinson	1981	22,100	Metro
Metro			

Name of shopping centre/ department store	Founded (year)	Size (m²)	Department store / other main enterprise
Phrakanong Asia Phrakanong Bangkok Co-op	1980 1984 1984	3,887	Landmark
City Landmark Robinson Thai Daimaru	1985	3,312	Robinson Thai Daimaru
Bang Rak Central Silom River City Robinson Charm Issara	1968 1984 1984 1985	11,311 20,804 14,000 14,000	Central Royal Orchid Robinson
Samphanthawong Cathy Yaowarat Daifha Macukham	1981	3,186	Cathay
Bang Kapi Central Ramkamhaeng Ramkamhaeng Center The Mall Ramkamhaeng	1985 1983	 14,000	Central The Mall
Bangkok Noi Bangkok Co-op Pata Pingklao	1980	16,000	Pata
Klong San Bangkok Co-op Central Ladja	1980	13,352	Central
Bang Khen	1982	106,000	Central/Hotel

Name of shopping centre/ department store	Founded (year)	Size (m²)	Department store / other main enterprise
Central Plaza			
Thonburi Cathay Wongwien The Mall Wongwien	1987		Cathay The Mall

Source: Korff (1990: 222–23)

Supaluck Umpujh, is Executive Vice-President of The Mall Group Co., Ltd. Her father began the company that is now the second largest department store operator in Thailand. There are eight locations in the city some spanning an area of 300,000m². The ninth is currently being designed. All "The Mall" complexes include amusement parks, water parks, and ice-skating rinks (Licuanan 1995: 47).

Some mega-malls, like those described above, resemble the "West Edmonton Mall," which focuses on leisure activities (see Hopkins 1991a, 1991b). Nearly all have extensive and elaborate food centers and food floors featuring a full range of Thai, Chinese, and Western foods. To some, this may appear like a straightforward process of "Westernization." On closer examination, however, it seems as though Thai cultural practices, including foodways, are being re-contextualized and are far from being "malled" out of existence. Rather, the context in which Thai and Sino-Thai foods have habitually been sold, such as small food shops, is facing intense competition from new institutions such as food centers.

Much of Bangkok's retailing activity in the food-sector is clearly expanding from public places such as streets and street fronts to privately owned and controlled indoor places, for example, shopping centers and new air-conditioned restaurants and in food centers and food-floors. This reflects the tastes of the emerging well-heeled classes. The spatial shift in public eating—as street restaurants are forced to close to make way for more automobiles—has been bemoaned by one of the city's restaurant critics. He cites an example near Yaowaraj (Chinatown): "[I]t was one of the few parts of the city where a large number of people gathered spontaneously, met friends, and had a good time: the kind of thing that is always welcomed and cultivated by those who are administering a properly-run city, and that gives the city a good name among visitors" (*Bangkok Post* 1993).

Thai urban streetscapes are under threat by these developments. Public eating is increasingly taking place in privately owned space, more or less open to the public. On the other hand, shopping center and department store owners argue that their food services are more hygienic and adhere to the labor code. Regarding food safety, newspaper articles have dismissed this claim, at least for "pre-prepared" food packages in supermarkets, which are neatly presented on foam and covered in plastic wrap (*Matichon* 1994). Information on the enforcement of labor standards is more difficult to obtain. Food center and shopping plaza managers reported that food-shop owners on their premises make their own arrangements for staffing and often hire family members. It is unlikely that family members were paid minimum wage or other benefits associated with the labor code.

Evidence presented here suggests that as the gap continually widens between the rich and poor in Bangkok, we are witnessing the emergence of a dual food-system resembling trends identified in neighboring Malaysia (Salih et al. 1988).[9] The wealthy have a range of choices available to them in terms of eating arrangements. These consist of eating food prepared by servants at home, catering networks, neighborhood food shops and food centers, suburban "food gardens"—large restaurants with a *sala thai*[10] design—as well as expensive restaurants. The second system is for the poor, including those who actually transport, sell, and prepare the food. Here, the range of eating establishments is limited. Their eating places include their humble living quarters and shops, street foods, and, in some cases, meals provided by their employers. As summarized by Askew and Paritta:

> The shopping centers of the outer areas symbolize the development of a newer culture based on modern convenience, shopping and transportation by private motor vehicle. At the same time, the neighborhood markets and the cheap street-side restaurants in the *soi*s and more congested neighborhoods point to the persistence of a less modernized life-style reflecting the continuing significance of public life in less formally regulated public spaces, especially for the urban poor. (1992: 164).

The inhabitants of these far from separate worlds often converge, not only because of transactions between vendor and customer or maid and employer but in the many intermediary eating venues that cater to a wide range of income groups. The above representation, then, requires some qualification.

The shift in retailing structure is intricately related with the growing availability of convenience and ready-to-eat foods. For Taiwan, this has been identified as related to the high number of women in the workforce (*Bangkok Post* 1993: 20) and the same certainly holds true for Thailand.

Gisèle Yasmeen

Why Eat Out?

The added contemporary impetus for buying prepared food in Thailand and Southeast Asia comes from rapid urbanization and industrialization and concomitant changes in family structure and the roles played by women. As Suntaree Komin explains, socio-economic change has completely altered the food-system:

> The decline of family functions is clearly visible in Bangkok. As there is an increase of women working outside households, this trend is almost inevitable. Family functions have been taken over by various specialized organizations. For example, working mothers leave their household chores to the servants. Meals preparation [sic] are taken care of either by servants, or by subscription to the meal-catering services (*pinto*),[11] or by buying those ready-made foods each day on the way home. (1989: 86)

Suntaree is primarily describing middle-class food habits as the poor in Bangkok can ill afford to hire servants; however, the general explanation for the growth of public eating is sound, that is, the changing roles and occupations of women. Also, with large numbers of men coming to the city to find employment, especially those separated from their families, there is increased demand for prepared food emanating from the male population, a trend evidenced elsewhere (Klopfer 1993; Savara and Everett 1991). There are several other interrelated explanations for the general emergence of public eating in Bangkok, namely, the labor-intensivity of Thai cuisine, demographic change, kitchenless housing, and general "cultural" preferences explained in detail below.

Labor-intensive Cuisine

The preparation of Thai food involves a lot of chopping, grinding, and pounding and thus takes much time and effort to prepare. It also involves combining many ingredients. Paradoxically, however, noodles are easy to prepare, yet noodle shops are the most ubiquitous and highly frequented eating establishments in Thai society. This may be because they were originally part of the "coolie food-system" catering to migrant Chinese laborers and also due to the importance of proper broth preparation, time-consuming if one wants good results. People rarely cook noodles at home except for the packaged type, which, except for "Mama's" brand, are not considered tasty. Nevertheless, the labor-intensivity of Thai food preparation is a determinant in the development of Bangkok's food-system.

Demographic Change in Bangkok

Since the Second World War, migrant workers, students, and others have come to Bangkok to earn a living or study. Many come on their own without their families. According to the National Economic and Social Development Board (NESDB), a total of 892,000 people migrated to Bangkok or its five surrounding provinces of the Extended Bangkok Metropolitan Region between 1975 and 1990 (Table 4.4). Government figures grossly underestimate actual migration because temporary residents of Bangkok who return to their homes in the countryside for part of the year are not counted and number in the tens of thousands (Keyes 1996). These people either live in housing where it is impossible, if not difficult, to cook (see below) due to lack of space, or find it inconvenient to cook for just one or two people. Most of these migrants are poor and in need of income, which leads to the opening of a small enterprise such as a food shop. Vendors and their employees are willing to work long, hard hours for very little by way of financial compensation.

Table 4.4 Migration to the Extended Bangkok Metropolitan Region, 1975–90

Years	BMA	Five surrounding provinces[*]
1975–80	190,000	96,000
1980–85	184,000	122,000
1985–90	149,000	151,000

[*] Nonthaburi, Samut Prakan, Pathum Thani, Nakhon Pathom, and Samut Sakhon
Source: Cited in Greenberg (1994: 104)

Kitchenless Housing

Dolores Hayden in *The Grand Domestic Revolution* (1981) described how nine-teenth-century American apartment buildings were often kitchenless with a central cafeteria or dining-room frequented by tenants during mealtimes. A similar trend has emerged in late twentieth-century Bangkok with many apartment blocks typically providing one-room suites (see Fig. 4.1) that do not contain cooking facilities. *In toto*, more than 20% of Bangkok's housing stock is kitchenless. This can be inferred from the fact that 23.4% of the city's housing stock consists of rooms, the majority of which do not have cooking facilities (NSO 1990). This is attributed to the ease of purchasing meals but also because cooking is prohibited in apartments to prevent odors and hygienic problems. At the same time, people do not have the space to entertain at home. Thais do not usually invite guests to their homes unless they have lavish furnishings and a beautiful home (Walker 1991). Since nearly a quarter of Bangkok's housing stock is comprised of rooms and 12.6% is classified as "other," it is possible that nearly half the population of the city does not have access to a full kitchen.

Table 4.5 Type of Dwelling (% of Housing Stock), Greater Bangkok

Detached House	44.0%
Room or rooms	23.4%
Row house	20.0%
All other types	12.6%

Source: National Statistical Office, Office of the Prime Minister, Preliminary Report of the 1990 Household Socio-Economic Survey

"Luung" (meaning uncle[12]), a 60-year-old duck-noodle shopowner, explains the relationship:

> People like to eat out because they can't cook in the apartments. There are only bedrooms so they have to buy already-prepared food. Therefore, as I explained earlier, there are many food shops and vendors. At the beginning of this *soi* until the end there are at least ten businesses.

Usually, a food shop selling made-to-order food (*ahaan tam sang*) is located on the ground floor of an apartment building. Tenants can phone the shop to place orders, usually noodles or fried rice, and sometimes can eat in the shop if it is large enough and provides tables and chairs. Typically, however, the vendor and her or his family will live in the shop rather than use it as an eat-in establishment. It is more common for tenants to have food delivered directly to their rooms after placing an order by phone. Many landlords design the suites without kitchen facilities to prevent residents from preparing food in their rooms. The pungent odors of Thai cooking are considered inappropriate in high-density housing.[13] Despite these regulations, rented-room dwellers often use rice-cookers to steam rice and make other simple

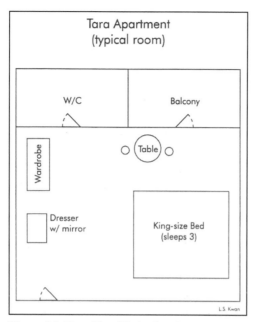

Figure 4.1 Floor Plan: Kitchenless Apartment

dishes. A hot-plate or kettle can also be used to make packaged noodle soup. The wealthier increasingly own microwaves. A conversation between Luung and one of his customers illustrates one perception of the phenomenon:

> *Customer*: Now there are microwaves, people with money can buy them.
> *Luung*: But, microwaves can only re-heat food, isn't that right?
> *Customer*: No, you can cook in that machine. When you put the food inside, it cooks! Ordinary people can't buy it because it's expensive. Only the rich can have it.

Here, it is evident that Luung and his customer are conscious of the income stratification of Thai society and the limits it imposes and privileges it grants. The microwave oven, if purchased by or made available to a large enough group of people, could radically transform the Thai urban food-system by making small food shops partially obsolete. Lunchtime customers could purchase their food in supermarkets and "cook" it at the office, or else, cook food at home and re-heat it elsewhere.

Consumerism

Thailand's rapid industrialization has led to growth in disposable income, especially in Bangkok. The society has moved from a subsistence to a cash economy in urban areas and to a certain extent in rural parts of the country.

People now have to buy the things they need to survive, even prepared food. In addition, eating and related activities, such as shopping, are important parts of the leisure habits of Thai urbanites. The infamous nightlife of Bangkok, which often involves prostitution, mostly for local men, includes drinking alcohol and eating meals in "cafés."[14] This ties in with Thai patterns of gendering.

"Cultural" Preferences

Thais appear to be preoccupied with convenience and make great use of labor-saving strategies and devices when affordable. For example, a maid I met from Isaan would buy pineapple from the market for her employer to save him money but would purchase one already cut up for herself and her husband because it was more convenient. A Sino-Thai shopkeeper I met described the Thai preponderance for purchasing prepared food as evidence of a lack of "discipline." "They don't know how to budget their money," he remarked. Luung made similar comments.

Like other parts of Southeast Asia, Thailand is a snacking culture where several small meals per day are common rather than the "three square" requirement of Westerners.[15] Perhaps this is the most logical eating pattern in a tropical environment. Thai are fond of repeating: *khon thai kin khao talot wela*, or "Thai people eat all the time!"[16] It is a well-established cultural practice to eat out of doors, which results in a lively street and *soi* life. Leisure habits of Thai urbanites focus very much around commensality in public places. "Have you eaten yet?" (*Kin khao rue yang?*) is a typical greeting on meeting friends and co-workers.[17]

According to Walker's *Food Consumption Survey*, 11% of Bangkokians never cook at all. NSO figures are even higher, at 27% (NSO 1990). The figure is no doubt even more impressive if one includes people who limit "cooking" to using a rice-cooker or hot-plate for steaming/boiling rice and noodles. True cooking "from scratch" is becoming rare in Bangkok. Furthermore, a growing number of markets sell "semi-prepared" food that can be "cooked" in a microwave and eaten immediately with no additional labor. This further complicates definitions of cooking and food-preparation.

The following illustrates some of the arrangements made at the Asian Institute of Technology:

Field Notes 4.3: The Asian Institute of Technology's Student Food-system

Wednesday, 30 September 1992: Found out the South Asian students have a food-system of their own on campus. Many (most) have Thai women hired as cooks. These women cook Indian food for them, either on an individual household basis (for those living in the "village" housing complexes) or on a "mess" basis. Apparently there are several messes that are divided on an ethnic/region and a gender basis. The Indian students refer to their cooks as "The Khuns" and report that they make delicious food in almost any regional style. I met one of these women and asked her where she learned to cook Indian food. . . She said she just watched someone and learned. She claimed not to like the food herself.

Others have a "contract" with the Thai-Muslim manager of the little snack bar in the cafeteria. The snack bar provides subscribers with two meals per day (or whatever one arranges) for Bt 20 per meal. This includes a chicken or vegetable curry, a dal, rice, dessert, yoghurt, and a drink. Subscribers get served by the young Thai women at their tables or help themselves cafeteria-style. They pay in advance for the term. You can also get meals on an individual basis if there's enough. All these arrangements are in addition to the formal cafeterias and dining-rooms of the university.

The practice of forming "messes" is quite common on a number of South Asian university campuses (Pendakur 1992). Students from China were known to do the same, and to join a mess was to make a statement about one's ethnic allegiances.[18] I am unsure to what extent the Thai students at AIT formed similar arrangements. The practice is no doubt less widespread due to the wide availability of Thai food and the fact that eating a "home-cooked meal" in a domestic setting does not appear to have the same cultural importance as it does in South Asia, or traditional Europe and North America.

Public Eating

Thailand boasts the highest female labor force participation rates (FLFPR) in Southeast Asia, a region already known for the high economic activity levels of women. The curve in Figure 4.2 representing Thai FLFPR is consistently the highest

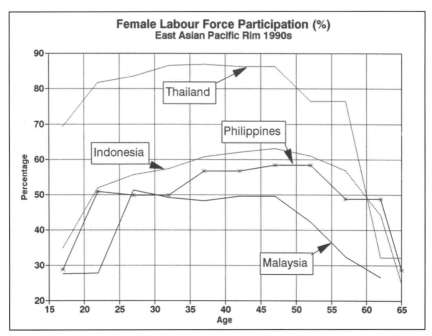

Source: International Labour Organization, 1994

Figure 4.2 Female Labor Force Participation Rates in Southeast Asia (%)

at 87% and demonstrates a "central peak" or plateau pattern indicating that women do not withdraw from the labor force during child-bearing/rearing years (Jones 1984: 28). This is characteristic of the Malay and T'ai cultural realms where women play an important economic role earning money for their families.

Although the poorest urbanites continue to cook for themselves when possible (de Wandeler 1990), most women and men have no time to cook and have income available for prepared food. As indicated in Table 4.6, 48% of the monthly food budget in Greater Bangkok is spent on pre-cooked comestibles. The trend of purchasing prepared food to take home and eat began in the post-Second World War period and has grown significantly in the last twenty years with large numbers of women entering the remunerated urban workforce (Van Esterik 1992).

The 1990 Household Survey of Greater Bangkok found that in a seven-day period, take-home food consisted mostly of rice and curry (*khao gaeng*) and noodle dishes. Table 4.7 provides a breakdown of expenditures for this time period. Fried

Table 4.6 Average Monthly Expenditures per Household
by Type of Food Consumed, 1990

Type of food consumed	All-Thailand	Greater Bangkok
Food prepared at home	1,494 Bt (76%)	1,616 Bt (52.3%)
Prepared food taken home	173 Bt (8.8%)	457 Bt (14.8%)
Food eaten away from home[1]	300 Bt (15.2%)	1,014 Bt (32.9%)

Source: National Statistical Office, Office of the Prime Minister, Preliminary Report of the 1990 Household Socio-economic Survey
[1] Excludes alcoholic drinks away from home

Table 4.7 Average Weekly Expenditures for Prepared Food Taken Home,
Greater Bangkok, 1990

Type of Food	Expenditure (baht)	% of total
Rice and curry	85.93	73.8%
Noodles	16.65	14.3%
Fried rice	4.97	4.3%
Meals (pinto food)	4.03	3.5%
Snacks	3.26	2.8%
Other Prep. Food	1.58	1.3%
Total	116.42	100.0%

Source: National Statistical Office, Office of the Prime Minister, Report of the 1990 Socio-Economic Survey: Bangkok Metropolis, Nonthaburi, Pathum Thani and Samut Prakan, 1994: 17

rice, "meals" (referring to catered tiffin food), snacks, and other prepared food total up to the remaining 12% of weekly take-home prepared food expenditures. On average, 116.42 Bt per week is spent on take-home food.

Table 4.8 shows that most meals, especially breakfast and dinner, are still eaten at home rather than in stalls or restaurants. Although much of this food may be purchased from an outside source, the domestic setting remains the preferred locus of commensality. Eighty-seven percent of respondents to the Food Consumption survey indicated that they eat dinner at home "everyday or most days" with 65% answering the same for breakfast. Only lunch appears to be the meal taken most frequently outside the home with less than half (46%) indicating that they eat lunch at home "everyday or most days."

Table 4.8 Frequency of Eating Meals at Home, Greater Bangkok, 1990

Respondents' reply	Breakfast	Lunch	Dinner
Everyday or most days	65%	46%	87%
Occasionally / rarely	35%	54%	13%

Source: Marilyn Walker, *Food Consumption Survey* 1990

The household survey confirms Walker's data and found that 63% (163.04 Bt) of the total expenditure on prepared food consumed outside the home is spent on lunch with breakfast coming in second place at 16.2% (41.97 Bt). 13.4% (34.56 Bt) was spent on the evening meal. Table 4.9 provides information on other expense categories for food eaten away from home. Walker's data confirm this trend and show that most respondents ate out at lunch and breakfast and for snacks; 87% still reported eating dinner at home "everyday or most days." Concerns about the impact of eating away from home on family life need not be exaggerated because evenings are still reserved for family commensality. Prepared food is therefore a frequent substitute for home-cooked meals whether or not the food is actually eaten at home or elsewhere. The following section defines and describes the various food strategies employed by Bangkok residents to obtain cooked food outside the home.

Table 4.9 Average Weekly Expenditures for Prepared Food Eaten Away from Home, Greater Bangkok, 1990

Expense Category	Expenditure (baht)	% of Total
Breakfast	41.97	16.20%
Lunch	163.04	63.00%
Dinner	34.56	13.40%
Snacks	3.01	1.16%
Alcoholic Drinks	14.81	5.73%
Other Food and Beverage	1.30	0.50%
Total	258.69	100.00%

Source: National Statistical Office, Office of the Prime Minister, Report of the 1990 Socio-Economic Survey: Bangkok Metropolis, Nonthaburi, Pathum Thani, and Samut Prakan, 1994: 17

Everyday Food Strategies

A "traditional" strategy common throughout Southeast Asia is the subscription to neighborhood catering networks where food—normally one soup, one vegetable, and one dish (often a curry) –is delivered at a regular time every day in a tiffin-carrier (*pinto*) (Fig. 4.3). The tiffin-network strategy is seemingly being eclipsed by the small food shop sector where food is available anywhere, anytime—an important attribute in a city where traffic is grid-locked during rush hours. Women are seen stopping at a food shop in the evenings on their way home from work to pick up dinner for the family—main courses are placed in small plastic bags, the accompanying rice being prepared easily at home in a rice-cooker. More recently, foam containers have been introduced; it is now common to hear people request "*say foam*" or "put it in a foam box." Bangkok residents hence refer to *mae baan tung plastic* or "plastic bag housewives" (Van Esterik 1992). Obviously, women consumers are rarely "housewives" as most engage in remunerative employment. The arrival of this newcomer in the foodscape signals the blurring of boundaries between public and private space. Food shops act as semi-private or semi-public spaces where urbanites meet their daily food needs. What traditionally took place mostly within the home is now contracted out to micro-entrepreneurs.

The owners of D'jit Pochana, considered the first "proper" Thai restaurant, started with a family-run tiffin network and later, a curry shop. This expensive establishment now has three locations in suburban parts of the city and is popular with military officers. D'jit Pochana is but one example of Bangkok's elite food-scape, which includes both Thai and expensive "international" restaurants where businessmen and a few businesswomen woo customers (Walker 1991).

Bangkok's contemporary foodscape, where cooking and/or eating quite often takes place outside the home, is a reminder of the haphazard way in which ostensibly public and private activities and spaces are grouped together.

The following summary description of one of my acquaintances provides an example of upper middle-class eating habits:[19]

Ajaan (Professor) Prinyathip teaches at a university in central Bangkok and is married to an engineer. She has no children and lives in a housing estate in a suburban area of the city. At lunch time, if she doesn't have time to go to the faculty cafeteria, she asks the janitor to bring lunch back to her office. Everyday, on her way home from work, she stops at a small roadside curry shop and picks up dinner—usually a curry and a vegetable dish or a soup. Since she drives a car, she often frequents one of the shopping centers on

อาหารปิ่นโต
คุณตุ๋ย + คุณต้อย

239 ซ.อินทามระ 16 สุทธิสาร กรุงเทพฯ โทร. 270-0339

ชื่อ_____ บ้านเลขที่_____ ซอย_____ ถนน_____

โทร.(ที่ทำงาน)_____ (ที่บ้าน)_____ ราคา_____ เริ่มรับวันที่____ เดือน_____ พ.ศ._____

รายการอาหารเดือน มิถุนายน 2536

	แกงเผ็ด-แกงส้ม	ต้มยำ-ต้มจืด	ผัดเผ็ด-น้ำพริก	ผัดจืด	ทอด-ลบ-ย่าง
1.	แกงป่าไก่	หน่อไม้ซี่โครงหมู	ยำถั่วพลู	ผัดดอกกระหล่ำ	น่องไก่ทอด
2.	แกงกระหรี่หมู	ต้มยำไก่พริกเผา	กระเพราเครื่องในไก่	ผัดเปรี้ยวหวาน	ไข่พะโล้
3.	แกงส้ม	ต้มยำไก่	ปลากระพงผัดพริกขิง	หมูผัดซีอิ๋วฉอย	ปลาสลิดทอด
4.	แกงเขียวหวานเนื้อ	ไข่เจ้าซี่โครงหมู	พะแนงหมู	ผัดผัก	ไก่ทอดกระเทียม
5.	แกงเผ็ดไก่ฟักทอง	ผัดจับฉ่าย	น้ำพริกกะปิ	หมูผัดขี้ไก่	ปลาทูทอด
6.	แกงเลียง	ต้มจืดฟักหมูกุ้งแห้ง	ไก่ผัดพริกเผา	ปูผัดเผ็ดเจี๊ยว	เต้าหู้น้ำแดง
7.	แกงอ่อมมะระปลาดุก	ชูปไก่	หมูผัดพริกหยวก	ผัดถั่วลันเตา	ทอดมันปลากราย
8.	แกงคั่วสับปะรดหอย	แตงกวายัดไส้	ย้ากุ้งเขียว	ไก่ผัดกระเทียมดอง	ปลาหมดพริกน้ำปลา
9.	แกงเหลืองปลากระพง	ต้มเค็มน่องไก่	ห่อหมกปลาช่อน	ผัดเต้าหู้ยอดไส้	หมูอบซ็อส
10.	แกงส้มมะละกอกุ้ง	ผักกาดดองซี่โครงหมู	ปลาช่วยทอดราดพริก	ผัดหน่อไม้ไข่หมู	ปลาเค็มทอด
11.	แกงหมูเทโพ	ต้มยำซาหมูพริกเผา	เต้าเจี้ยวหลน	ผัดกระเพราใบโปล	ไก่เจะโล้
12.	แกงป่าปลาดุก	หัวไชเท้าปลากุ๋สด	ลาบหมู	ไก่ผัดมันหอย	ปูจ๋า
13.	❀❀❀❀❀❀❀		หยุด 1 วัน		❀❀❀❀❀❀❀
14.	แกงเขียวหวานไก่	มะระยัดไส้	กระเพราหมู	ผัดจับฉ่าย	กุนเชียงทอด
15.	แกงเผ็ดหมู	เกี๊ยมฉ่ายซี่โครงหมู	พะแนงไก่	ผัดบวบ	เครื่องในไก่ทอด
16.	แกงป่าเนื้อ	เต้าหู้หมูสับ	น้ำพริกปลาร้า	คะน้าหมูกรอบ	ไข่ดาวหน้าหมู
17.	แกงส้ม	ต้มเลือดหมู	ผัดเผ็ดไก่	ผัดรุ้นเส้น	เนื้อเค็มหวาน
18.	แกงเผ็ดปลากราย	ต้มยำเนื้อตุ๋น	ขนมจีนน้ำยา	ปลาทอดคดผัดขึ้นฉ่าย	หมูตอดกระเทียม
19.	แกงโปะปลา	คำลึงหมูสับ	กระเพราเนื้อ	ผัดผักกาดดอง	ปลาดุกย่าง
20.	แกงเขียวหวานหมู	ไก่ตุ๋นกระหล่ำปลี	หอยนบเต็ม	คลกกุ๋ยช่ายผัดหมู	หมูทวาน
21.	แกงลาว	ผักกาดขาวปลาดุก	ผัดเขียวหวานหมู	ผัดพักทอง	ไข่ตัดไส้
22.	แกงคั่วหน่อไม้ดองไก่	ต้มโต้งปลากรอบ	ยำวุ้นเส้น	ใช่นหกระทาผัดหนังหมู	หมูนึ่งไข่เค็ม
23.	แกงเป็ดย่าง	โป๊ะแตก	ปลากรอบผัดพริกแกง	เกี๊ยมฉ่ายผัดหมู	ปีกไก่น้ำแดง
24.	แกงเผ็ดปลาช่อน	ต้มหน่อไม้จีน	กระเพราไก่	ผัดมักกะโรนี	กุ้งอบวุ้นเส้น
25.	แกงส้มผักรุ้ง	ไข่ป๋าซี่โครงหมู	ผัดเผ็ดหน่อไม้ดอง	ผักกาดขาวหมูกรอบ	ปลาหมึกแห้งทอด
26.	แกงป่าหมู	ไก่ตุ๋นมะนาวดอง	น้ำพริกอ่องแค้มหมู	ปลาผัดหมอมใหญ่	ไข่ลูกเขย
27.	❀❀❀❀❀❀❀		หยุด 1 วัน		❀❀❀❀❀❀❀
28.	แกงลูกชิ้นไก่	ปลาหมึกยัดไส้	จู้ฉี่ปลาดูล	ผัดถั่วผักยาวหมู	เนื้อย่าง
29.	แกงเผ็ดเนื้อ	ต้มยำปลากระพง	ไก่ผัดพริกสด	ผัดถั่วงอก	ปูชุบแป้งทอด
30.	แกงมัสมั่นไก่	เกาเหลาลูกชิ้นเนื้อเปื่อย	ผัดเผ็ดหมูถั่วผักยาว	ผัดไช่โป๋	ขาหมูพะโล้
	... ทุก ๆ วันอาทิตย์ เรามีขนมหวานบริการฟรี สำหรับสมาชิกทุกท่านตลอดเดือน ...				

รับประทาน 2-3 ท่าน ราคา 1,100 บาท อาหารมีให้ 5 อย่าง แต่ให้เลือกทานได้ 3 อย่าง

อัตราค่าบริการ

	4	"	1,300	"	5	"	"	4	"
	5	"	1,500	"	5	"	"	4	"
	6	"	1,700	"	5	"	"	4	"

เพิ่มขึ้นท่านละ 200 บาท อาหารต่างๆ จัดให้ปริมาณ | กรุณาขีดเครื่องหมาย ลบ (-) ลงหน้าเชิ้งที่ท่านไม่รับประทานด้วยค่ะ

=กรุณาสั่งจองล่วงหน้า 3-4 วัน จะเป็นพระคุณยิ่ง=

Figure 4.3 Menu from a Tiffin-catering Network, Bangkok

the way home where she can park her car and purchase from a large selection of take-home food in small plastic bags—or foam containers—on the "food floor." When asked whether she ever sits down to eat in roadside food shops or stalls, she answers: "Never, not with the heat, dust, and noise. . . It's so unpleasant." If she's going to spend time eating out, Ajaan Prinyathip would rather go to a nice restaurant with air-conditioning and beautiful surroundings.

Eating in stalls is associated with unpleasant environmental conditions that can be avoided in an air-conditioned restaurant or a quiet middle-class home. For typically middle-class Bangkokians, particularly women who tend to be impeccably dressed, frequenting a cool, comfortable establishment is the most desirable option. Pollution and the noise of traffic make the food shop experience less aesthetically pleasing and even a health hazard.

Middle-class men such as government workers on Friday evenings enjoy "slumming" in stalls and outdoor restaurants where they can sit at long tables and drink vast quantities of whisky. Working-class men (e.g., tuk-tuk drivers) do the same but in less expensive venues. Since "proper" Thai women do not drink alcohol, they engage in a slightly different pattern. Their habit is to go out with a group of friends (women or mixed) to a *suan ahaan*, or "food garden," such as "Bua," a chain of open-air restaurants.

Walker's Food Consumption Survey (FCS) (1990) clearly demonstrates that the ideal locus of everyday commensality is the home. Special occasions, however, merit an outing to a "special" restaurant, funds permitting. The same holds true for entertaining guests, as previously mentioned.

For the most part, the urban masses have very low incomes and either cook for themselves and/or purchase food on the streets and *soi*s from vendors, both mobile and stationary, and small food shops specializing in noodles, curried dishes, or other fare (see Yasmeen 1992).[20] The FCS confirms this observation, as indicated in Table 4.10, by revealing that noodle shops and small Thai restaurants are the most highly patronized eating establishments in Bangkok with 91% and 84% of the 4,198 respondents reporting that they frequent these places (Walker 1990: 6).

Small restaurants are quite diverse in terms of the food is sold, access to clientele, and the types of functions they perform in the city and cannot, therefore, be classified in the manner of the many studies that focus on the so-called "informal sector" or "street food" (see Amin 1991; FAO 1988; McGee 1971; Napat and Szanton 1986; Tinker 1987). The differences between small eating-establishments in terms of ethnicity, income-ranges of the clientele and, perhaps

Table 4.10 Most Highly Patronized Eating Establishments, Bangkok

Type of establishment	Respondents (%)
Noodle shops	91%
Thai restaurants	84%
Garden restaurants	65%
Regional Thai restaurants	63%
Chinese restaurants	47%
Western fast-food	44%
Western restaurants	27%
Others	3%

Source: Marilyn Walker, *The Food Consumption Survey* 1990 (Designed by Walker and administered by Frank Small and Associates)

most importantly for this volume, their various locational environments in the city are the focus here.

The food shop sector is now quite ethnically differentiated as result of migration from the provinces, especially from the Northeast resulting in the emergence of various types of Isaan food-vending establishments for migrant workers such as taxi-drivers and construction workers (see Van Esterik 1992). Considered the most "macho" men of Thailand, male patrons of these places can be seen drinking "whisky" and eating spicy dishes late into the night in various parts of the city where Isaan men traditionally congregate (for example, the boxing stadium, gas stations, and night-markets). Massive migration from the Northeast has resulted in most of the city having examples depicting this behavior. For instance, between 6 p.m. and 3 a.m., a night-market (*talat to rung*) off Sam Sen Road in Banglamphu hums with activity as Isaan taxi- and *tuk-tuk*-drivers snack and drink at food-stalls and shops run mostly by women micro-entrepreneurs. It appears as though Central Thai men are beginning to participate in these rituals in stark contrast to the past when things Isaan were more thoroughly denigrated by mainstream Thai society. Details for the Victory Monument Areas are illustrated in Chapters 5 and 6.

The majority of small food shops are patronized by a wide range of income-groups and therefore inexpensive. A number of extremely small restaurants in Bangkok are geared toward a wealthy consumer. An example of this is the "one-woman" operation, *phrik yuak*, where wholesome, artistically presented Thai food is served in a home-like setting (Puntana 1992). Small eating establishments can therefore be differentiated on the basis of the income levels of entrepreneurs and their customers. Discussions of "food shops with one to four employees" mask the fact that some of these places may actually be expensive restaurants. Other examples are the small "health food" restaurants in Bangkok and Chiang Mai that are beyond the budget of most Thais.

A more important remark, however, concerns the diverse locations or operating environments of small food shops and the contractual opportunities to which these micro-entrepreneurs can have access (see Naruemol and Oudin 1992). First, many food shops are now located indoors where they are integrated in settings as diverse as privately owned luxury shopping plazas (Fig. 4.4), educational institutions such as universities, and, even the United Nations Building on Rajdamnern Road.

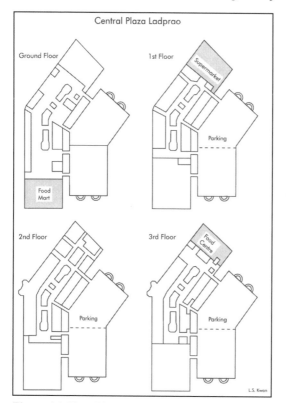

Figure 4.4 Floor Plan: Central Plaza Ladprao

Hence, small shops—by obtaining exclusive contracts with business or government—become directly involved with politico-economic structures at national, regional, and even international scales.

This is a clear example of what Gregory, following Giddens, has labelled as the "local-global" dialectic (1990). It is considered "one of the most far-reaching consequences of modernity" and is defined as the simultaneous globalization of social life, which is the result of "time-space" distanciation afforded by widespread travel, advances in communication and technology and the resulting disembedding of "traditional" life-worlds that were, for the most part, rooted in a restricted space:

> The reverse side of the local-global dialectic is thus what Harvey calls *time-space compression*. He sees this as the compulsion to "annihilate space by time" under capitalism. . . For Harvey, "the foreboding generated out of the sense of social space imploding in on us is wired to a crisis of identity: "to what space/place do we belong?"(Harvey 1990: 427; cited by Gregory 1994: 121)

The most humble, simple, and vernacular food shops in Bangkok are part of the local-global dialectic, not only through their purchasing patterns and locations but also through the routine flows of customers that come in and out of their shops. Bangkok is an extremely cosmopolitan city, and even the most "Thai" of neighbourhoods, such as the Victory Monument Area, contain long- and short-term foreign residents.

In Daeng's small shop, for example, I routinely encountered and interacted with people from all over the world. Whereas Daeng, her mother, and their assistants (most of whom are relatives) had rarely ventured from Bangkok and their home province of Roi-Et, there were customers who came from Japan and Burma as well as Thais who had lived and traveled abroad.

The place was often filled with people from other parts of the world as the following vignette illustrates:

Field Notes 4.4: The "United Nations" Food Shop

Tuesday, 15 December 1992: Tonight, there was an interesting Japanese couple there eating Isaan food and drinking "whisky." The woman (who doesn't speak much English) has been here four or five months and is learning Thai so we communicated in Thai. . . The man has only been here for two weeks. . . He speaks English. At one point, an older (50-ish) *farang* man came by (take-out) and spoke Thai. At another point, a Thai-looking man came in, but Daeng said that he was from India (?). I said that the food shop is like the UN!

Clearly then, the Thai example of a mass-based daily strategy that relies extensively on the small food shop is not a simple, standard phenomenon. The preceding discussion has attempted to elucidate the complexity of the system by pointing to the differences in the types of eating establishments frequented by most Thai urbanites every day. Terms such as "street foods" and "informal sector" are not appropriate for the description of this sector because many shops are no longer located on the street and do, in fact, comply with licensing regulations making them technically, "formal."

Bangkok houses many small ubiquitous food shops that act as a life-support system for many urbanites. Small restaurants serve a number of latent social functions in addition to providing meals. For example, children are often cared for in these environments, and young people spend time and "help" thereby learning skills and meeting others. Food shops are also a source of information on local affairs for customers and helpers; some learn of jobs or read the newspaper in these spaces.[21]

Field Notes 4.5: Food-Shop-based Childcare

Sunday, 11 October 1992: Went out to run errands. Lunch time approximately. Went into a poor residential neighborhood with lower density housing near my place between Rajavitee and Rangnam.[22] Had fried rice in this woman's small stand, which has a few tables and chairs. There were chickens and roosters all round me. I had fried rice with egg and veggies and a coke. Her daughter (or perhaps younger sister) was working there also. Her baby boy (or someone's baby) was scampering around the place and his grandfather was keeping an eye on him. Their house seemed to be attached. The grandpa would sometimes bring stuff from the house to the food-stall. The food was good. I didn't chat. I will next time.

Unfortunately, there was no "next time." Upon my return a few weeks later, the stall was no longer there. Many of the families in this zone had moved following the awarding of a BMA relocation allowance. The row-houses were in the process of being demolished to make way for a public park that had been "in process" for at least twelve years (Vespry 1994).

There are numerous other examples of children, from babies to school age youngsters, being cared for in food shops. This is not only the case in small informal stalls of the type described above but also applies to more expensive, air-conditioned restaurants. Childcare in food shops is an example of the multi-functionality of such spaces.

Small eating-establishments can be interpreted as realms of femininity where women are employed, and to a great degree, remain in control of their micro-enterprises. This topic requires further exploration. Small food shops are unique "everyday" spaces for the majority of urbanites whereas larger establishments cater to the "occasion" and are, at times, idiosyncratic or else fit a pattern that can be more easily typologized.

The smallest food establishments can be classified as semi-public/private spaces. Here, behavior associated with the home is relocated to commercial spaces. Local residents are sometimes seen sitting in food shops near their homes in their pyjamas having breakfast. This resembles the observations of de Certeau's students in Lyon, France (Giard and Mayol 1980). Housewives in the Croix-Rousses Quarter were seen emerging into the neighborhood bakeries in the early morning clad in house-coats, slippers, and curlers. The bakery was seen as an extension of the home and the private sphere and gendered patterns of activity were commensurate with this view. In many food shops, regular customers sometimes prepare food themselves, wash their own dishes and even help serve the clientele. Regular customers are sometimes originally from the same village as the shopowner or may be kin. The food shop, then, is both a private homespace and a public commercial place. These neighborhood eateries blur the socio-spatial boundaries of public and private and are extensions of the home sphere. This leads to the partial domestication of public space where home becomes part of the neighborhood. Traditional cooking activities and kinship networks are recreated within a commercial establishment. Bangkok's small food shops are instrumental in establishing contemporary Thai public life similar to the roles played by pubs and coffee houses in industrializing Europe: "Habermas argues that . . . it was the growth of an *urban* culture—of meeting houses, concert halls, opera houses, press and publishing ventures, coffee houses, taverns and clubs, and the like . . . which represents the expansion of the public sphere" (Howell 1993: 310).

Small food shops are products of urbanization and industrialization and con-comitant social change but, at the same time, reproduce traditional social relations. As such, they represent the simultaneous modernization and post-modernization of Thai urban society.

Similarly, food shops located in "modern" environments such as shopping center food courts, office buildings, and educational institutions are instrumental in re-orchestrating spatial relations. Again, mostly women micro-entrepreneurs and small restaurant owners enter into a contract with larger scale commerce but often continue to rely on unpaid family labor and cook the same types of food. Differences with the informal pattern of organization revolve around price, payment arrangements (sometimes involving a coupon-system), and more formalized relations with customers who are not "regulars" making themselves "at home" as is the case in many *soi*-based food shops.

Eating in a food center is a more expensive proposition than eating on the street and takes place in a highly controlled environment replete with security cameras, air-conditioning, and music. Whereas street and *soi*-based food-shop owners are constrained by property owners and the police who condition access to space, those who locate in privately owned indoor environments are subject to the rules and regulations of the authorities who own the property. Both are operating in a competitive environment where market shifts play a decisive role. Micro-entrepreneurs and small-restaurant owners, much like their counterparts elsewhere, are relatively powerless actors compared to the agency exercised by state officials, property owners, and large-scale commerce (Jellinek 1991). This is certainly not to imply that they are without power but that their agency is limited by the lack of economic and political resources.

Food shop outlets in shopping centers represent a transitional space between the "mass-based" strategy associated with the small neighborhood stall and larger formal restaurants that cater to the wealthier middle-classes.

Bangkok's Elite Foodscape

Southeast Asia's "City of Angels"[23] has an astounding array of unusual restaurants such as "Cabbages and Condoms" (C&C) (Fig. 4.5), owned by the Population and Development Association, which has the mandate to promote condom use.[24] The restaurant is a well-known venue catering to Thai families as well as foreigners. "C&C" even has a branch in China.[25] The founder of the Population and Development Association, Meechai Veeravaidya developed the idea of a restaurant as a fund-raising and educational venture and is a well-respected Thai politician and activist. The example of "C&C" points to the latent social function of the expensive, elite restaurant. A standard typology of expensive eating establishments (as opposed to the ubiquitous food shop) will simplify the complexity of this arm of the food-system.

In a personal communication, Thai economist Pasuk Pongpaichit recalled growing up in Bangkok in the late 1960s when there were only a handful of "proper"

Figure 4.5 "Cabbages and Condoms": A Family Restaurant with a Family-planning Theme

restaurants where families would dine on special occasions. Most of these were Chinese, and some, such as *Somboon Pattakarn* and *See Faa* were successfully in operation at the time of writing.[26] Van Esterik (1992) completes the picture by identifying the four or five hotels where the only "proper" formal restaurants were found in the city until the mid-1970s. Since that time, formal establishments modelled on the Chinese and Western traditions of restaurants catering to special occasions have emerged and specialize in Thai cuisine as well as other culinary traditions.

As documented by Van Esterik and Walker, there is the development of hundreds of open-air mega-restaurants located in the suburbs referred to as "food gardens" (*suan ahaan*). These are often designed in a *sala thai*, or open pavilion style. The use of this style is reminiscent of Thai traditional architecture, yet, as a recent invention, encloses "untraditional" activities. The world's largest restaurant, *Tum Nuk Thai* (Fig. 4.6), which closed shortly after the onset of the Asian economic crisis in the latter half of 1997, had a staff of a thousand, many on roller-skates, is the most extreme example of Thai restaurant gigantism. The restaurant grounds

Figure 4.6 "Tom Nuk Thai": Formerly the World's Largest Restaurant

include *khlongs*, replete with fish that can be fed by customers who purchase bread from a vendor. Thai classical and folk dances are staged at regular intervals to taped music, and souvenir shops located at the exit. Most food gardens are slightly less spectacular and cater to Thai middle-class families and groups rather than tourists. They are generally decorated with bright lights and many plants or trees. Fresh fish and seafood are on display in cases at the entrance for customers to examine and choose.

Discussions of post-modern architecture and design cite the use of vaguely traditional architectural and lifestyle references as a key element often resulting in the production of "depthless images" or *simulacra* (Baudrillard 1981; Jameson 1983; Dear 1993). Simulacra are fanciful "re-creations" of the past that never, existed, much like "Main Street USA" in Disneyland or "Europa Boulevard" in the West Edmonton Mall (Warren 1994; Hopkins 1990). The post-modern experience is also framed by the use of *pastiche* or exaggerated representations that mock the original form being alluded to:

> Post-modern design aims explicitly at expressing specific localities and their history and tradition. . . This use of past styles, which is simultaneous with a tendency to erase style as a consistent and distinctive set of features, incorporates a certain nostalgia and leads to a kind of pastiche, revealing, maybe, innovative and unexpected combinations. . . It goes without saying that all these aspects of post-modern design point to some different conception and experience of space on the part of its producers, while also calling its consumers to participate in this new experience. (Lagopoulos 1993: 260)

Patrons of suburban garden restaurants are participating in a new experience of place inspired by traditional Thai spatial design. This phenomenon is reproduced elsewhere as well. For example, a well-known housing development in Central Bangkok, *Suan Parichat*, is designed in a "traditional" Thai style with all the "mod cons" of air-conditioning and indoor plumbing. The houses have sloping roofs and floors made of polished teakwood. Mini-canals are found throughout the walled and guarded compound for the aesthetic enjoyment of residents and guests but are not used for obtaining water, transportation, fishing, or dumping waste, the practical uses of canals in Central Thailand. Traditional images, void of function and content, are therefore used to add symbolic capital to both restaurants and other new spaces in Thai society. The development of suburban mega-restaurants also closely parallels Bangkok's pattern of mega-urbanization, a theme that has drawn considerable attention over the last decade (McGee and Robinson 1995; Greenberg 1994).

Elite restaurants cater to the social and cultural needs of elites as well as their gastronomic preferences. The FCS indicated that 65% of respondents thought that "Eating out provides a more pleasant atmosphere" and 80% believed that the practice "gives you more variety." Other relevant responses are summarized in Table 4.11. It appears that eating out is a family activity, allowing one to spend more time with spouse and children, and that it is a suitable activity for special occasions.

Expensive restaurants, and other forms of conspicuous consumption, contribute to the construction of an elite identity (Walker 1990). These spaces are instrumental in the creation of a new Thai middle-class aesthetic and lifestyle. This identity revolves around the accumulation of wealth and status, worldliness, and a reconstruction of "Thainess" that emphasizes the traditional arts such as cooking, classical dancing, and certain religious images, such as, for example, spirit houses (Askew 1994; Walker 1991). This is part of the pluralistic value-system in Siamese society:

> A Buddhist-based secular tolerance of what are considered to be matters of individual moral choice has contributed to the development of plural value-systems among the Thai. At one

Table 4.11 Attitudes Toward Eating Out, All-Thailand

Statement	Agree	Indifferent	Disagree
Eating at home is better than eating out	88%	8%	4%
Eating out provides more pleasant atmosphere	65%	23%	13%
Eating out allows more time with family	94%	4%	1%
Eating out gives more variety	80%	12%	8%
Home food is higher quality	94%	13%	3%
Like to eat out on special occasions	69%	15%	17%

Source: Marilyn Walker, *The Food Consumption Survey* (1990)

end of the spectrum, there is a subculture made up of those who have not internalized any of Buddhism's emphasis on temperate behavior and who pursue the hedonistic pleasures of drink, drugs, and sex. At the opposite end of the spectrum is the sub-culture of those ascetic monks who have turned their backs on all worldly temptations. Of particular interest are those sub-cultures—found especially among the Sino-Thai, the Lao of Northeastern Thailand, and perhaps among other groups as well—that emphasize tempering desires for immediate gratification in order to accumulate capital to be invested for a future goal. This latter view has been instrumental in promoting economic growth. (Keyes 1987: 207–08)

The middle-classes, following rapid industrialization and resulting disposable income, engage in conspicuous consumption to purchase, partly, the gamut of "modern conveniences" that make life more comfortable and to display new wealth and status. A case in point is elite eating establishments.

There is a contradiction in the responses summarized in Table 4.11. On the one hand, it is considered 'better' to eat at home where food is higher quality. On the other hand, pleasant atmosphere, variety and special occasions are associated with eating out as well as convenience. For this set of questions, no distinction was made between the types of restaurants under scrutiny, food shops (*raan ahaan*) or formal restaurants (*pattakarn*). Certainly, pleasant atmosphere and special occasions are to be associated with the grander establishments described in this section as opposed to the humble food shop.

One conclusion to be drawn from these data is that elite restaurants are spaces where special events are marked, clients are entertained, and guests are invited. Small food shops and stalls, on the other hand, are associated with quotidian experiences of home and family. Many other restaurant types, however, are located between these two characterizations.

The Future of Street Foods

The worst thing that could happen in the future, in my opinion, would be the disappearance of working-class street food. The street-stalls and tiny hole-in-the-wall restaurants that used to make noodles, won ton, pao, congee, stuffed dumplings, steamed meatballs, fried pastries, and thousands of other snack items could be at risk in the new, affluent world of the future. They are in no danger of disappearing, but they are becoming rarer and are being influenced by the big restaurants' corner-cutting and sodium-loving ways. Much interest has belatedly been devoted to these wonderful foods, among the high points of Chinese cooking. Yet people seem less than aware of the foods in question. Chinese are apt to write them off as poverty food, and Westerners often are never introduced to them. Countless tourists have complained to me about the quality of food in the People's Republic; all of them, it turned out, had dutifully eaten only in the big West-oriented hotels and restaurants, which have altered their food to please the Western palate and which feed hundreds at a meal. I even heard that the old food stalls are gone and one can no longer get 'small eats' in China. But on my travels, I found that small eats existed in every form. Street pushcarts, small cafés, workers' dining halls, and snack bars sold them, as good as anything comparable in Hong Kong or Taiwan—certainly the best food I ate in China outside a few private homes.

E. N. Anderson, *The Food of China* (1988)

Anderson wrote this alarming comment as a critique of the emerging industrial palate in 1980s Hong Kong. Nevertheless, there is a message of hope in the final two lines of the passage, which provides evidence of the persistence of "hawker food." Bangkok's foodscape is being threatened in similar ways due to the emerging middle-class and its tastes. To aggravate the situation, the food served in more expensive Thai/Chinese restaurants is sometimes of much poorer quality than the comestibles in the humblest food shop.

I do not believe, however, that the types of food sold on the streets and lanes of the city are under threat *per se*. Rather the informal context in which the food is usually sold is apparently being eclipsed by indoor food centers and highly capitalized restaurants. The comfort and convenience associated with air-conditioned restaurants and food centers is beginning to drive demand. For this trend to continue, however, the indoor formalized environments will be required to provide equal or better quality food than the roadside stalls and eating establishments. The continuum between the informality and formality of eating establishments in the Victory Monument Area will be scrutinized in the following chapters.

In keeping with the final two lines of the opening quotation, there appears to be a renewed interest in street foods and the heritage of the hawker tradition. Scanning the local newspapers suggests that people have taken an interest in discovering street foods where up-scale hotels hold "street food festivals" in fully controlled situations. For example, the Stable Lodge Hotel on Sukhumvit *soi* 8 holds a "traditional" Thai street food buffet every Saturday evening "but with the Stable's special flair (*Bangkok Post* n.d.). The Martino Coffee Lounge, located in The Mandarin Hotel, advertised its addition of "Authentic Thai coffee prepared from our coffee cart as you watch" (*Bangkok Post* 1992). Figure 4.7 reproduces the advertisement containing the "quaint" drawing of a traditional coffee cart. Ironically, Thais increasingly consume Nescafé as a status symbol following years of vigorous advertising. Gastronomes who pride themselves on their good taste, however, reject instant coffee and look either to Thai "traditional" filtered coffee or quality coffee from abroad.

The interest in street foods is also borne out by the publication of (now, out-of-print) handbooks for foreigners such as *Thai Hawker Food* where "authentic" street food is the object of interest (Pranom 1993). The guidebook contains colorful drawings of the different types of street vendors, their goods and Thai phrases designed to aid the foreigner through Bangkok's foodscape.

Figure 4.7 An "Authentic" Thai Coffee-cart

Chapter 5

Food Micro-entrepreneurs
and Eating Establishments

What do we know about Thai foodsellers and their regional counterparts? The stereotype of the self-employed woman does not apply in certain situations, even in Thailand. Men are involved as well. The complexity of both women's and men's positions in the food-system as cooked-food vendors is conditioned by the ethnicity of entrepreneurs and their customers, the size and type of enterprise, class (or income group), and the nature of the goods sold. This chapter combines an examination of the existing literature on Thai food-sellers with my own quantitative survey of food-vendors and restaurant owners in the VMA.

This chapter examines the socio-economic characteristics of this occupational group and contrasts the situation found in other cities of the country and region. A typology of eating establishments is a necessary part of the description of this income-earning activity. Last, and certainly not least, the gendering of this type of (self-) employment will be discussed with reference to the emergence of new eating patterns in the city. A discussion of debates on Thai and Southeast Asian sex/gender systems informs the entire chapter, particularly with respect to the concept of nurturing (*liang*).

Thai Hawkers and Cooked-food Sellers

The lone hawker, itinerant or stationary, has long been the subject of fascination for researchers of Southeast Asian cities (Geertz 1963). Foreigners romantically delve into the world of the peddler of cooked-food and label this type of entrepreneur as a proud, independent, and quintessential inhabitant of the Southeast Asian city. Certainly, night-markets are distinguishing features of life in urban Southeast Asia, and the cooked-food seller finds a prominent place in this locale. Fixed-pitch stalls and small restaurants such as noodle houses and curry shops have also been looked at as "charming" features of everyday life in this part of the world. It is important, however, to try and sort out what the salient features of life as a cooked-food seller and small restaurateurs are in historical and contemporary Southeast Asia before making generalizations about the profession in Thailand.

Typical Southeast Asian Food Entrepreneurs

Even though the region of Southeast Asia is often characterized as one where female entrepreneurialism far surpasses that of women in other parts of the world, particularly in cooked-food retailing, there is a great degree of variation with regard to the ways and degrees in which women versus men occupy public space. There is a stark contrast between the Chinese man selling *yong tao-foo* in Singapore and a woman from Minangkabau operating a *warteg*[1] selling Tegal-style food in migrant *kampung* in Jakarta (Murray 1991: 58–59).

Studies of hawking, food vending, and restaurants in Chinese societies, including Singapore and Malaysian cities, have concluded that selling on the street is ideally a male occupation:

> A possible cultural explanation is perhaps rooted in the Chinese aversion to letting their women into situations which involve frequent interaction with strangers. . . While this cultural aversion must have moderated greatly as increasing labor participation is being utilized in various capitalist enterprises, it remains true today that some jobs are less desirable than others because of this factor of what is known as [sic] *paau tau lo min* (showing one's face in public). Street hawking is considered an unsuitable vocation for women (Smart 1989: 25).

Women in Chinese societies still play an important role as cooked-food vendors and restaurant co-owners as part of family-run businesses. In Taiwan, for example, they still dominate informal markets (Keyes 1996). Their contributions are therefore difficult to generalize across the very diverse landscape of Chinese influence. Indeed, Anderson (1991) argues that it is essentialist and empirically inaccurate to categorize a group of people as "Chinese." "Chinese-ness" has very much been a construction developed by Westerners and others who do not trace their ancestry to mainland China.

In Vietnam, the situation is slightly different despite the common Confucian heritage. Nguyen Xuan Linh explains why even restaurant cooking is typically performed by women in Vietnamese restaurants: "Vietnamese cuisine, be it within Vietnam or abroad, served at home, or in a public place such as a restaurant, cannot be prepared without women who control the entire gastronomic heritage" (Nguyen 1993: 190; translation mine).[2]

Men refuse to have anything to do with "women's work," which is denigrated. Women are the only ones who know how to cook. In the same volume, Krowolski demonstrates that men tend to be considered less financially responsible than women. Indeed, women's income tends to assure family survival (Krowolski 1993: 162). As Drummond's study clearly shows, since *Doi Moi*, much of this crucial income arises from women's small enterprises, notably in the domain of prepared food (Drummond 1993).

In the indigenous societies of Southeast Asia—among the various Malay speakers, Tai-Lao groups, Khmer, and Burmese, for example—the idea pertaining to the seclusion of women has had far less currency, except among elites. Women play far greater roles as independent vendors; however, they often occupy specific niches in the local foodscape.

Jakarta's restaurant culture provides interesting examples of the specialization of roles in prepared food vending according to gender. *Warteg* are often run by women, but also by men, and are typically frequented by male migrant workers in larger Indonesian cities; "women are almost never seen sitting in them" but are important take-out customers (Murray 1991: 59). In addition, Murray remarks that *kampung* stalls are a women's domain, whereas those on main thoroughfares tend to be male-owned and operated.

The mix of factors that lead to specific types of micro-entrepreneurialism in the prepared-food sector are based on a mix of cultural, class, and gender relations of the locality being studied. Age and the family situation of individual sellers are also of consequence as they indicate prior business experience and access to labor.

Thai Food-Sellers

The socio-economic attributes of Thai food-sellers vary somewhat depending on the type and size of establishment in question and the nature of the food sold. This section constructs a typology of prepared food sellers ranging from the mobile *hab re* (shoulder-pole vendors) and *paeng loy* (street-stall) entrepreneurs to eating establishments with a fixed pitch. Studies conducted outside of Greater Bangkok will be summarized. The city's *raan ahaan* or "food shops" are dealt with in greater detail below.

Renu's (1994) thesis dealt with women *hab re* and *paeng loy* vendors in Bangkok. Her principal conclusion was that 84% of the women studied were earning money for the needs of their children or parents. Renu found that nearly 47% of those engaged in this occupation were originally from Isaan and were from farming backgrounds. Most of the operations surveyed (62%) were managed by one or two people.

The study of sanitation conditions of street foods in Prabuddha-bath municipality provides much broader information than the main objective of the research (Sunanthana and Sriprat 1993).[3] The researchers discovered that 88% of the enterprises selling cooked-food surveyed were owned and operated by women, who usually earn extra income for the family. Owner's husbands tend to be employed in permanent white- or blue-collar occupations. The average age of the vendor's studied was 43 with 75% between the ages of 30 and 60. Nearly half of the informants had received formal education up to *Prathom* (primary) Four. Most food-sellers came from outside the municipality with the majority (78%) from the north. Forty-three percent reported being in the business less than five years and 36% for more than ten.

An important piece of research for the objectives here is the EPOC- and CUSRI-sponsored study of street foods in the once provincial town of Chonburi[4] (Napat and Szanton 1986). This survey of "traditional fast food s" portrayed the gendered nature of production and consumption of street foods. The research team found that, consistent with the studies summarized above, around 80% of the vendors selling processed (i.e., cooked) food were women. Men specialized in the selling of traditional Chinese snacks or light meals (*moo daeng, kha moo, khaaw man gai*) and were themselves of Chinese background. Ethnically Thai men were "almost completely absent" (Napat and Szanton 1986, 23). Sixty-four percent of the female vendors were between the ages of 26 and 45; some younger women sold sweets, and male vendors were often older than the women: "Over 20% of all women were the main household supporters at the time, another 21% were unmarried and earning their own subsistence or sustaining older parents and young siblings" (Napat and Szanton 1986: 23). This income-earning role and sense of responsibility for the family's well-being appears to be one of the critical factors explaining Thai women's high level of micro-entrepreneurialism in the prepared-food-system, a phenomenon discussed in depth below.

Food Vending and Thai Women's Sense of Responsibility

Thai women have long played an important income-generating role in the family and have a history of micro-entrepreneurialism. This trend is shared with other societies of the region. The selling of raw and prepared food by market women is a long standing tradition in Southeast Asia and is particularly highlighted in Thailand. Women in Kelantan (Jamilah 1994), parts of Indonesia (Manderson 1983), and Burma (Spiro 1977) also exhibit this pattern of activity. Why is this? And how can we interpret this phenomenon? This behavior has typically been interpreted by foreigners as a sign of Thai women's strength and independence and that of Southeast Asian women generally. It is often cited alongside an impressive list of other factors that lead one to believe in the equality of the sexes in this region:

> Chiang Mai women are impressive. They have the strength of character, independence, and self-assurance of women who live in a society where they are in a strong position. Residence here is matrilocal. The daughters stay at home and their husbands come in to live with them. Inheritance is bilateral, and the women share equally with the men; daughters inherit the parental home and matrilineal ancestors. In case of divorce, it is the man who leaves and the woman who stays home. Women work in the fields, rear the children, keep house; they are also the merchants who earn money for the family selling in the markets. They are the ones who keep the money, for fear that their men will waste it on gambling or drinking, or on other women. There are many strong men in Chiang Mai village, but what impresses a Western outsider is the strength of the women. (Potter 1976: 24; emphasis added)

In this quotation, we see that Thai women are considered more financially responsible than men. They are trusted with the family wealth. This is a stereotype, and there are plenty of examples, including some drawn from my field research, that challenge this gender ideology. It is generally true, however, that women tend to earn and keep money for the family, especially for food and school fees. A married man is expected to provide the house. Men, particularly in their younger years, tend to squander money for recreational purposes: in gambling, drinking, and prostitutes (including mistresses for the more powerful). Sometimes women are well aware of this problem but continue to provide sons and husbands with money, hoping they will spend it responsibly. However, as I evaluate toward the end of this book following presentation of research results, this general situation may be changing for both women and men.

Foreigners may have exaggerated and misinterpreted the meaning associated with the income-earning abilities and public presence of Thai women. Kirsch, for example, argues that in the Thai Buddhist ascetic value system, the handling of money and other "worldly" occupations are denigrated. Westerners tend to equate economic prowess with social power, an erroneous assumption in several cultural contexts. Thai writers tend to be more sober when commenting on the position of women in their society. Pasuk Pongpaichit, a well-respected woman economist, has observed:

> The easiest way to describe the Thai rural household is as a corporation of kinswomen who induct males through marriage. The rural family is built around its women, and this central role imposes rights and duties. Women traditionally manage the finances of the household, take (or help take) many of the most important decisions about household expenditures, and have a great degree of personal responsibility for managing and maintaining the family's wealth. As we have noted above, it is that *sense of responsibility to the family* which propels many of the girls to migrate in search of income. (Pasuk 1984: 256; emphases added)

It is this social structure and female responsibility that drives women to Bangkok to sell prepared food. The gender relations present in the urban milieu with which these rural migrants are faced presents a sharp contrast to their home environments:

> Within this urban culture men have many more privileges and pre-emptive rights, often at the expense of women. Taking courtesans or minor wives or simply just going out on the town is not only legitimate but somehow rather admirable—a mark of status. The ability to dominate women, many women, becomes inextricably bound up with concepts of commercial and political power and success. (Pasuk 1984: 256)

There is therefore a significant urban/rural divide distinguishing the ways in which femininity and masculinity are constructed and practiced. This hinges on issues of responsibility toward one's family and the ways in which power is used to dominate others, as illustrated in the case of urban men displaying status through philandering. Thai urban women, according to Pasuk and others, are, generally speaking, less socially and economically equal to urban men compared to their rural counterparts. One conclusion that can be made is that both femininity and masculinity are differentiated in rural and urban areas with the "modernized" city centers actually showcasing regressive gender relations. The traditional Thai sex-gender system that persists in rural areas can therefore be seen as more or less complementary, whereas the urban situation is more hierarchical.

Keyes (1987) attributes the predominance of women in "care-giving" activities such as cooking and working as market-women (and, by extension, food vendors) as a result of the symbolic association between femininity and nurturing (*liang*). Indeed, he argues that the essence of femaleness in Thai society is nurturing, whereas the essence of masculinity is "potency" (Keyes 1987: 123). He qualifies this by referring to the various images in Thai and Buddhist folklore that typologize women as nurturers, ideally, while also symbolizing "foil," or opposite, characters such as the "passionate/suffering woman" and the "demanding mistress" (Keyes 1984). This indicates there are, indeed, a range of options in Thai culture for definitions of and practices associated with femininity (see also Keyes 1987: 124; Van Esterik 1994).

Certainly, the Thai language, folktales, and epics abound with images of "mother nurturers" and include metaphorical uses of the term to refer to water, rice, fertility, and elements in the natural world. Attempts to discover "essences" of femininity and masculinity in any society strike me as problematic. Gender-systems are in a constant state of negotiation, and redefinition and essentialist approaches, like those toward "culture" or "race," are heavily criticized (Fuss 1992; hooks 1990). Searching out stereotypes and archetypes has metaphorical utility nevertheless.

"Nurturing," unlike in many Western contexts, is not exclusively female. Van Esterik (1992) clearly explains the gender neutral use of the term and plenty of examples of men engaging in behavior where the term *liang* is used. The term has a wide range of meanings besides the literal connotation, "to feed," and cannot be associated with the English term "nurture" with its attendant notions of femininity, duty, and domesticity (Mies 1986). In Thai, *liang* also means "to treat" (invite guests for a meal or sponsor a banquet) and to "raise" or "foster," such as when adopting a child. One can *liang* orchids, for example, whether male or female.

Liang carries a sense of power; those who want to be influential treat others to build debts of gratitude. Powerful politicians and officials, for example, guarantee the loyalty of their entourage by hosting elaborate meals/festivities. To raise a child (*liang luuk, liang dek*), and by extension feed it, involves reciprocity as part of the bargain whereby a child "owes" something to its parents, particularly the mother. Hence, the Thai practice of the bridegroom paying "milk money" (what anthropologists have called "bride price") is meant to compensate a bride's mother for feeding the daughter during infancy (Sharp and Hanks 1978).

Thai men, like their counterparts in the rest of the region, participate a great deal in child-rearing (see Van Esterik 1992). Men are often good cooks and participate in food-preparation tasks, even those from Isaan who are considered the most "macho" of Thailand. The cooking of meat outdoors, in keeping with what appears to be a worldwide trend, is defined as men's work (Keyes 1996). When describing cooking as women's work, Formoso qualifies the extent of the gender division of labor in the kitchen: "among the Isaan, these types of activities are not exclusively part of the feminine sphere and it is admitted that men can take over the daily tasks of preparing rice and side dishes whenever the female labor force is insufficient or temporarily absent" (Formoso 1993: 109; translation mine).[5] In addition to the activities listed above, there is certainly a case to be made for the presence of nurturing men and boys as evidenced in the following chapters. Van Esterik lists the many symbolic images of masculine nurturers, notably the king who is a supreme example of the *pau liang* archetype (see Wijeyewardena 1971).

We cannot turn to Theravada Buddhism to explain the fundamentals of the Thai sex-gender system; in some ways the patterns resemble those found in the region as a whole, including among Thai Muslims in the south (Chavivun 1986) and in Malay society (Firth 1966). The importance of religion has been a "stumbling block" for those studying women in Southeast Asia (Manderson 1983, 3). Manderson states that scholars assume the regions "have adopted foreign religions wholesale," and this "ignores how religion has been integrated with local beliefs." She suggests that the predominance of matrilineality in Southeast Asia is a more powerful explanatory factor than official religion. Looking for the "one great cause" to explain gender relations in the region is bound to be unproductive.

My position is that Thai gender-relations on a mainstream, basic level tend to be idealized and practiced dichotomously in Thailand with femininity quite sharply distinguished from masculinity. Here, appearances and "surfaces" seem to be of greater importance than "essence." For example, in same-sex relationships, which are relatively tolerated in Thailand, one partner always cross-dresses. Keyes reports attending a lesbian wedding in rural Thailand where this was the case, with Buddhist monks officiating at the ceremony (Keyes 1992)! There are, however plenty of other options that allow an individual to be "butch" or "feminine" or to adopt a range of in-between identities.

Femininity is generally considered inferior to masculinity, which prohibits women from achieving significant power on a national scale (Vitit 1985). Erosions of traditional female equality began hundreds of years ago. Vitit argues that, in the Sukhothai period, women's status was quite high compared to the subsequent Ayutthaya period (14-17th century AD) during which a series of laws were introduced that eroded women's rights (for example, allowing polygamy and permitting the beating of wives). Thai women today do not see themselves as "equal" to men in their society and are organized in a struggle to change their material and legal positions (Decade 1992). In sum, women's income earning responsibilities toward their families, in addition to the fact that they are more trusted with money, combined with women's child-rearing responsibilities, and a huge demand for prepared food leads many Thai women to open food shops.

Food Establishments in Bangkok

In her MA thesis, Bhavivarn (1993) describes the small businesses selling cooked food in the distinctive riverside market at Tha Prachan (Moon Pier) near Thammasat University. She notes that places selling Thai food were generally run by women whom she viewed as knowledgeable and skilled agents specializing in producing a range of ordinary as well as unusual Thai foods.[6] Thais, she notes, traditionally view this type of occupation as women's work. Shopkeepers tended to be longstanding figures in the market culture of Tha Prachan. *Hab re* and *paeng loy* vendors tend to come from outside the district and do not consider themselves part of the community. She also describes how made-to-order and take-out food is now in greater demand for nearby university employees and students.

As far as food shops are concerned, daughters and sons of vendors are not interested in taking over their mother's (and sometimes father's) businesses (Bhavivarn 1993: 125). This is a serious problem and will likely lead to the decline of small food shops in Tha Prachan. Bhavivarn noted the encroachment of Thai-owned fast-food chains and convenience stores such as "7–11" as well as foreign food.

Naruemol and Oudin's study of "restaurants" as part of a larger study of the informal sector in Bangkok provides detailed information about the operations, income-levels, and concerns of small food-shop owners. They found that three quarters of the "restaurant" owners surveyed were women.[7] Their average age was 39, relatively older than the entrepreneurs in other domains of the "informal sector." The average number of employees in restaurants was 0.9. In other words, entrepreneurs tended to be self-employed and worked on their own or with one other person. Only 16% of businesses selling food had employees.

Typology of Eating Places

Eating establishments in Bangkok can be distinguished on the basis of size (floor area or number of seating places), number of employees, type of food sold or according to the linguistic categories used by Thais to speak of food shops and restaurants. I prefer the latter method but also deal with the other criteria in this section and the following parts of the chapter. Other typologies certainly exist and are possible (Pranom 1993).

It is clear when examining Table 5.1 that small food shops with one to four employees form the majority of cooked-food enterprises in Thailand. They form 70% of all establishments in the country and 67% in the Bangkok metropolis.

Table 5.1 Number of Eating and Drinking Establishments by Location and Number of Employees, Thailand 1990

Number of Employees	Bangkok Metropolis	Five Provinces around Bangkok	All-Thailand
1–4	4,387	393	11,808
5–9	930	115	2,648
10–19	625	53	1,417
20–49	426	35	815
50–99	111	6	150
100–299	41	2	53
300–499	4	0	4
All establishments	6,524	604	16,895

Source: Thailand Ministry of Labor: Labor Force Survey, 1990

The second largest category of restaurants, those having 5–9 employees, form only 16% and 14% of all establishments in the country and Greater Bangkok, respectively. At the other end of the spectrum, mega-restaurants with more than 300 employees are limited to the primary city, Bangkok, where there were only four as of the early 1990s. The number of mega-restaurants has certainly increased since.

The smallest and most ubiquitous food establishments of Bangkok and the rest of Thailand are by no means uniform, as argued previously. In addition to the locational, ethnic, and economic differentiations previously identified, the Thai language can be a tool for defining how Thais themselves typologize food shops.

Stalls, known in Thai as *paeng loy*, are defined as eating establishments located outside a fixed building, such as on a sidewalk or in a lane. A stall usually has tables and chairs, set up at the beginning of the selling period and taken down and put away at night. Quite often, a stall will include a pushcart—in addition to tables, chairs, and other furniture—as part of its basic equipment.

Pushcarts, or *rot khen*, are a crucial piece of equipment that are either part of a stall or exist independently to serve take-out customers only. Vendors who operate pushcarts are at times itinerant, but, more often, set up at a fixed location every day. Sometimes a number of stalls will group together in one place and share tables and chairs creating an outdoor, informal food center. McGee referred to this as a bazaar-type agglomeration, a variation of which is the night-market (McGee 1973: 84–85). Smart writes: "Of all the different types of hawking agglomerations, the night markets or night bazaars are the most colorful. There is always an air of festivity at these night-markets, also known as the "poor man's nightclub" (*ping mun ye jung wooi* in Cantonese. (Smart 1989: 49)

There are several lively night markets in the VMA where the sale of prepared food in street restaurants plays a dominant role (see Fig. 5.1). When a pushcart has tables and chairs it becomes a stall and can therefore be considered a small food shop.

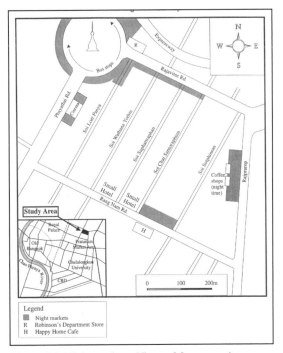

Figure 5.1 Night-markets, Victory Monument Area

Likewise, *pheung*, is a term referring to an awning-covered or loosely built semi-permanent structure. It is a type of stall with a distinctive design, sometimes including features of other establishments such as a pushcart. *Pheung* are most often located on vacant lots where they are not required to set up completely and set down the food shop every day or night. As such, they usually squat on someone else's property, with or without the owner's consent. Establishments such as this were referred to by one scholar as "interim land-use restaurants" (Archer 1992).

Shophouses (*deuk taow*) are distinctive features of cities with a strong Chinese influence such as Bangkok. These two- to five-storey structures typically have a business located on the ground floor and housing for the merchants on the upper levels. There are many variations on the use of floor space, however. Many older restaurants in Bangkok are located in shophouses. These structures are, for the most part, 50–60 years old in the VMA. Many are being cleared for the construction of higher density office or residential buildings. In Singapore, however, many old shophouses have been renovated in the past ten years as part of inner city revitalization schemes, a type of Asian gentrification. This renovation trend may be forthcoming in Bangkok but is not yet evident in the study site.

Food shops in apartment buildings or in food-centres are examples of the newer additions to Bangkok's foodscape, as previously outlined. Shops either have facilities for customers to eat inside the restaurant, or outside "café style," while the vendors sleep inside the premises, or the "restaurant" may be strictly for take-out or phone in/delivery. As explained in Chapter 4, most rental apartments, rooms for the most part, lack proper cooking facilities stimulating demand for prepared food. Figures 5.2 and 5.3 reproduce a floor plan and menu from an apartment food shop.

A franchise is an enterprise with a recognized brand name such as KFC or the local "Isaan Classic," which closed in the late 1990s. Strictly speaking, a franchise is an operation whereby the owner pays for rights to use a trade name and agrees to employ standardized production techniques. I use the term to refer to established chain restaurants regardless whether the individual operation is a franchise outlet or a part of a centrally owned chain. In the case of KFC, some locations are franchized to a third party, whereas others are owned directly by either the Central Group or Charoen Pokhpand, which divide up the franchise rights.

Finally, *pattakarn*, are expensive restaurants with formal menus, full service, and decorated, comfortable surroundings. The term refers to establishments that specialize in catering to "grander occasions." Many of these places have conveniences such

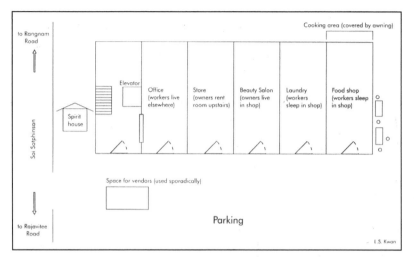

Figure 5.2 Floor Plan, Ground Floor: Tara Apartment

Breakfast	Price in Baht
Coffee, Soft boiled egg	20
Set breakfast (coffee, fried egg, bread)	25
Large breakfast (coffee, fried egg, sausage, jam)	45
Bread, Canned orange juice	20
Rice porridge with chicken or pork	20
Rice porridge with prawns or squid	25
Chok moo with egg	25
One dish meals	
Fried rice with salty beef and fried egg	25
Rice with scrambled egg and chopped pork	20
Rice *khlukapii*	25
Fried rice with *namprik langreua*	25
Fried rice with pork or chicken	20
Fried rice with catfish	20
Khun Siang's fried rice	25
Fried rice with *naem* sausage	20
Fried rice with basil and chicken, pork or beef	20
Fried rice with basil with prawn or squid	25
Fried rice *poh kaek*	25
Spicy stir fry *pa laaw* with rice	25
Spicy fried rice with fresh pork, chicken or beef	20
Rice with rad beef and oyster sauce	20
Fried Rice with crab or prawn	25

Figure 5.3 Menu from Tara Apartment Food Shop, 1993

as air-conditioning, a large staff, and a division of labor for employees. Examples of *pattakarn* are discussed throughout this book. It is not linguistically improper to refer to grand establishments as *raan ahaan*, but, for the sake of clarity, they will be called *pattakarn*.

The typology described is by no means exhaustive, and categories used are certainly not discrete. There is often overlap and confusion when it comes to defining the nature of a specific enterprise. These categories are used in the quantitative survey analysed below are presented in order to clarify the meaning of terms rather than present the entire range of eating establishments available in Thai society.

Large vs. Small Establishments

Department of Labor statistics indicate that as an eating establishment, or restaurant becomes larger and more lucrative, men become involved in greater proportions (Table 5.2).[8] In the smallest food shops, with one to four employees, women account for 83% of employees whereas in those with more than ten employees, women account for only 51–58% of all workers.

A closer examination reveals that a gender division of labor emerges in the larger establishments whereby men or boys, and sometimes girls, work as waiters and women work as cooks, or, in expensive establishments as hostesses and entertainers. Two good examples are Bussaracum [Fig. 5.4][9] and Than Ying, located in the new World Trade Center. Note that these restaurants specialize in Thai cuisine. Large, expensive Chinese restaurants, like their smaller, more humble counterparts, tend to employ men as chefs and cooks.

An extreme example of the specialized role of women in food-establishments are the "no hands" restaurants where young women employees spoon- and hand-feed adult male customers. This introduces the relationship between the commercial sex industry and Bangkok's restaurant sector.

"Respectable" Thai women (*phuying dii*, "good women") do not participate in "bar culture" and other activities associated with the consumption of alcohol as this is relegated to prostitutes (*phuying mai dii*, "bad women"; see Mills 1990). I comment on these night-time institutions based on information gleaned from discussions with Thai urbanites and instances of participant-observation. A first example is the contrast provided by lunchtime versus evening dining experiences in one of the Victory Monument's former Isaan entertainment restaurants.[10]

**Table 5.2 Number of Employees in Eating/Drinking Establishments
by Sex and Size of Establishment, Bangkok Metropolis**

Number of employees	Female employees	Male employees
1–4	7,319 (83%)	1,542
5–9	3,858 (64%)	2,131
10–19	4,741 (57%)	3,552
20–49	7,016 (58%)	5,159
50–99	3,676 (52%)	3,353
100–299	2,975 (51%)	2,916
300–499	736 (56%)	586
Total	30,321 (61%)	19,239

Source: Thailand Ministry of Labor: Labor Force Survey, 1990

Figure 5.4 Bussaracum Restaurant Serves Food in the "Royal Style"

Field Notes 5.1: Friday, 9 October 1992: Lunch

We went to an air-conditioned place across the street from Robinson's. It was a large restaurant with space for a band. I think the owners are from Isaan because the food is northeastern and the waitresses are dressed in a style reminiscent of the region. It was good. A bit more expensive than on the street. A group of Thai men behind us were consuming massive quantities of beer with their meal. Their faces were very red! I'd like to return there in the evening when there's music.

Field Notes 5.2: Wednesday, 21 October 1992: Dinner

Jean, Meera, and Lekha arrived around 7 p.m. We went to eat at the Isaan restaurant across from Robinson's. It was noisy. There was a band playing horrible music, and the drunken male customers were talking loudly and singing terrible karaoke. The food wasn't extraordinary.

This vignette describes encounters between our international group and a "modernized" provincial culture, replete with state-of-the-art sound systems. We also entered a male space, one oriented toward consumption of whiskey and mind-numbingly loud entertainment. The establishment was not the preferred haunt of "good" women but neither was it a place, such as a *café*, featuring young women entertaining male customers.

Rangnam Road (Fig. 5.5), a part of the research site, is well known for its *cafés*, for Thais a specific type of establishment usually featuring young women singers dressed in flashy (usually gaudy) costumes. Women act as "hostesses" or "partners." These types of venues are the descendants of "hostess bars" that made their appearance in Thailand several decades ago:[11]

> Still another manifestation of the Thai way is found in cabaret life. In Singapore the Chinese have organized cabarets so that there is no dancing with the taxi dance-girls without tickets, and the whole procedure is well organized to give a steady financial profit to the management. Bangkok also has cabarets—but no manager has succeeded in running one Singapore-style. Each girl (sic) comes or does not come on a given night as she pleases; she may or may not require a guest to buy a dance ticket; and if she goes home with him afterward she may or may not be mercenary about it, depending on how she feels. A man from Singapore with some experience in cabaret management commented unfavorably to me on the casual way in which these things are done in Bangkok. Cabarets are, of course, an innovation in Bangkok

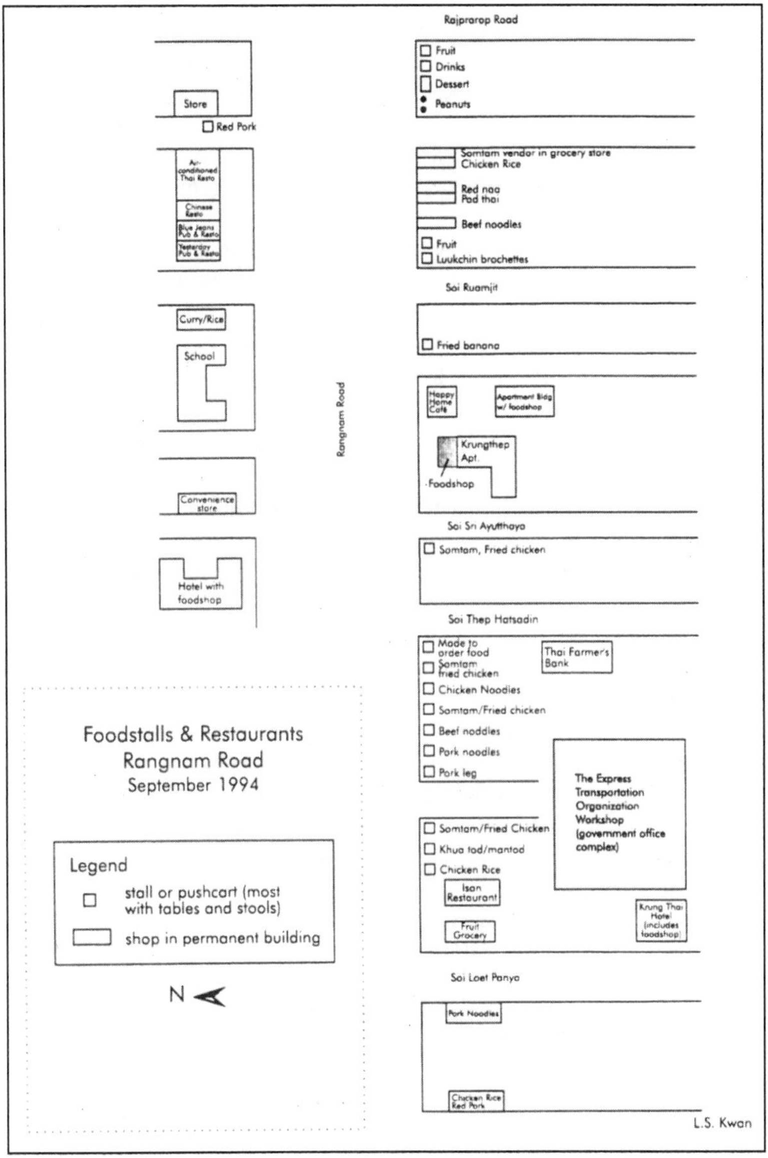

Figure 5.5 Food Stalls and Restaurants, Rangnam Road

from the West, but the permissive behavior pattern of managers and the individual behavior of the girls are characteristically Thai. Even if the manager is Chinese or European he finds it necessary to adjust his management to the Thai way. (Embree 1950: 8)

In a Thai-style "café," the customers give garlands of flowers pinned with money (500 Bt and up) to the singers of their choice in return for their company after the solo.

In transvestite cabarets and gay bars, "partners" are usually young men who may or may not cross-dress (see Field notes 5.2). Hosts/hostesses are required to entertain (mostly Thai male) customers by providing them with pleasant conversation, singing, and perhaps dancing. Mostly their function is to encourage customers to buy expensive alcoholic drinks for themselves and their partners.[12] Cafés are a fascinating aspect of Bangkok's foodscape and encompass very specific gender relations related to the city's commercial sex industry.

Field Notes 5.3: Two Cafés in Bangkok

Wednesday, 14 October 1992: We decided to go to the little drag cabaret on Rajprarop Road.[13] The shows were scheduled to start at 11 p.m. and 1 a.m. We arrived about 10–15 minutes before the 11 o'clock performance. We were the only non-Thais in the audience. A large bottle of Thai beer was 200 baht . . . very expensive. 95% of the customers were young men. There were young male "waiters" [partners] wearing red jackets, small bow-ties and black trousers—normally they sat with the customers (but not us). Very soon after we entered a cross-dresser who looked *Luuk Kreung*—very beautiful and nice (sincere)—came to speak to us in English (she spoke very well). It appears she was a customer who knew the staff. She said that we could call on her if we needed anything. She was dressed like a casual "chic" young woman in white trousers and a blouse . . . not too much make-up either. The show was very good—choreographed with many people (mostly lip-sync). Except there was one act consisting of two overweight guys dressed (mockingly) like women from Isaan. . . It was disgusting. They wore skirts under which they had pinned fake male genitals (flashed on occasion). . . Implying that the women they portrayed were really men. They harassed us in various ways as the "odd trio" in the audience. Apparently there were three different shows. We left after the first. During the break, the "waiter-boys" danced in couples—each did the same slow "jive" routine.

Thursday, 29 October 1992: We drove around and went into this place near the Democracy Monument, which we thought was called "Jazz Club" but it was actually

"Lolita's." There were young Thai women singing popular Thai songs with a band. People would give them garlands with two 500 baht notes pinned on to show appreciation. *Ajaan* "P" told me that these were men who wanted the singers to go and sit with them after. He also said the Thai bars hire young women—called "partners"—to chat with customers and make sure they have a good time. They charge by the hour, and the client must buy drinks and food for the partner. . . Apparently, a comedy show and drag act were scheduled for later on (1 a.m.), but we couldn't stay so late. The drag act was a lip-sync and a special show from Pattaya where that sort of entertainment is very popular. *Ajaan* "P" said that all sorts of people go to see drag shows, women, children, couples, etc. It's a very popular form of entertainment in Thailand. On the way out we noticed that the lounge upstairs had an Elvis impersonation show that evening.

The first passage describing the transvestite cabaret gives yet another example of the subordination of *khon Isaan* by mainstream Central Thai society. It is a type of "symbolic violence," drawing from Bourdieu and a form of cultural imperialism (Chai-anan 1991). The moments described point to the socially constructed nature of gender as something that is, above all else, "performed" (Butler 1990). This is not specific to Thai society but is a generalized trans-cultural process. Rather than concluding from this passage that masculinity is somehow "ambiguous" in Thai society, it alludes to the ambiguity of both masculinity and femininity ideologically and in practice (Keyes 1986).

The second passage puts forth examples of interaction between the sexes as feminized and masculinized individuals. Here, economic relations are interwoven with gender relations in that men buy the time of aestheticized women. The widespread existence of "partners" points to the sexual and spatial unavailability of mainstream Thai women to men. "Respectable" women do not usually frequent the types of places described in the vignette for fear of being construed as bold, and with their reputations therefore sullied (Kamolrat 1994; Mills 1990). Food, but especially alcohol, sets the stage for the encounters and mediates the relationship. The first image of the drag cabaret gets re-played in the second scene where it becomes clear that cross-dressing, rather than being relegated to the margins of society, is something in which mainstream Thais participate mostly as spectators. Male cross-dressers are known as "women of the second type" (*phuying prapet song*) (*Bangkok Post* 1994). In the West, drag cabaret is an underground phenomenon. Preoccupation with surface appearances and aesthetic images again comes to the fore in representing experiences of gender in Thai society.

Women in the larger establishments, which serve a latent leisure function (as well as sites of the business lunch or dinner), are being more firmly recast as nurturers and pleasure-giving objects and that their historical capacity as entrepreneurs is being overlooked. However, there are a number of very prominent Thai women in the restaurant business, for example, Patara Sila-On, owner of the successful "S&P" chain and also the wife of a prominent general. A Thai-Philippina owns the chain "Little Home Bakery." Several others could be named. This is in keeping with the generally high proportion of Thai women in managerial roles in business, government, and academe compared to their counterparts in other parts of the world including North America and Europe (see Licuanan 1992: 199).

It is difficult to generalize about women in the food-system owing to their complex positions in the restaurant and food shop sector. Women tend to dominate micro-, small, and medium enterprises yet are not absent from the upper echelons of the restaurant industry where they often play leadership roles. Likewise, Thai men's greater involvement in the restaurant sector, particularly in large, lucrative eating establishments might superficially appear to be a shift from the ascetic ideals of masculinity outlined by anthropologists Keyes (1984, 1986) and Kirsch (1982, 1985). Thai men, as opposed to Chinese or Sino-Thai men have not, until relatively recently, played important roles in commerce presumably due to the low status of such "worldly" occupations in the Theravada Buddhist value system (see Khin 1980). Keyes' position is that middle-class culture in Thailand is largely Sino-Thai in character (Keyes 1995), in other words, a cultural hybrid.

Further scrutiny suggests that the changing situation of masculinity can be interpreted as contradictory whereby the law of Karma stipulates that one is born into a higher station in subsequent lives following acts of merit and *vice versa*. Theravada Buddhism's asceticism is not absolute, and material wealth can even be admired in certain circumstances. Walker's thesis (1991) indicates clearly the desire of middle-class Thais to acquire the trappings of aristocracy, and this could, in fact be related to a Buddhist influence rather than solely to "materialism" and "Westernization." Kirsch's argument on the links between Buddhism and the Thai culture of gender may need to be revisited yet again.

Distribution of Eating Establishments

Table 5.1 indicates that small food shops with one to four employees are the most ubiquitous eating establishments in Bangkok and the five surrounding provinces of the Extended Bangkok Metropolitan Region (EBMR) where they represent

65–67% of total restaurants. The statistics likely exclude the smallest and least formal food shops, which can easily escape government canvassers. Realistically, then, the proportion of small food shops is certainly much higher than 65–67% of total eating establishments.

Figures 5.6 and 5.7 are maps depicting the percent distribution of small food shops with one to four employees within the EBMR. Concentrations of 80% or more are

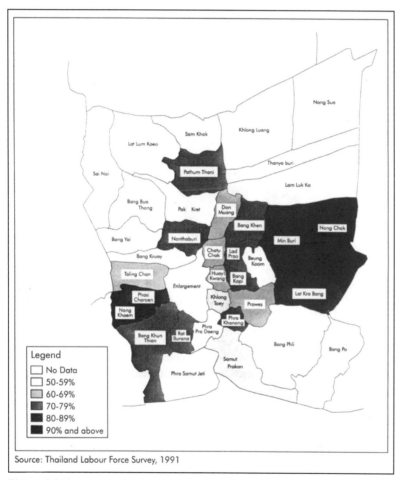

Source: Thailand Labour Force Survey, 1991

Figure 5.6 Percentage of Eating Establishments with 1–4 Employees: I

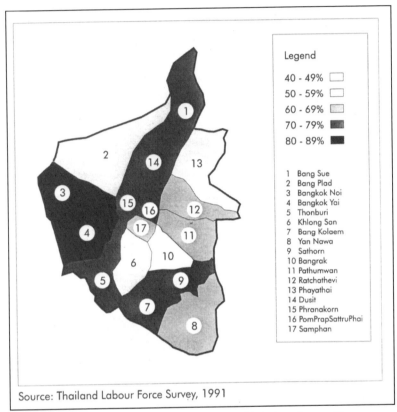

Figure 5.7 Percentage of Eating Establishments with 1–4 employees: II

found in the districts of Bangkok Noi, Bangkok Yai, Min Buri, Lat Kra Bang, Phasi Charoen, Nong Khaem, and Nong Chok. These are generally wealthier suburban areas of the city where middle-class housing estates have been constructed over the past twenty years. The findings run contrary to my assumptions that the oldest, central quarters of the city would have the highest proportion of small food shops compared to larger establishments. For example, the infamous slum of Klong Toey located near the port has one of the lowest relative concentrations of small food shops. As noted by de Vandeler (1990), it may be that the poorest families in Bangkok cannot afford to purchase prepared food and therefore do most of their cooking themselves.

Older central parts of the city have a greater diversity of food shop types, perhaps in keeping with the diverse land use compared to large tracks of lands converted to standardized housing estates in the suburbs. The report of the 1990 Household Socio-Economic Survey indicates that 18.6% of all households in Greater Bangkok do not cook at home. More recent statistics related to public eating are cited in the concluding chapter.

Table 5.3 indicates the percentage of total households that do *not* cook according to household type, as revealed in the 1990 Household Socio-economic Survey. Prefatory remarks in the survey explain (rather unclearly) that worker categories were divided into sub-classes. In the case of own account workers this resulted in three categories: professional, technical, and administrative enterprises.

Table 5.3 Households Where no Cooking is Done

Farm Operators	Owning Land 5.8%
	Renting Land --
Own-Account/Non-Farm	Entrepreneurs[a] 12.5%
	Professional[b] 55.6%
Employees	Professional 10.9%
	Farm workers 1.9%
	General workers 39.3%
	Clerical 22.3%
	Production workers 22.2%
Economically Inactive	Economically inactive 16.6%

[a] This category is defined as "Entrepreneurs, Trade and Industry" and is the occupation of the household head (as defined by family members).
[b] "Own account" refers to those who operate enterprises on their own and hired no employees.
Source: National Statistical Office, Office of the Prime Minister, 1994, Report of the 1990 Household Socio-Economic Survey: Bangkok metropolis, Nonthaburi, Pathum Thani, and Samut Prakhan

Own-account entrepreneurs in trade and industry report not doing any cooking at all at an astounding rate of 55.6%. Employees in all categories are the second most highly represented occupational groups that do not cook. Even the "economically inactive," which includes "housewives,"[14] students, and others report that 16.5% *never* cook at home. Finally, it is clear that the few farmers remaining within Greater

Bangkok continue to cook at home with only 5.8% reporting that they do not cook for themselves.

Results of the Quantitative Survey

The remainder of this chapter summarizes the results of the quantitative survey of 58 food shops in the VMA. The findings echo other research on the prepared food delivery system. The case study site therefore resembles the rest of Thailand with respect to the socio-economic characteristics of cooked-food vendors and restaurant owners.

Socio-Demographic Characteristics

Consistent with results of other studies outlined in this chapter, two-thirds of the cooked-food sellers in the study area are women. I suspect that my omission of night stalls and establishments specializing in the sale of alcohol excluded more male respondents. Likewise, most informants are individuals between the ages of 26 and 44 with an average age of 39 (median and modal age is 30) (see Fig. 5.8). In total, 69% of the informants reported being married and are assisted on a volunteer basis by immediate family members (38%) or, less frequently, by relatives from the extended family (21%).[15] The remainder either have employees (41.4%) or report working alone. There is sometimes a combination of the two phenomena with both paid employees and volunteer helpers. Indeed, the conceptual distinction between "helper" and "employee" is difficult to ascertain.

Household income

Half of respondents claimed to be the sole income earners in their households (52%), and performing solely this occupation (93%).[16] Nineteen percent responded that another family member worked in trading as well (selling clothing, for example), and another group (21%) had households with another person working as a company employee or a civil servant.[17]

Length of time

Two patterns are visible when considering the length of time an establishment has been open. First, there are the long standing cooked-food sellers and small restaurant owners who have been in business ten or more years. The second group

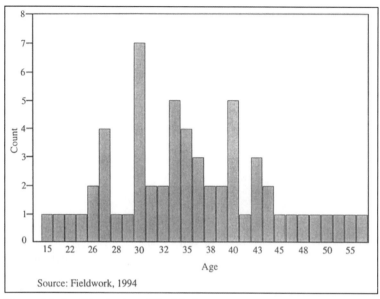

Source: Fieldwork, 1994

Figure 5.8 Age Distribution of Food Sellers

consists of those who have operated two years or less. Indeed, 9% of respondents reported opening less than half a year prior to the survey. One small food-shop owner was unable to answer our questions because we arrived for the survey on his opening day!

The mushrooming of cooked-food enterprises appears to be related to the real estate boom in the area, which created opportunities for vendors and small restaurant owners at the time of the field survey. Higher density construction of kitchenless apartments for young, single people has resulted in a higher resident population and thus has accentuated the demand for prepared food. On the other hand, as the next chapter explains, small food-shop owners were, at the same time, being displaced by massive real estate development in the mid-1990s.

Educational levels

Figure 5.9 represents the educational level of respondents. The majority (53%) of cooked-food sellers have some primary education.[18] Nineteen percent attended secondary school, with 21% of respondents having post-secondary training either

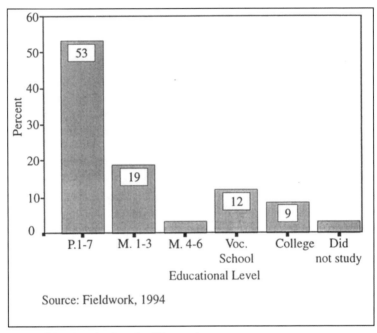

Figure 5.9 Education Levels of Respondents

at the college level or in a vocational program. This runs contrary to the findings of other studies. The main reason for the high level of education is due to my inclusion of indoor, "formal" restaurants such as KFC and The Noodle Garden complex. In these establishments, managers typically obtain a bachelor's degree or a diploma from a technical or business school. Results were also biased by family helpers, especially teenagers, who were sometimes interviewed. Generally speaking, the children of informants are better educated than their parents.

Place of birth

The majority of respondents were born in Bangkok (53.4%). In total, 34.2% were born in the provinces of Isaan with the remainder from southern and northern regions (6.9%).[19] Like migrant workers in other sectors of the economy such as construction, domestic employment, and light industry, people from Isaan migrate to the city in

116

order to sell prepared food. People from Isaan are the butt of ethnic jokes in Central Thailand and are stereotyped as stupid, unsophisticated, and even lazy. A discussion between a food vendor (Daeng) from Roi-Et Province in the northeast, one of my assistants, and myself illustrates these stereotypical views.

> *Daeng*: Many people from Isaan come to find jobs in Bangkok. People from Isaan are looked down upon. [We laugh amongst ourselves.]
> *Morn*: At first, many people think Isaan people are lazy.
> *Daeng*: Not lazy.
> *Gisèle*: Not lazy at all.
> *Daeng*: Northerners are lazy. They like comfort.
> *Gisèle*: Northerners? [Laughter.] What about Southerners?
> *Daeng*: Southerners are rich . . . good economic status. Southerners don't work very hard.

Although Daeng is a victim of prejudice against Northeasterners, she also perpetuates generalizations about Thais from other regions. People from Isaan form Thailand's largest ethnic minority and are systematically discriminated against and negatively stereotyped by mainstream society. They and their region are considered culturally and economically "backward," although their status is improving somewhat (Cohen 1991). Nevertheless, jokes are continually made about their supposedly "vulgar" ways, darker skin (considered unattractive), and "lesser intelligence." *Khon Isaan* form the underclass in Bangkok society partly because of this prejudice.[20]

Shop Types and Food Specialties

A breakdown of shop types is found in Table 5.4.[21] The majority of respondents own or are employed in establishments located in a shophouse (*deuk taow*) (n = 18), or own pushcarts (*rot khen*) (n = 15), stalls (*paeng loy*) (n = 8), food shops located in apartments (n = 6), or those located in food centers (n = 5).[22]

"Other" types of shops include stalls using awnings (*pheung*) (n = 3), one food shop in a hotel, one expensive restaurant (*pattakarn*) and two franchises (KFC and Noodle Garden). Twelve percent (n = 7) of the establishments studied have branches at other locations or the proprietor owns other restaurants. These branches are examples of medium-scale Thai businesses.

Distinctions between these types of enterprises are sometimes difficult to ascertain for a shophouse restaurant may actually contain a pushcart and a stall may also have a pushcart as part of its equipment. Classification involves deciding which feature is to be given precedence. Through consultations with Napat Sirisambhand-Gordon, author of a previous study on Thai food establishments, and research assistants, it was found that the above categories coincided with Thai categorizations of eating-places.

Table 5.4 Shop Types, Victory Monument Area, 1994

Shop Type	%
Shophouse	31.0
Pushcart	25.9
Stall	13.8
Food shop in apartment	10.3
Food shop in food center	8.6
Other	10.3

Source: Field Survey 1994

Most enterprises specialize in the sale of certain types of food. The largest category is that of noodle shops (18 cases),[23] which are either located in shophouses (n = 8), or on the street in stalls (n = 5), or sold in hotels, food centers, or apartment food shops (n = 5). Noodles are especially popular at lunchtime with office workers and students. There are several varieties of noodle dishes both in soup and stir-fried. According to the survey, noodle shops are no longer the exclusive domain of the Sino-Thai. Many are run by people born in Isaan who are ethnically Lao.

The second major group sell "made-to-order" food (*ahaan tam sang*), that includes specialties such as fried rice (*khao pad*), fried noodle dishes (*pad si ieuw, kwayteow latna*), varieties of salads (*yam*), fried eggs and omelettes (*khay dao, khay jieaw*), and borrow highly popular additions to the Thai menu such as Thai-style *sukiyaki*.[24] Food "made to order" is therefore prepared according to the specifications of the customer and served piping hot. According to some, *tam sang* is becoming the preferred fast food of the area.

Wira: Thai people don't like food like this. . . They prefer fried dishes.
Wira and Goy: Very Hot.

118

Gisèle: *Tam sang*.
Wira: We've lost a lot of customers because they go to the *tam sang*.

Wira and Goy, a husband and wife team managing a student residence and food center, are commenting on the decline in popularity of lukewarm, pre-prepared food such as curries, soups, and vegetable dishes. According to Walker, however, Thais are not fussy about food temperature and are willing to eat lukewarm or even cold food.[25] My observations coincide with Walker's given the popularity of room-temperature curries. This is rooted in the ways in which meal taking is informal and less ritualized than in other cultural traditions:

> Because a Thai cook knows that while the food may be ready at a certain time, not everybody will be there to eat it. The husband might be in the bathroom, the wife talking on the phone, the children watching television, unlike the Chinese who seat everybody at the table and then bring the food. . . Thai food can be eaten whenever you're ready. (Walker 1991 citing informant "PN," 105)

Middle-class Thais exhibit cultural traits borrowed from Chinese foodways. The more disciplined Chinese eating tradition leads to greater degrees of commensality. The general situation in Bangkok is flexible, and families may or may not eat together at the same time depending on circumstances or family custom.[26] The informal Thai meal system may be a factor explaining the popularity of purchasing prepared foods and is also related to the ways in which Thais perceive and use domestic space flexibly (see Walker 1995).

Curries and rice (*khao gaeng*) are the third most important type of food sold in the VMA. Curry/rice shopkeepers prepare dishes in the morning and place the curries, soups, and vegetable dishes in large aluminium pots on a table for sale throughout the day. Customers look and see what is available and choose items. If they are friendly with the shopowner, they may serve themselves. This is also the case with shops specializing in other types of food, such as made-to-order dishes. I would often enter Daeng's shop, make my own *som tam*, serve it to myself in a dish, rinse the dish, and then place the money owed in the small basket on the counter. Daeng teasingly referred to this as "self-service"!

Food from Isaan is a very important type of food sold in the neighborhood. Of the shops enumerated, 12.1% specialize in this type of food, which includes green papaya salad (*som tam*), various other salads with ground meat, herbs, and spices (*lab*), grilled chicken (*gai yang*), and the ubiquitous "sticky rice" (*khao niew*) of the

Northeast and Laos. The range of establishments serving Isaan food span from the mobile vendor with a shoulder pole and baskets (*hab re*) catering to construction workers and passers-by to the large restaurants on Rangnam Road. The latter are often decorated with small white lights and are open late at night serving "whisky" to male office workers in the evening. The combination of meat, alcohol, and male patrons lends a particularly ludic quality to these restaurants (Formoso 1993: 99). Perhaps this is because the food served, consisting of meat dishes for the most part, is symbolically related both to masculinity and festival food (Keyes 1996). The last Friday of each month, immediately after pay day, is the most popular time for many Thai men to frequent restaurants as a group.

Field Notes 5.4: Isaan "Evening" Restaurants

Wednesday, 14 October 1992: We went for dinner in a super Isaan restaurant on Rangnam Road, close to my place. It got very busy about an hour after we arrived. . . There was a superb ambience. On that end of Rangnam there are plenty of interesting food shops/restaurants that are frequented mostly in the evening. They are "open air" and are decorated with strings of little white lights. Typically, the serving staff consists of young women (mid- to late teens) dressed in Isaan costumes (baggy, indigo, pyjama-type outfits).

Friday, 30 September 1994: I invited a group from the Chulalongkorn University Social Research Institute (CUSRI) for dinner at *Saap Ilie Resto* on Rangnam. It was Friday and the end of the month (i.e., payday). The place was jam-packed with men eating and drinking "whisky" sitting at long tables. There were very few women present. They were very loud. Two of the people serving were obvious transvestites (men dressed as women). We ordered a lot of sticky rice, *som tam*, *gai yang*, *lap gai*, and *plaa tod mamuang*. It was very inexpensive.

The behavior of patrons exhibited in these establishments contrasts the sober, polite, and soft-spoken middle-class Thai male idealized in romantic movies, television shows, and encountered routinely in Bangkok. Instead, male customers are drunk, loud, and lewd.

In 8.6% of cases surveyed, Chinese specialties such as chicken rice (*khaaw man gai*),[27] pork leg, and barbecued red pork (both with rice) are the house specialties. Other categories of food (6.9%) include "foreign" food, deep fried chicken, sweets, grilled meat or fish-ball brochettes (*luuk chin ping*) and stalls selling drinks only.

The category marked "other" would include other types of foods such as *khao tom* (rice porridge) and a popular breakfast food of Chinese origin also referred to as *jok* (a Chinese term), as well as Chinese "doughnuts" also eaten in the early morning. Other specialities in this category would include sweets of various kinds as well as fruit.

Clientele and Daily Selling Patterns

Half of the respondents estimate receiving 50–100 customers per day and a third (31%) serve more than 100. For the vast majority, customers come at lunchtime between 11:00 and 14:00 (72%). By cross-tabulating food type and time of day, it is evident that noodles are the most popular lunchtime food. The majority of curry/rice shops and establishments selling food made-to-order also report 11 a.m. to 2 p.m. as their peak selling time. In general, public eating is a lunchtime phenomenon though a study of night-stalls and restaurants might reveal a different pattern. I am told, however, that Thais who have kitchens still tend to eat their evening meals at home whenever possible.

Locational Patterns

Others studying hawkers and shophouse restaurant owners have observed that people in these occupations tend to live close to their workplace. Indeed, 48% of the interviewees lived adjacent to their shops. In some cases, cooked-food sellers actually live in their shops and simply roll out a mat for sleeping. Other small shopkeepers, such as hairdressers, often do the same. Most of those who live adjacent to their businesses dwell in shophouses (n = 14). Seven stall and pushcart owners lived near their shops, and all of the apartment food-shop owners resided in their workplace. Three respondents from a hotel, food center, and expensive restaurant also lived adjacent to their workplaces. Many stall owners also (n = 6) dwelt in the VMA and therefore walked to their work avoiding the city's legendary traffic jams. The inexpensive area of Asoke-Din Daeng-Huay Kwang, a short bus or *tuk-tuk* ride to the VMA, was the second most popular place of residence for micro-entrepreneurs. The others travel fairly long distances to reach their businesses. They either used motorcycles or public transit to reach their shops.

The contiguousness of home and workplace has been remarked as something beneficial as it enables people to work more efficiently and combine domestic tasks with income-earning activities. On the other hand, as will be seen in Chapter 6, the integration of home and workplace can also make some people feel trapped, especially women who tend to have greater domestic responsibilities.

Initially, I speculated that women micro-entrepreneurs in the prepared-food sector were ghettoized in the lanes or *sois* in small, home-based food shops as opposed to the main thoroughfares where men would supposedly have a greater presence. This is the case in certain Indonesian cities (Klopfer 1993: 301; Murray 1991: 39). After having cross-tabulated sex of informant with location, however, this does not appear to be the situation in the study site (Fig. 5.10).

Women were the majority of business owners at all locations (main streets, minor streets, lanes, and a housing project under re-development). Proportionately, women consistently accounted for between 58% to 77% of entrepreneurs in all locations. Since I suspect that the Labor Force Survey under-enumerated the number of food shops in the *sois*, which are nearly always owned/operated by women, the proportion of women micro-entrepreneurs (82%) should likely be even higher in government data.

On the formal/informal axis, women dominated all types of enterprises, even at the helm of larger, more formalized establishments in the VMA. Women are the

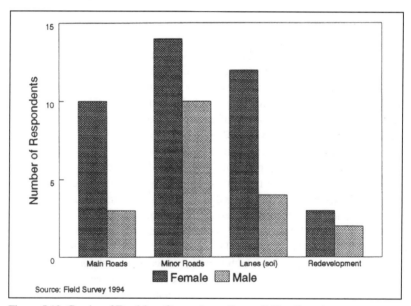

Figure 5.10 Gender of Foodshop Owner According to Selling Location

majority of managers (or "head of food sector") as well as renters of spaces in the Rattana Food Center. Women employees and family helpers also outnumbered their male counterparts.

Survey Conclusions

The significance of the urban/rural divide for gender relations is one of the main points that emerge from the survey. Rural gender relations reflect more egalitarian traditions where femininity and masculinity are generally complementary. Urban Thailand, unfortunately, is associated with asymmetrical gender relations where women are more subordinated. This is reflected in the practice of urban men taking "minor wives," frequenting prostitutes, drinking, and spending money irresponsibly. Thai urban middle-class women, in some ways, are more subordinated than their rural sisters due to the male behavior described above and the more conservative gender ideologies borrowed from India and China that seclude women in the home.

The combinations and permutations of gender according to domicile (urban or rural), class, ethnicity, education, and age result in a rather contradictory position for women in Thai society where they are both independent, mobile money-earners and subordinated within the social system. These characterizations are, nevertheless, abstractions, and Thai women and men, in reality, are presented with a range of ideological and practical options for their identities and behaviors.

The results of the quantitative survey in the VMA resemble the findings of other researchers with respect to the socio-economic characteristics of cooked-food sellers. One exception, however, is the high level of education of small-scale food vendors due to the inclusion of formalized eating establishments. Another interesting contribution of the survey is the flexible ethnic differentiation of micro-entrepreneurs with respect to food type, particularly noodles. Whereas noodle shops were traditionally a Chinese domain, many noodle vendors in the VMA, originally from Isaan, are ethnically Lao.

Chapter 6

Lives and Voices of Food-shop Owners

This chapter traces the life histories and daily activities of food-shop owners who were interviewed in-depth. Self-employed micro-entrepreneurs are compared and contrasted with managers/owners and employees of larger establishments. I begin by profiling the thirteen informants interviewed at nine establishments. Observations on a tenth business, a food center, were made. Official permission to study the premises was denied, but the manager was briefly interviewed.

Profiles: Key Informants

The qualitatively interviewed informants fall loosely into two categories based on the nature of the business: micro-entrepreneurs, and owners or managers of more "formal" establishments. A firm definition of "formal" and "informal" is difficult and resembles the problems associated with identifying "traditional" and "modern" economic sectors. As a model, the "two-circuit" system is conceptualized as a continuum with informal or traditional enterprises and formal sector activities at opposite ends and helps sort out the types of eating establishments found in the Thai food-system.

The conceptual divide between putative formal and informal sectors has been sharply criticized as a spurious dichotomy based on Western systems of national accounts (Laquian 1993). Many activities do not conform to the two "sectors." Boundaries are fuzzy and examples of semi-formal or informal activities abound. Furthermore, there are links between the two circuits (Salih et al. 1988).

Like the public/private sphere framework, the informal/formal distinction is a useful conceptual tool for grouping types of food shops and restaurants under study. I use this division metaphorically, as a type of shorthand, because of general distinctions between the two types of food enterprises. The purpose of using this conceptual framework is to point out the many examples of businesses that are not only roughly formal or informal but also at some point between the two poles. McGee and Yeung proposed semi-formal/informal enterprises as a salient feature of the Southeast Asian urban "bazaar" economy in the 1970s: "Between these two polar types many Southeast Asian cities have intermediate forms of economic organization that are owned and operated largely by local Chinese or Indians" (1977: 20). One of their conclusions was that the "traditional and modern sectors make conflicting demands on urban space" (1977: 20). The study did not, however, focus on the types of spatial demands made by hybrid enterprises. The discussion of food centers and other intermediate forms of eating establishments here contributes to this discussion.

"Micro-enterprise" refers to a business generally operated by one or two people where owners/operators fall into the category of the self-employed. Micro-enterprises are generally "informal" as they are more often than not unregistered and do not pay taxes or follow regulations specified by the local state. Many also depend to a large extent on unpaid family labor. Sethuraman provides the standard definition of the informal sector characterized by ease of entry, small-enterprises, status not recognized by the state, and dependence on family labor among other factors (Sethuraman 1981).[1]

"Informal" Food Establishments

Daeng and Ying's Shop

Aunt Ying, 49 years old, is originally from Isaan where her family is engaged in farming. She never married but raised one of her nieces, Daeng, since babyhood. Ying moved to Bangkok in her early twenties when she was recruited to work as a maid for a Thai woman married to an Italian. Then, she had various positions as a cook and nanny for several other families, including a Thai aristocrat living on prestigious soi Ratchakruu. Through these occupations she learned how to cook a great variety of dishes.

Soon, however, it became clear that she could no longer support her extended family in the countryside with her meagre salary, so she opened a pushcart on the soi next to her employer's house and, with her patron's blessing, quit her job. Ying was forced to relocate following complaints from her former employer's daughter, who saw customers as having too great a view of the family property. Daeng, her adopted daughter and niece, began working as her assistant and they were fortunate to find a new location in a newly constructed building on the same *soi* where they have been since 1988. She and Daeng operate a food shop that sells curry and rice as well as stir-fried and other made-to-order dishes on a *soi* in the VMA. Ying's relatives and friends, who live nearby, come to help on a regular basis. Daeng's younger brother is enrolled in a local business college and tends to spend his sister's and aunt's hard-earned money in snooker halls rather than on his studies. Still, Ying continues to give him money, hoping he will use it for tuition as he always promises to do.

At the time of field research, Daeng was in her early 30s,[2] unmarried, and lived with Ying in a small room adjacent to the shop. The rent for their shop and sleeping-room is very expensive compared to competitors in the neighborhood. Ying and Daeng may now be forced to move because of the proposed re-development of their building into a high-rise apartment building. To make ends meet, Daeng has been working at a series of jobs as a cafeteria cook and helps Ying, in the evenings. Most recently, she was employed at the headquarters of the huge agri-food conglomerate, Charoen Pokphand. "I'm tired of working and discouraged. Sometimes I sit down and cry," Daeng confided. Her adoptive mother is having difficulty keeping up with the demands of the food shop as she suffers from diabetes, hypertension, and back-aches. "Some days, I don't want to sell. . . It's difficult," Ying laments, "I'm tired. After I wake up in the morning and open the shop, I ask the security guards [from the apartment next door] to help me carry the cooker and water." Daeng, though often depressed, still has hope for the future. She likes cooking and would like to own a shophouse restaurant one day.

Samrit and Lek's Chicken Noodle Soup Shop

Samrit and Lek, a young married couple, operate a stall selling chicken noodle soup on a busy street in the Victory Monument Area. At the time of the interview in late 1994, they had been operating their stall for a year already. Lek and her husband had tried operating a restaurant before, though unsuccessfully. They rented a shop in Bang Pho for 4,000 Bt per month but eventually gave up because they were not selling enough At the time, they sold noodles and had invested quite a bit of money in a pushcart, dishes, tables and chairs . . . a total of approximately 15–16,000 Bt obtained from their savings. "I lost more than 20,000 baht," lamented Samrit. "We couldn't sell; we were losing money. We changed our selling location just on time," he explained. Now, their sales are enough to build up their savings again.

Lek previously worked as a seamstress for three years in a factory in Din Daeng that fabricated clothing for export. Prior to that, she worked at various jobs including having to return to her home in Kalasin Province (Isaan) to help her parents on the family farm. Lek and Samrit met as children since they were neighbors. After completing his military service, they got married and Samrit worked as a *tuk-tuk* driver but was having difficulty making ends meet due to the constant traffic jams. His friend was doing well in the food shop business so Samrit decided to change occupations. He worked as an apprentice for a while to learn how to manage a similar operation. Despite the misfortune in the earlier food shop venture, Samrit remained motivated to earn money to send his children to school. Their daughter was born in 1991, and at the time of the interview they had a four-month old son. Their mothers take turns coming to Bangkok to help care for the children.

Samrit and Lek keep a bank account, but their funds have depleted after experiencing financial trouble and because of their families' debts in the countryside. They lend family members and friends money when it is available. They also give free meals to beggars and those too poor to buy food. The two do not participate in rotating credit circles (*len share*). "Others can leave with your money. . . It's enough to drive you crazy. I don't want to have to think about such things," said Samrit. Both are interested in locating in a food center or bidding for a contract in a school or other institution but missed at least one opportunity due to the timing of their son's birth. Their long-term goal is to own a shophouse with a ground-floor restaurant. A more immediate concern in late 1994, however, was to find a new place to live as the house where they rented a room was scheduled for demolition in 1995 to make room for a high-rise apartment building.

Tip's Stall

Tip is originally from Chiang Mai Province where her family used to farm. She lived there until 1972 at which point she moved to Bangkok. She is in her mid-forties and finished her schooling in Grade 4. After moving to Bangkok, she stayed with an aunt and uncle in a small hotel and got a job in a food shop on the premises. This is where she learned about the business and learned to cook. Her family eventually sold the farm, and Tip's widowed mother came to live with her. She is married and has one daughter, who was thirteen at the time of the interview. Her husband and daughter help her with the business along with one paid employee, Oy. Once in a while, a nephew then attending Ramkamhaeng University, would lend a hand.

Tip's shop sells all types of made-to-order food such as *latna, pad si iew, tom yum*, fried-rice dishes, macaroni, and several soups. Most dishes are sold for 15 Bt. She has extended credit in the past but discourages the practice. "One person who lives in a nearby apartment borrowed money from me then moved away," she warned. Tip does not play *len share* (rotating credit) because she cannot afford to contribute regularly. Instead, her daughter deposits savings in a bank account. She has eight brothers and sisters, who still live in Chiang Mai: "My younger sister is married and stays with her husband; my younger brother works; and one brother is unemployed. Another sibling is still single," she explained. The unemployed brother is disabled so Tip provides him with 300 Bt per month: "He can't use his legs because of a car accident. He stays in a government nursing home."

Tip is interested in bidding on a contract in an institution: "I've never been, but my younger sister-in-law offered to take me to a school to ask for information about cooking food there. But I found out that the bidding was over so I couldn't get the space." She's never thought about locating in a food center. Her goal, like that of Samrit and Lek, would be to own a shophouse with a food shop on the ground floor. "Shortly, this place will be torn down," she told us pointing to a more pressing concern. "If the owner is offered 25 million baht, he will sell."

Noo and Her Father's Pork Noodle Stall

Noo's family is from Surin Province, Isaan. The pork noodle stall she operates with her father opened in September 1994. Prior to this micro-enterprise, they operated a similar stall near the Coliseum on Phetchaburi Road. There, she ran into problems with the *tesakit*, who nearly arrested her and began to confiscate her tables and chairs until she realized she had to pay them "rent" for the space.

Noo was 19 years old at the time of the interview, her father in his mid-fifties. There are five children in the family, all girls, Noo being the second oldest. She and her father accompanied her sister to Bangkok, then 17. "My younger sister passed the entrance exam for Sri Ayutthaya School. I came to live with her" explains Noo. Sri Ayutthaya is a prestigious secondary school in the Victory Monument Area and her sister eventually hoped to go to university. They moved to the neighborhood in order to be close to the school. The eldest daughter was finishing her last year of teaching college in Surin in late 1994. The other younger daughters were all enrolled in school in Surin. Noo's aunt owns and operates a street-stall on nearby Rangnam Road. They also have other relatives in the city.

Noo and her father invested about 20,000 Bt to start their first food shop on Petchaburi Road to buy the pushcart, tables and chairs, and utensils. In their present shop they earn about 350–500 Bt per day on daily expenses of approximately 600 Bt. They manage to send 3,000 Bt per month back home to help with expenses. "My older sister is still studying, we have to send money for her as well" explains Noo. Her mother operates a small dry-goods shop, while her father used to sell wholesale rice at retail price to various customers. They are also engaged in rice farming.

"I like selling things" explains Noo, who used to help her mother in the store prior to moving to the city. "I have big dreams," she said to us with laughter. "I'd like to have my own shop." A problem facing Noo and her father in the neighborhood is the high rate of re-development. "People have to move, so there are fewer customers," Noo concludes.

"Formal" eating-establishments, as described later in this chapter, tend to be located within a proper building and comply with some of the licensing and inspection regulations of the local municipality. They are larger in scale and may have several paid employees. A more complex division of labor appears in these types of establishments. An interesting hybrid, though, is the appearance of the food center in which "semi-informal" shops are located within more formalized structures such as shopping centers, educational institutions, or office buildings. They are semi-formal as they are registered with local authorities yet continue to rely on unpaid family labor and sometimes prepare food at home for later sale. This blurs the boundaries between "informal" versus "formal," "private" and "public." The following passage describes Central Plaza Ladprao where I interviewed both the center's director and property manager.

Field Notes 6.1: Central Plaza Ladprao's Food Park and Food Center

Tuesday, 12 January 1993: We had a drink in the "Food Park," which only has eleven shops, all independently owned. Main dishes are priced from 20–25 Bt. The coupon system is in operation whereby Central Plaza retains 30% of all sales for use of dishes, service, and rent. Apparently, the mall has a team that does market research to monitor the tastes of potential customers and decides, based on that information, what types of shops they should have. They then send agents to various cities in Thailand to sample (traditional) indigenous food shops and, if they are good, invite them to set up a stall in the food park or food center. Khun Pornchalee, the first person I interviewed, said the stalls are owned, operated, and staffed mostly by women and usually have three to five employees. One "famous" noodle vendor from Khon Kaen set up her stall in the food park. Several places have the *shell chuan chim* endorsement. I didn't count the number of food shops in the larger food center, but there were approximately thirty. Pornchalee pointed out the great number of "traditional" dessert vendors in the food center. A shoulder pole with baskets (*hab re*) was one of the props used to market the sweets.

The manager of Central Plaza stipulates that the food shops must adhere to state regulations, such as cleanliness standards and the labor code (Chongrak 1993). It is claimed that Central Plaza Ladprao's food center was the first of its kind in Bangkok, but other shopping plazas such as the gigantic Mah Boon Krong (MBK) complex dispute this.[3] Opening the food center was risky because Thais were unaccustomed to self-service and preferred being served by waiters.[4] Chongrak Tripakvasin, Central Plaza's manager, explained that its food center was a success because many comestibles were on display, encouraging customers to "take a look" and try the food.[5] The food center has shops representing the country's varied culinary traditions, including Muslim (*halal*) and vegetarian counters. Chongrak asserted that other food centers in the city had copied the Central Plaza prototype. Design of food centers is jealously guarded and taking pictures strictly prohibited (Pitch 1994). Some even include a pictogram forbidding photography in the shopping plaza and food center.

Micro-entrepreneurs

The owners and operators of the smallest food shops studied opened their businesses in order to earn the principal source of household income. They not only support their immediate families but also contribute to the welfare of parents, siblings, and more distant relatives. The micro-entrepreneurs engage in two types of nurturing, or *liang*, behavior: first, they are literally feeding urbanites through a transactional medium; secondly, they are nurturing their own families, nuclear and extended, financially and contributing economically to the poorest regions of the country, particularly the Northeast.

Selling prepared food is the most feasible way for vendors to earn daily revenue. "I came [to Bangkok] to help care for my family" explains Ying. She worked as a cook and maid for nearly seventeen years before finally opening her first micro-enterprise. "My employer said to me, 'If you want to open a shop here I don't mind. If you stay with me your salary will not be as high'," Ying revealed. She explains that her salary as a domestic employee was not high enough to support her family any longer.[6] Daeng adds: "It's an independent occupation. Also, you can get money everyday." Ying's first pushcart operation was forced to close because of a conflict with the adjacent landowner. She then opened a larger food shop with her niece. For Ying and Daeng, however, what used to be a successful micro-enterprise is now suffering because of increased competition from new neighboring shops and what they perceive as a poor economic situation.

Another small vendor, Noo, operates a pork noodle stall with her father (Fig. 6.1). Slightly wealthier than Ying and Daeng, they also own a small dry goods store, managed by Noo's mother and siblings, in a market town in Isaan. Noo and her father came to Bangkok for the youngest sister to get a better education. Aided by her father, Noo looks after her sister and regularly sends money home.

Figure 6.1 Noo's Pork Noodle Stall

"Formal" Establishments

The formal establishments studied indicate a range of reasons why a shop was first opened.

Luung's Restaurant

Luung, meaning "uncle," is 60 years old and was born in Bangkok of Chinese parents. He spent many years as a traveling salesman in the provinces where he sold natural foods such as wild corn and nuts. His first wife died suddenly when their five children were still young so Luung decided to change occupations. Seventeen years ago he bought the restaurant where he still sells *bami* noodle and rice dishes with duck and Chinese-style red pork. He remarried and has a 10-year-old daughter. Most of the adult children have gone to the country's most prestigious universities and studied engineering, sciences, and medical technology. Four have good jobs, and one adult daughter still lives at home in their leased three-storey shophouse where the restaurant is located.

Luung's small restaurant, which can seat 20–25 customers, was once busy and successful. He had several young employees and was able to produce a greater variety of dishes. In the early 1980s, Luung even appeared on television cooking shows to demonstrate his skills! Today, however, business is slow. He wakes up to go to the market at 6 a.m. and closes at 5 p.m. "In the old days there weren't any shopping centers," where people now spend time shopping and eating, explains Luung. Labor is more expensive, and he complains that young people these days don't want to work hard. Luung's wife helps him at lunchtime, the only busy part of the day. The shop closes before dinnertime.

Luung considers himself to be quite poor. He does not keep a bank account. "I don't have enough money to deposit! I earn money and then it gets spent. I have many children. They have to be taken care of. Four have finished their studies. Expenses are very high and I only have a small business" he laments. At the age of sixty, Luung no longer enjoys his business and would like to retire.

Mister Donut

Although this internationally known franchise chain of doughnut shops is now Japanese-controlled, the Thai operations are owned and operated by the Central Pattana Group. This Sino-Thai family-controlled corporation owns the chain of Central department stores and has controlling interest in Thai Baskin-Robbins, half the KFC outlets, and Burger King. The first Mister Donut in Thailand opened at Siam Square fifteen years ago; the Victory Monument branch, the second, is thirteen years old. There are now almost 40 branches throughout the country, 33 in the BMA.

Mister Donut sells sandwiches and pastries other than donuts as well as a wide selection of cold and hot beverages. Its main competitor is the Dunkin' Donuts chain. Both companies are involved in extensive marketing campaigns on television, radio, and in the print media.

The Victory Monument shop has been renovated and occupies two floors in a prime location on long-term lease near the main bus stop near the monument.[7] It opens at 5:45 a.m. and closes at midnight. The renovated location seats close to 130 customers. The shop manager, Khun Wisaanu, explained that employees are generally in their twenties, work full or part-time, and receive the minimum wage. The VMA store has fourteen employees, two part-time. The store is busy and receives approximately 600 customers per day including a large number of students (approximately a quarter of all customers by Wisaanu's estimate).

Only the most successful Mister Donut locations have their own kitchens. Others, like the VMA branch, have doughnuts delivered twice a day. The first delivery is at 4 a.m. and is received by the cleaning staff. The 29-year-old manager of the VMA store has a degree in political science from Ramkamhaeng University. He has worked two years for the company but does not expect to be promoted to a high rank: "Here, the system is family-based. Thai people know this!" Non-family members have difficulty making their way through the ranks of the Chiratiwat family's operations. "It's better to work as a government official," concludes Khun Wisaanu.

Wira and Goy's Rattana Food Center

Wira and Goy, a married couple in their mid-thirties, opened the Rattana Food Center in July 1993. It was an complement to the student residence they had opened a year before. The residence and food center were constructed from old renovated shophouses. Wira, who also works for United Airlines as a maintenance engineering supervisor, was educated in California for fourteen years, completing high school and university there. His family is wealthy, being the area's old landlords. They own 28 shophouses, 26 of which were renovated for the residence and food center; the remainder was divided into 25 small lots rented to clothing and accessory merchants and a "7–11." His family has generated its principal income from rent for over thirty years. Wira's mother is the official owner of the property.

Wira and Goy find employees from the neighborhood to clean up, wash dishes, and work in the soda pop and juice stand that they operate in the food center. "It's more convenient for them," says Goy. They've hired eight people ranging in age from 18–50. All employees are originally from Isaan. Some of the younger employees live on the premises and are paid 75 Bt per day to start, less than minimum wage. Their housing is paid for, but these employees are responsible for their own food expenses. Wira and Goy supervise the employees and the center. "Really, these days, it isn't clean enough," according to Goy. "When we aren't here, the cleaning staff doesn't work." Rattana Food Center has a certificate from the district office certifying cleanliness of the premises and the requisite number of washrooms and sinks. It was the first place on the *soi* to obtain the required grease trap to avoid ground-water pollution.

"It was a deteriorated slum" before Wira came back from the US and decided to make some changes, explains Goy. Now, the food center and residence generate considerably more revenue. There are over a hundred rooms in the residence, normally two to a room. The food center is continually busy though there is some competition from food shops further down the *soi* and from the nearby "Home Food Center." Rattana Food Center does not advertise. "We don't put up any signs," explains Goy, "but people find out about it by word of mouth." In the next five years, Wira and Goy plan to tear down the shophouses to build a high-rise apartment. "This building is already 25 years old" explains Wira. "We've had major problems with the plumbing." "The life of the building is finished," adds his wife, Goy. "The bank would like it if we invested [in a high-rise]. It's our goal but we've never done anything like that before," Wira concludes.

The Professor's Pub

Professor Chaichana has been teaching in the Department of Interior Design at King Mongkut Institute of Technology (KMIT) since 1976. He finished a Master's at the Pratt Institute of Design in Brooklyn. He and Vipawan, one of his students at KMIT, got married in the early 1980s. Chaichana, whose family is originally from Sukhothai though he grew up in Bangkok, was in his late-forties at the time of the interview, and Vipawan, from Thonburi, was in her mid-thirties. Chaichana is one of nine siblings, Vipawan one of five. The two work as a team. They jointly own and operate the restaurant as well as the furniture-making factory in Navranakorn, which Chaichana has had since he came back from the United States more than twenty years ago. They also work in partnership as design consultants.

Fong Kee

Fong Kee, one of the oldest restaurants in Bangkok, has already been in business for sixty years. The present location is its fourth. The original owner came from Hainan Province, China, and his children operate the establishment today. Chinese food in the Hainanese style is the house specialty. "Hainanese food resembles Thai food because Hainan is quite close, in Southern China. . . It's a strong taste," explained Viwan with a school teacher's clear pronunciation. The original owner's niece, she studied languages in university. Viwan has been involved with the restaurant since her childhood but worked elsewhere for ten years after finishing her studies. After her father died, she quit her job and went to work at Fong Kee. That was in 1975.

The first location of Fong Kee was in a medical school for the military. After six or seven years, they were forced to change location when the hospital decided to expand. The second location lasted only five or six years due to construction of the Victory Monument, which displaced the restaurant. Finally, a third location was secured for the next forty years next door to their present location. Viwan's aunt, the wife of the original owner, suggested a final change of location after consulting a geomancer. Their fourth and present location is intended to be the restaurant's permanent home. The family owns the property outright.

In the old days, Fong Kee was surrounded by guava orchards, some rice paddies, and many royal palaces. The clientele consisted mainly of military officers and government officials, men for the most part. Today, it is a family restaurant for middle-class Thais and is a preferred venue for small wedding banquets of 50–80. Those who work nearby continue to frequent the restaurant at lunch. There are twenty full-time employees, and family members who work in the restaurant receive a salary. "Regular" employees are provided with housing, transportation, three meals a day, and a uniform. The two chefs are Sino-Thai men. Operations in the kitchen are very modernized, the equipment including a dishwasher and dryer. Fong Kee is a legal operation that has obtained all necessary permits from the district office, is regularly inspected, and has the mandatory "grease trap" to prevent sewage water pollution.

Fong Kee is now a large, formal restaurant. The cashier explained how her Hainan-born uncle decided to open a small restaurant:

Gisèle: Why did the owner open a restaurant?
Viwan: I think that in the old days, for the Chinese who came to Thailand, it was the easiest thing to do . . . cook. They had the knowledge.

According to G. W. Skinner, the Hainanese were at the bottom of the hierarchy among the Chinese in old Siam. The most successful and powerful speech groups were the Teochiu, followed by the Cantonese, and then the Hakka and Hainanese, who worked as manual laborers and hawkers (Skinner 1957). The Teochiu-speakers came to own prosperous rice-mills and controlled the rice export trade in the late nineteenth and early-twentieth centuries (Pannee 1995). Siam's wealthiest families who developed and still control trans-national corporations such as Central Pattana

Group and Charoen Pokphand are of Sino-Thai Teochiu origin. In fact, Teochiu is still one of the important business languages in Thailand:

> Hakkas and Hainanese, on the other hand, were almost entirely unrepresented in the occupations of higher standing. Hakkas in particular were the petty tradesmen, especially those dealing in sundry goods; the lesser artisans, including silversmiths, leatherworkers, and tailors; manual laborers, *hawkers*, and barbers. Hainanese were the hand sawyers, market gardeners, fishermen, domestic servants, *waiters*, *tea-shop operators*, and, not infrequently, "coolies," miners, and *peddlers*. They were the poorest of all the speech groups, and their general low social standing was undisputed. (Skinner 1957: 136; emphasis added)

Skinner explains that Hainanese were sometimes hotel and coffee-shop proprietors and employees. The owners of Fong Kee were examples of these types of entrepreneurs when their small food shop opened. Fong Kee's owners have, within a few generations, experienced a great deal of upward mobility. Though the owners readily admit they are of Chinese ancestry, they see themselves as Thai:

> *Viwan*: We trained the chefs. They are the grandsons of the first chef, *luuk ciin*, children of Chinese. They were born here.
> *Gisèle*: You don't have any Thai chefs? I mean, a chef that only looks after the Thai dishes?
> *Viwan*: They are both Thai. Both are men.[8]

Thailand is often characterized as a country where the Chinese rapidly assimilated into mainstream society partly by force but mostly due to the fact that the country was not colonized. Pannee, citing a study from the 1970s, explains the dynamics of Chinese assimilation:

> It is the characteristic of the Chinese in non-colonial Thailand to look up to and not down on the "foreigners" among whom they live in contrast to the behavior of their congeners in colonial Southeast Asia. In Thailand, the Chinese have been attracted to their hosts who being masters in their own house, have not labored under the disadvantages of Malays or Indonesians as subject peoples. (Freedman 1978: 48; cited by Pannee 1995: 35)

Compared to neighboring "plural" societies, Chinese immigrants in Thailand practiced a great deal of inter-marriage and adopted the Thai language and

Theravada Buddhism. Nonetheless, a strong Thai-Chinese identity conditioned by speech-group affiliation and income grouping, persists and is being resurrected in 1990s Bangkok.[9] G.W. Skinner's classic position on the Chinese in Thailand (and Sino-Thai) has been critiqued and refined by more subsequent scholarship on the subject (Chan and Tong 1995; Szanton 1983).

Fong Kee serves Hainanese specialties as well as Thai food. It is frequented by government officials, as in the old days, and physicians from the nearby hospitals at lunchtime and families in the evening. Retired civil servants are another main group of customers. Because the elderly patrons represent an earlier generation of government officials, these customers are mostly men. Viwan gives nuance to the composition of the clientele:

> *Viwan*: In the old days, there weren't many women. Now, we have all types. At lunch, it's workers, and in the evening primarily families. On weekends, there are many families. Nowadays, toward the end of the afternoon, we get young teenagers who eat while waiting for their parents in order to go home with them.

Fong Kee now caters to a wide range of middle-class Bangkok residents. It is, for the most part, a family restaurant that is a safe space for women and children. An example that contrasts with Fong Kee is the Professor's Pub. The owners are of Sino-Thai background. Professor Chaichana and his young wife Vipawan as interior designers decided to start a restaurant as an experiment in aesthetics:

> *Vipawan*: First time, we never thought about the investment, but we wanted to do our own restaurant because I designed many restaurant for my customers, but sometime I wanted to design this, this, this, but my customer "no, no," so we wanted to do our own.[10]

The restaurant is meant to be in a style reminiscent of an English pub. The winner of numerous design awards, the restaurant has been featured in a number of Thai home-decorating and women's magazines. A home-like decor is evident with the restaurant cabinets displaying personal curios and family photos (see Fig. 6.2). The couple, their children, and some of their employees live upstairs in the five-storey shophouse. Their children are often cared for by restaurant staff. Informality pervades the restaurant when it is not too busy where the two young boys play in the dining-room.

"Our parents are rich" explained Vipawan, the professor's wife and former student. No need ever existed for this couple to worry about providing for their

Figure 6.2 The Professor's Pub

parents, themselves, or their two young sons. Professional and artistic interest dominated the reasons for launching the business. Vipawan herself has appeared on television to demonstrate cooking techniques. House specialties are of Thai and Chinese origin. Service is polished and professional, and prices are expensive by Thai standards. The ambience resembles that of a Western formal restaurant.

The large-scale, multi-million dollar chain operation like Mister Donut is controlled by the Chirathivat family who own the Central Pattana Group. These operate under a paternalistic "family-system" that is considered typical of overseas Chinese conglomerates (Hamilton 1996; Redding 1995). It is difficult to ascertain if this family dominated business system is distinctive to the overseas Chinese. Canada's McCain and Bronfman families can be argued to manage their corporations in a similar fashion.

The small Rattana Food Center located on a narrow *soi* further straddles the "traditional/modern" or "formal/informal" division. It is managed by Wira and Goy, a married couple in their 30s. The center was created following the renovation of old shophouses that were redesigned as student residences. The small food center houses eight independent food shops that used to sell in the shophouses prior to renovation. "We're like a family," Wira explained when describing the management practices of the food center that include paying medical expenses for employees and hiring members of the same family. Young people are hired to clear tables, clean up, and sell cold drinks. This center is explored in greater detail later in this and the following chapter.

Everyday Lives and Spaces

The quintessential "one-woman-shop" selling prepared food occupies a vastly different social space than the person owning/managing or employed in a more formal eating establishment. The cooked-food micro-enterprise involves the strenuous work of one or two people. Even more formal establishments demand 12-hour shifts of employees with few, if any, days off. This pace makes it difficult for small- and medium-sized food-shop owners to find employees willing to work on those terms in good economic times. Limited economic opportunities make finding employees easier. Times have changed considerably as remarked by Luung, a Sino-Thai food-shop owner of 60:

> *Luung*: Before, I cooked a lot of things. For example, *salapao, khanom jeep, kha po paa* (steamed buns, Chinese dumplings, and fish stomach). I made a lot of things. I had many

assistants. Now, I don't have any assistants. Young people don't like working that way. They prefer a more comfortable job in a factory where you get a day off. So, they get a day to go out. Here, there weren't any.

In the old days, Luung's employees lived with him on the premises of his shophouse restaurant (Fig. 6.3). "Salaries were very low" he explains. If he sold well, he was able to hire four or five people. "But today I can't find any. Even if I could find some they wouldn't want to work," he concludes. It is ironic that factory work is considered by Luung to be an easier way of life given depictions of highly disciplined industrial labor, especially by feminist authors (Enloe 1989; Heyzer 1986; Ong 1987; Wolf 1992). Again, the typical scholarly response to the booming economy of Southeast Asia is to focus on industrial labor at the expense of the service sector. As Peter Bell argues, the two sectors are intimately related and depend on low-paid female labor.

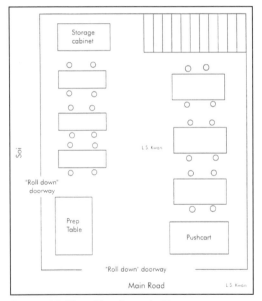

Figure 6.3 Floor Plan: Luung's Shop

In 1988, 14.3% of women in Thailand worked in services, and another 14.5% in commerce. "Women's work" includes employment as maids, secretaries, nurses, school teachers, waitresses, shop assistants, and street peddlers. Also much of the subsistence work of poor women consists of this type of "women's work" as it is essential to subsidize low wages paid in factories. (1992: 66)

Despite Luung's comments implying that working in a factory is an "easy living," service sector employment (and self-employment) may be a greater site of exploitation than industrial factory employment. The image of Dickens's Bob Cratchitt comes to mind as an example of service-sector drudgery (Ley 1996).

For other small food shops, where gratuitous family labor is unavailable, finding and paying for employees is difficult. The smallest stalls cannot possibly afford to pay the legal minimum wage of 135 Bt per day and instead provide their employees with room and board or other payments in kind. Wealthier establishments are able to hire many employees who are often tied to the firm through patron-client bonds. Fast food restaurants tend to hire teenagers for low wages, in line with Western practices.

Daily Routines

In order to prepare fresh food in the morning, someone must go to the market between 5–6 a.m. Usually, the shopowner will go and must wake up between 4–4:30 a.m. to have time for bathing, dressing, and walking to the local market. The daily routines of Daeng/Ying, Tip, Noo and her father, Luung, and Samrit and Lek are summarized in Figure 6.4. Those who wake up later than 6 a.m. usually have someone else go to the market or own food shops that sell simple meals such as noodles, which require fewer fresh ingredients.

The formal restaurants delegate the task of going to the market to a specific employee. Some, such as Fong Kee, have modified the practice by faxing in orders to Yaowaraj (Chinatown) and having their assembled order picked up. One of the oldest restaurants in the country has entered the era of high-speed communication and enjoys the conveniences of space-time altering devices such as fax machines:

> *Viwan*: We order by fax at night. Afterward, we go and pick it up. The drivers check the list to make sure if it is correct or not. After, we have another person who verifies again at the restaurant.

Professor Chaichana and his wife Vipawan provide another example of re-formulating relations between the restaurant owner and places selling food supplies. They

Time	Daeng/ Ying	Luung	Samrit/Lek	Tip	Nong and her father
4 a.m.		Wake up	Wake up		
5	Wake up			Wake up	
	Market		Market		
6	Preparation of food (goes on all day, with Mother Ying)	Market	Set up and preparation of food	Market	Father wakes up at 6, goes to market til 7. Nong wakes up at 7.
7		Preparation of food (ongoing through day)	Opening of shop	Preparation of food	
8	Opening of shop			Opening of shop (daughter helps)	
9					Preparation of food
10		Opening of shop			Opening of shop
11					
12 noon					
1					
2					
3					
4			Shop closing		
5		Shop closing	Set down and cleanup		
		Set down and cleanup			
6			Supper, put children to sleep	Shop closing	
7		Bathe, supper, watch t.v. (news)		Set down and cleanup. Has supper too.	
8					
9	Shop closing	Bedtime	Bedtime		
10	Set down and cleanup				Shop closing
					Set down and cleanup
11	Bedtime			Bedtime	Bedtime

L.S. Kwan

Figure 6.4 Daily Activities in Five Small Food Shops

shop at a mega-store called Makro, the Thai equivalent to Costco or Price Club, a self-service wholesaling warehouse in the suburbs serving a growing clientele and owned by the mammoth Charoen Pokphand (CP) conglomerate:

> *Gisèle*: So, can you please explain where you get your dry goods like rice, oil, and all those things you don't need everyday.
> *Vipawan*: Some at the market and some Makro.
> *Gisèle*: Oh, you go to Makro? But that's a new store isn't it? So before that you went to another wholesaler?
> *Vipawan*: Yeah.
> *Chaichana*: First [before] we go to Yaowaraj.

The "Wal-Mart" phenomenon is happening to the detriment of older traditional wholesalers, many of which are in Chinatown (Yaowaraj). The interior design couple send their employees to a well-known but expensive market near Chulalongkorn University daily for fresh produce, meat, and fish.

Preparing ingredients is a time-consuming task in every business studied. It involves chopping meat and vegetables and preparing items that are on sale throughout the day such as curries, fried fish, and deep-fried chicken. Much of the work is done before the shop opens, although it may be conducted on and off whenever there is a spare moment. Tip explains how her daughter helps the occasional customer first thing in the morning before going to school while Tip is preparing ingredients:

> *Tip*: Usually I open at 8:30 a.m., but people come as early as 7 to buy food and my daughter sells. Phi Oy comes to help, but I'm still preparing in the house.
> *Morn*: So, really your shop opens earlier than 8:30. Your daughter is really great, she can do it.
> *Tip*: She can do it.

Similar to the quantitative survey data presented in Chapter 5, informants report experiencing peak periods at lunch and dinner times. Many state that their primary customers are women who work at night time. Daeng was too polite to bring up the issue directly, but her implication is clear when she states: "I don't know what they do, but they work at night [giggles]." Thai-style cafés and bars are popular in the area and are places where many young women work as "entertainers" or "hostesses." Many are no doubt involved in the sex industry and/or are *mia noi* (minor-wives or mistresses) for wealthier men who pay for their apartments and living expenses. There was much gossip in the neighborhood and among food vendors about the extent to which certain women were subsidized by their lovers or customers.

Closing time for the establishments vary from Luung's duck noodle shop, which closes early at 5 p.m., to those who wait until the dinner-time rush is over and put away their materials starting at 9 p.m. Sometimes, set-down can take one or two hours. Tip explains that she begins to put everything away at 9 p.m. but sometimes is not finished until 11, when she promptly goes to bed.[11] Many of the micro-entrepreneurs interviewed sleep four to five hours per night. Daeng is exhausted as a result of chronic sleep deprivation. Most do not complain but are clearly suffering physically from the pace of their schedules. The long-term health of small food-shop owners due to lack of sleep, combined with the effects of air pollution and other environmental factors, are a concern.

The pace for managers of more formalized establishments is less strenuous than that of micro-entrepreneurs. Viwan of Fong Kee works a set shift and only does overtime when the restaurant is very busy. The same can be said for the manager of Mister Donut. Professor Chaichana and Vipawan work long hours because they not only manage a restaurant in their shophouse, but also have a consulting business and a furniture factory in the suburbs. This, along with the raising of two children, is a result of ambition rather than economic necessity. In the case of formal establishments it is the employees who put in the longest shifts by going to the early morning markets, receiving deliveries before dawn and closing the restaurants in the evenings.[12]

Operating Budgets

The micro-entrepreneurs, being principally responsible for most of the operations of the business, know exactly how much is spent for supplies on a daily, weekly, or monthly basis. The larger enterprises work differently and owners/managers are more secretive about revenue and expenditures. When interviewing the owners or managers about regular expenses, typical answers only generalized total figures. They were also less willing to provide financial data so these questions were not asked of them in detail. This section begins by profiling the monthly budgets provided by two micro-entrepreneurs. (See the Appendix for the other budgets collected.) The first food shop is a street-stall and the second is located in a building. I conclude by making general comparisons with the limited budget information provided by larger scale restaurants.

Tip has a *paeng loy* in a lane near her rented room where she lives with her husband, mother, and teenaged daughter (see Fig. 6.5). The stall includes a push-cart, a table, and a parasol in the area where food is prepared and sold to take-out customers. The seating area, a small walkway between two buildings, is covered by an awning. The tables are kept very clean, and the service is professional. This is attributed to Tip's fifteen years of experience working as a waitress and later as a cook in a local small hotel.[13] By 2001, Tip's stall had expanded to include the lower floor of a shophouse.

Figure 6.5 Tip's Stall

Tip's expenses are representative of the lowest costs associated with running a stall because no rent is paid for her place of business. In addition, the rent for the room where she stays with her family is only 1,500 Bt per month because she has lived there for sixteen years and knows the landlady well. Like the other vendors on the *soi*, Tip has never had to pay fines or bribes to the municipal police. The relationship between food-shop owners and the local state is explored in greater detail in Chapter 7.

Table 6.1 details expenses for all the supplies needed to run Tip's shop. Her total outlays per month, including the rent of her room, are 41,000 Bt. The highest expense category is meat for which approximately 700 Bt per day is disbursed, resulting in 21,000 Bt monthly. Vegetables only account for 6,000 Bt per month

Table 6.1 Tip's Monthly Expenses

Item	Price (baht)	Times per month	From where
Rent	1,500	1	For housing
Salary-1 helper	2,100	1	Not applicable
Utilities:			
- water	120	1	House
- electricity	300	1	House
- telephone	-	-	-
- garbage		30	Pushcart service
Fuel			
- gas	161 /tank	10	Delivered
- charcoal	110 /bag	4	Delivered
Rice	5kg/day @ 11 Bt/kg	30	Pushcart delivery
Noodles	2kg/day @ 8 Bt/kg	30	Say Yut Market
Cooking oil	300 Bt/vat	1	Delivered
Meat/fish	700 Bt/day	30	Say Yut Market
Curry paste	150 Bt/day	30	Say Yut Market
Vegetables	200 Bt/day	30	Say Yut Market
Green papaya	7 jugs/wk @12 Bt/ea	4	Say Yut Market
Ice	25 bt/sack 2 x per day	30	
Drinking water	7 jugs/wk 12 Bt/ea	4	Delivered
Soft drinks	7 doz./day @ 92 Bt/ doz.	4	Delivered
Eggs	450 Bt/wk	4	Delivered

Source: Field Survey 1994

followed by spices, seasonings, and curry pastes (altogether 4,500 Bt per month). Soft drinks and rice are also large budgetary items accounting for 2,576 and 1,650 Bt, respectively. Fuel in the form of gas and charcoal was reported as costing a little over 1,300 Bt monthly. A crucial additional expense incurred by Tip is the 2,100 Bt per month salary of one employee, Oy. Tip estimates receiving 60–80 customers per day. Most spend about 21 Bt each, the cost of a meal and soft drink.

Soon after the interview with Tip, Oy decided to quit. She found a job working in the cafeteria of the American University Alumni (AUA). At the same time, Daeng obtained a job there as well working as a cook. She could not tolerate the horrid working conditions and later shifted to the cafeteria at Charoen Pokphand headquarters. These changes are elaborated upon in the following chapter. Oy was formerly employed by Daeng whose budget will be described next.

Daeng's financial situation is much more precarious than Tip's (see Table 6.2). Daeng and her Aunt/"mother" Ying operate the shop together and rent the shop and room behind it from the landlady, who lives next door. The rent for both was a hefty 5,000 Bt per month, not including utilities, at the time of interviewing in 1994.

Table 6.2 Daeng's Monthly Expenses

Item	Price (baht)	Times per month	From where
Rent	5,000	1	Landlady
Utilities			
- water	300	1	From City
- electricity	400	1	From City
- telephone	5 bt/call	n/a	Local payphone
Fuel			
- gas	161 /tank	4	Delivered
- charcoal	110 /bag	4	Delivered
Rice	10 kg/day @ 11 bt/kg	30	Delivered
Noodles	1 kg/day @ 8 bt/kg)	30	Say Yut Market
Cooking oil	300 bt/vat	3	Say Yut Market
Meat/fish	600 bt/day	30	Say Yut Market
Spices/curry paste	50 bt/day	30	Shop and market
Vegetables	150 bt/day	30	Say Yut Market
- green papaya	5 kg/day @ 4–10 bt/kg	30	Delivered
Ice	32 bt/day	30	Delivered
Drinking water	5 bottles @ 8 Bt/bottle)	8	Delivered
- soft drinks	8 doz./day @ 92 bt/doz.	4	Delivered

Source: Field Survey 1994

Like Tip, Daeng's largest expense category is for meat and fish. She purchases chicken, pork, squid, prawns, and fish for approximately 18,000 Bt per month. Beef is not sold because of her mother's religious devotion to the Goddess of Mercy, known in Thailand as *Chao Mae Guan Im* (Holy Mother Guan Im) and in Mandarin as *Guan Yin*. Thais think of Guan Im as a Chinese princess who became a devout Buddhist and vegetarian. Those who respect her either become vegan (excluding eggs and dairy as well as meat/fish), or, more commonly, exclude beef, lamb, and goat from their diet.[14]

Vegetables generally account for 4,500 Bt per month. The price of green papaya, the key ingredient in the popular *som tam*, varies depending on the season from 4–10 Bt per kilo though the price for *som tam* remains constant in the city's food shops.

Daeng and Ying report purchasing approximately 5 kilo of papaya per day. This is a sharp drop from a few years ago when business was good:

Daeng: I used to sell ten kilos of chicken but those days are over. Another example is papaya. . . I used to sell ten kilos per day but now it's usually five kilos, sometimes four.

Tip's shop is new in the neighborhood and is experiencing great success compared to Daeng's older, more established business. This may be due to the cleanliness and more professional service found at Tip's. Tip's location closer to Rangnam Road, where many local residents work, is also an advantage. Daeng's shop, on the other hand, is shabby, unorganized, and does not appear as hygienic. Flies abound and stray cats that Daeng and her relatives feed climb in and out of the supplies.

Detailed budget information was not requested of formal establishments as they are reticent to share this type of information. Instead, questions such as "How many customers do you receive per day" combined with estimates of charges per customer enabled estimating gross revenues and expenditures on a monthly basis. The Professor's Pub serves as a case in point.

Chaichana and Vipawan state receiving about a hundred customers for lunch on weekdays and 50–80 for dinner nightly. With estimates of 90 and 200 Bt being spent for lunch and dinner, respectively, daily revenues before costs are 25,000 Bt, or 750,000 Bt per month. I asked Chaichana and Vipawan to estimate how much

Table 6.3 Professor's Pub, Estimated Monthly Expenses

Expense category	Estimated cost (baht)
Food and Supplies[a]	300,000
Salaries	54,000
Utilities (estimate)	5,000
Total	359,000

[a] Not including alcoholic beverages
Source: Field Survey 1994

they spend on food and non-alcohol supplies per week. A profit of 200,000 Bt per month (the equivalent of CAD$10,000) does not include the large outlay for beer and spirits, certainly a very large expense category.

Mister Donut's Victory Monument branch's monthly expenses will not be reported upon as the figures provided by the managements did not appear accurate.

Rent for Housing and Business

Those operating micro-enterprises generally rent one room where the entire family lives and the larger establishment owners must rent their place of commerce. Rents for housing and vending location range from a low 1,500 Bt paid by Tip to 5,000 Bt per month rent for Daeng and Ying. For selling space alone, 8,000 Bt per month is charged to vendors in the Rattana Food Center serving students in a residence, *soi* dwellers, and local office workers (see Fig. 6.6). The least expensive situation is the one characterized by Samrit and his wife, Lek, who operate on the sidewalk. Although they used to pay "rent" to the police (see Chapter 7), the amount was minimal (300–400 Bt) compared to the rent paid by their colleagues at a fixed-pitch.

In addition to the typical month by month rental arrangement, which usually includes a deposit and sometimes a month's rent in advance, there are plenty of other options to secure access to selling places. Luung and Mister Donut both negotiated long-term leases for their premises. Professor Chaichana and the owners of Fong Kee, on the other hand, own the buildings in which their restaurants are located. The same holds true for the Rattana Food Center. Property ownership in Bangkok's booming real estate market almost guarantees financial security.

The micro-entrepreneurs have few high value possessions in their rooms unless they have managed to purchase them through years of saving or acquired them through the generosity of others. In the case of Daeng and Ying, a refrigerator, radio, and color television were given to them by a Japanese man who once lived in the neighborhood. He spoke Thai and had been a regular customer for quite some time:

> *Ying*: He was a Japanese man who moved to go to work in Europe. . . He took pity on me. He rented a room over there at Duang Apartments. I asked him if I could buy it but he said "no." He gave it to me. He was an older man. He had good habits. He gave me a fridge, fan, and television.

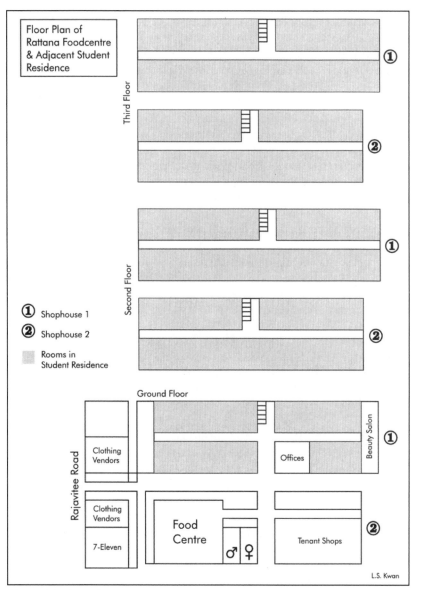

Figure 6.6 Floor Plan: Rattana Food Center and Adjacent Student Residence

The wealthier informants who own or manage more highly capitalized businesses either separate home and work space or follow a more traditional shophouse residential pattern. The Professor's Pub, for example, provides lodging on the premises for most of its employees who also double as domestic workers.

Low-level employees of Fong Kee are transported to and from work in a mini-van courtesy of the restaurant. Most live in a condominium owned by the proprietor and are required to pay utilities only since lodging is a form of payment-in-kind, as are meals and uniforms. Some smaller shops also pay wages lower than the required minimum set by the government because they provide employees with lodging and meals (Naruemol and Oudin 1992). Providing "welfare" to employees is a more cost effective strategy for small food shops and a way to reinforce patron-client relations for the larger restaurants (see Chapter 7).

Integration between Home and Wage Workplace

The shophouse strategy appears at first to be an ideal integration between home and work place. The shophouse is associated with the arrival and firm establishment of the Chinese on Thai soil. Historically, shophouses represent the economic and spatial expansion of Bangkok in the 1950s:

> The shophouse is a major feature of urban growth and character in modern Bangkok. The modern utilitarian box-shaped structure of the post-war shophouses (increased in height to four and sometimes five floors) proved versatile for a variety of business functions and can be said to have spearheaded much of Bangkok's urban expansion. (Askew 1994: 169)

Shophouses are not only a practical architectural form combining residence and workplace but also proved, as Askew argues, to be a profitable investment for what were suburbs at the time. Even in the extended periphery of Bangkok today, new shop-houses continue to be built, sometimes with grandiose Neo-Roman columns and other pastiche European features. Southeast Asia's "Levittowns" have a distinct style. Several of the micro-entrepreneurs interviewed dream of one day owning a restaurant in a shophouse where they could live with their families on the top floors. In Bangkok, residence adjacent to workplace is a way of avoiding the city's often grid-locked traffic.

Some feminist authors advocate the combination of home and work space as a solution to the disintegration of the two due to industrialization. Home-based businesses "eliminate the journey to work" and are seen as more flexible than nine-to-five office or factory employment (Christensen 1993). Dissatisfaction with the exigencies of the conventional workplace lead many women to explore the alternative of a home-based enterprise. Some rationalize this move as enabling them to combine the demands of housework, child-rearing and career. The so-called "electronic cottage," for example, has been the object of much scrutiny by many authors, including feminists (Gurstein 1995; Menzies 1981).

Upon further investigation, however, there appear to be some problems related to this arrangement. One of the chief complaints is not being able to leave work behind at the office (Christensen 1993: 71). Vipawan, the interior designer, faces this. Despite employing numerous domestic workers, she is having trouble juggling three roles. While her husband goes to teach at the university every day, Vipawan runs their design consulting company, manages the restaurant, and supervises their two young children and associated home-life. At 32 (at the time of the interview), despite her material wealth and employees, she feels as though she has no time to relax and re-charge for the next day. Vipawan explains that she and her husband purchased a condominium to move into once it is built. She needs a separation between home and work. This experience resembles the "double-day" of employed women in Western societies. Compared to micro-entrepreneurs who labor to make ends meet, Vipawan's double-day represents a choice guided by ambition rather than economic necessity.

A contrast is provided by the cashier of Fong Kee, Viwan, who is the niece of the original owner. She lives with her husband and two school-aged children in the suburbs. The construction of a new expressway means that when traffic flows well she can reach the restaurant in about twenty minutes. Prior to construction of the expressway, it sometimes took her two hours. For this reason, she would often stay in the rooms on the top floor that are available for employees to sleep on occasion or nap:

> *Viwan*: I finish around 6 p.m. . . . except for some days when the person in the other shift can't come in. On those days, I have to stay. Here, it closes at 10 p.m. If I don't want to drive home, I sleep here. I live in Changwattana. It's far but now there's the expressway. I get there in twenty minutes.

Viwan's two sons, aged 10 and 7, do not require the constant attention of pre-school children and the fact that she has a maid enables her to attend to the restaurant. Having a sleeping space for employees makes it possible to work late hours during busy periods. The restaurant acts as a temporary home for its employees when schedules demand it.

Shop Design and Patterns of Location

The shop designs of those businesses studied can be divided into three categories. First are small food shops and street-stalls that occupy the least amount of space; second, the formal establishments with separation from the street, air-conditioning and more complex seating arrangements; and finally the two food centers studied in the VMA where food shops are grouped around a central eating area.

Floor Plans

Figure 6.7 provides floor plans for Daeng and Ying, Noo, and Tip. Noo, the pork noodle vendor, obtained permission from the landlady to set up her small stall in the compound of the low-rise complex where she rents a room with her father and sister. These old buildings, made of teak, are of a traditional design. Noo located her pushcart immediately outside the gate of the compound in order to be visible and attract passersby. Here, take-out customers can get their noodles or buy the popular instant "Mama" brand to make at home. Eat-in customers step behind the gate into the courtyard where four small tables with stools are set up. Children living in the compound sometimes do their homework at one of the tables when business is slow. The serving and eating area is therefore a semi-public "family" space populated by tenants in the compound.

The layout of Tip's operations resembles Noo's in the sense that she does not occupy a fixed pitch. Her pushcart plus a work table, like Noo's, is on the *soi* adjacent to a wall surrounding the proprietor's house. Here, a menu is hung on the wall, and the food is prepared. Tip also sells dried noodles. She obtained the landlady's permission to sell in the alleyway between two houses: the first where her landlady lives, the second owned by the landowner's brother. Tip has erected an awning to shelter customers from rain, and the tables are covered with plastic tablecloths. The narrow laneway leads to the house where she rents a room with her husband, daughter, and elderly mother. The room, containing a fridge, is where Tip prepares some of the ingredients early in the morning and stores equipment at night.

Daeng and Ying's shop is incongruous with those described already. They rent both their room and their adjacent selling space. The food shop faces the *soi* and contains only two tables with stools. The shop is cramped, and it is an ordeal to

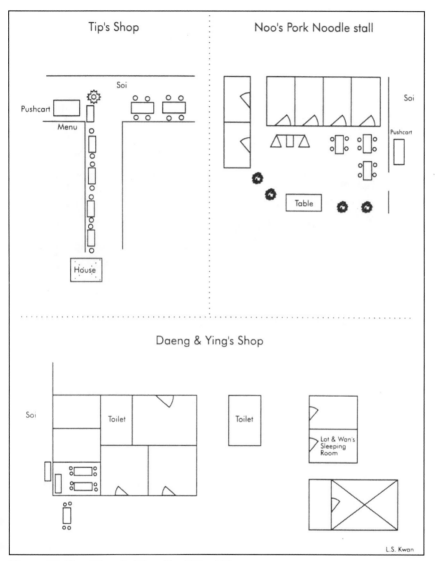

Figure 6.7 Floor Plans for Three Small Food Shops

get inside the shop when it is busy. There is a small table round the corner from the shop facing the entrance to their room, which is located next to a garbage heap where some tenants park vehicles. Children play in this area. The small yard next to the shop also serves as a spontaneous selling area: Ying once sold jackfruit there, and another person sometimes sells clothing from a rack (Fig. 6.9).

Figure 6.8 Buying and Selling in Front of a Food Shop

The shop is well equipped with a pushcart, "picnic stove,"[15] charcoal barbecue, work-table with display case, several shelves, and even a china cabinet. It has its own running water and electricity. Set down in the evening is not as difficult as it is for Tip because the shop can simply be locked up in the evening with perishables stored in the refrigerator in Daeng and Ying's sleeping-room.

The Professor's Pub is on two floors with the mezzanine open for seating only when needed. The typical shophouse structure is modified with the main floor being the amalgamation of two formerly separate buildings. Before the restaurant, the space was used as a showroom for designer furniture made in Professor Chaichana's factory. Sales were unsatisfactory so they decided to open a restaurant instead. At first, the mezzanine was Chaichana's office. The restaurant was initially only in one shophouse. The other shophouse contained the stairway to the second floor office and a small take-out bakery to attract customers. Today the restaurant is three times the size of when it opened in 1990 and has earned the attention of local interior designers. The kitchen is located on the third floor above their interior design consulting office. It is a hot room with two chefs (a Thai woman and a Sino-Thai man) and many assistants busily chopping and preparing ingredients. The fact that we were invited to visit the kitchen indicates the high standards of hygiene insisted on by Chaichana and Vipawan.[16] Food is sent to the main floor by way of a dumbwaiter elevator. The family lives on the top floor.

The floor plan depicted for Fong Kee represents the fourth and current location of the 60-year-old restaurant. When asked about the first location, Viwan explained:

> *Viwan*: Let's go back about fifty years. We were at the Saenarak Military Academy. In the old days it was a school for military doctors. It was near the monument in front of the Pramongkut Hospital . . . When they decided to develop the neighborhood we had to leave.
>
> *Gisèle*: Was it a shophouse?
>
> *Viwan*: In the old days, there were no shophouses. It was a *hong thaew* made of wood. It was a very long one-storey building. We were there about six or seven years. We moved to the corner where the Nakorn Luang Thai Bank is. Near the Monument as well.
>
> *Gisèle*: But there was no monument yet.
>
> *Viwan*: Not yet. We heard that they wanted to build a monument. So we moved again and built a *ruen taew* [wooden building]. We were there about five or six years too. Then we moved to where the bookstore is now on this corner. We were there about fifty years. We renovated and built a two-storey building, later four-storeys.

Fong Kee shifted from its last location because of *feng shui* (Chinese geomancy) which accounts it bad luck to be located adjacent to a bridge:

> In the year 2518 (1975 AD) they built the pedestrian bridge. It wasn't very nice. It looked like we were on top of the bridge. Chinese people believe that having a house on top of a bridge is bad luck. The mother said to move here because it was a better location. We had the opportunity to buy the property. We didn't have to move very far.

Fong Kee has been at its present location for nearly eight years. There is a dining area on the main floor where there are tables for busy periods, but the main restaurant area is on the second floor (Fig. 6.9). A dining room on the third floor has special rooms that can be closed off and reserved for weddings and banquets. The kitchen is on the fourth floor, and the top floor contains sleeping-rooms for

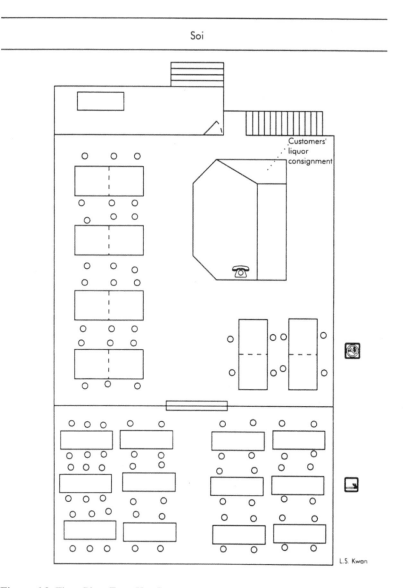

Figure 6.9 Floor Plan: Fong Kee Restaurant

occasional use by staff. Fong Kee is a traditional Sino-Thai dining establishment that has maintained continuity with customers and employees despite having relocated several times.

The Rattana Food Center contains eight shops, one of which is shared between two micro-entrepreneurs. Stalls specialize in selling noodles or curries. There are no stalls selling Isaan food or "made-to-order" dishes. Shops are individually owned and operated and were formerly located in the shophouses renovated to make the current food center. One exception is a noodle shop that formerly rented space in the gigantic Mah Boon Khrong (MBK) shopping center. A ninth outlet is operated by management and sells cold drinks. The food center seats approximately sixty patrons and is not air-conditioned. Customers pay cash directly to the vendors.

The Home Food Center (HFC),[17] which opened its doors in September 1994, presents a completely different picture of a food center (Fig. 6.10). It is located below the former location of Fong Kee. The space HFC occupies was previously the site of "Uncle Ray's Ice Cream Parlour." The corner location has experienced a great degree of commercial change during the past few years (see Fig. 3.4).

Sor Khon Kaen, a large Thai agri-food conglomerate, decided to launch a series of food centers in order to market its products and as a general revenue-earning operation. It contains a number of franchise shops such as "Chinese Express," "Noodle Duck," "*Saeb Isaan*," "Genghis Khan" (Chicken Rice), and "*Tae Jiew*," which specialize in *luuk chin* (fish and meatball brochettes). Other shops, however, are individually or family-owned small businesses selling dishes such as *latna* and *nam tok* ("water fall"), both fried noodle dishes. There is also a dessert outlet and a fresh juice bar.

Customers are required to buy coupons for their transactions from a central booth operated by the management. Coupons enable the management to retain 30% of all sales in lieu of rent. Most main dishes cost 20–25 Bt. The HFC seats approximately 150 customers and is air-conditioned. Loitering is discouraged. The HFC is a more formal environment than Rattana Food Center in terms of the food shops it contains, the service provided, and the expected behavior of patrons. It also engages in extensive and expensive advertising.

Soi versus Street

An important set of issues involves the nature of public eating on *sois* versus streets.[18] A further distinction is made between the foodways seen on major arteries as opposed to small neighborhood streets. Bangkok's *sois* can be characterized as semi-public (or semi-private) spaces where a certain informality prevails and the

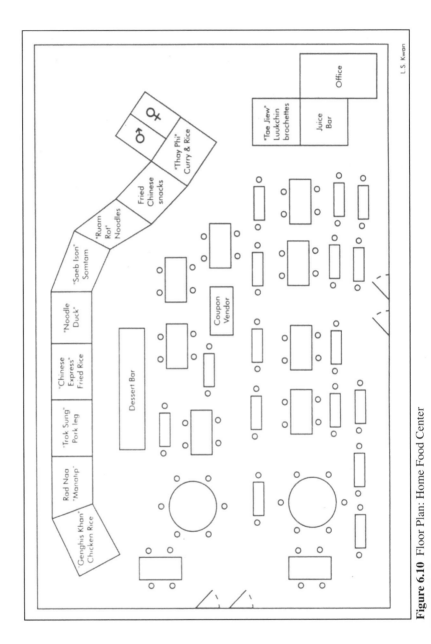

Figure 6.10 Floor Plan: Home Food Center

rules of society and of the state are not rigorously enforced. A first example is the ways in which *soi* dwellers routinely address one another, with "Have you eaten yet?" or *pay nay* ("Where are you going?"), exemplifying a certain sense of family. This resembles the porch-front repartee of some North American communities and the neighborhood familiarity of certain suburbs (Dyck 1989).

Residents share the *soi* as a living space and demonstrate informality not only in their speech but by dressing informally, even in pyjamas, as they eat in small *soi* food shops. Municipal rules regarding the use of space for commercial purposes or sanitary regulations are rarely enforced in the *soi*. Instead, the power brokers are the land-owners who set the rules for micro-entrepreneurs, giving or denying permission to sell in a given space. Rattana Food Center, located on a *soi* and family-managed, combines some of these elements of informality.

The street operates under more formal rules. The *tesakit*, or municipal police, make routine checks, and collect(ed) bribes. Generally, social interaction is less familiar and more formal. The main distinction between small and large streets is the scale and density of construction and the amount of human and vehicular traffic. For instance, in the VMA from 6–9 p.m., the south side of Rajavitee Road is so crowded with night-market shoppers than one has to squeeze through the crowd of customers and sellers. Vendors announce their prices in high-pitched voices using a blow horn (and thereby contravening city ordinances). Cars, buses, *tuk-tuks*, and motorcycles wait in endless traffic jams alongside the chaos.

On Rangnam Road, around the same time, a less chaotic scene emerges. The Isaan open air restaurants set out their tables and turn on their strings of small, white lights. Pedestrians stroll, the "cafés" open, and the day-time food shops close their storefronts. The setting is nostalgic of an older Bangkok.

Lives and Spaces

In the smallest and least formal food shops, economic survival is the *modus operandi*. In conformity with earlier discussions of *liang*, the mostly women micro-entrepreneurs struggle to assure their economic survival and nurture their families. This aspect of the food-system must be couched within an understanding of regional poverty in Thailand, particularly in Isaan, the home region of most small food-shop owners interviewed. Spatial and economic survival is a day to day affair; money is precariously earned and spent everyday in a place undergoing rapid physical transformation. Micro-entrepreneurs exploit themselves and their helpers/employees in order to survive.

The informality of an enterprise often relates to its location on a *soi* where informal social relations tend to be primordial and the power of the state is less visible. Here, traditional patron-client relations exhibited in patterns of interaction between land-owners and tenants affects the agency of individual food-shop owners. Those located on major arteries, however, must deal with the municipal police and larger-scale commerce.

I have demonstrated that the spaces associated with both small through medium to large-scale commerce in the prepared-food sector can assume a various forms. Even largely "traditional" architectural forms, such as shophouses, can be renovated to accommodate modern institutions such as the Professor's Pub. The HFC is located in a building that is at least fifty years old. Micro-enterprises can take on a variety of spatial positions and floor plans. Whereas the leitmotif of the small food shop sector is that of a "life support system," larger-scale establishments cater to the aesthetic needs of wealthier owners and their customers. Some, such as the interior designers' restaurant, are part of what Sharon Zukin named the "Artistic Mode of Production." Others, like Fong Kee, are part of a traditional Sino-Thai heritage tied to the military and bureaucratic power structure. Others still, such as Mister Donut and the Home Food Center, are clearly part of the Thai corporate structure.[19]

Middle-class entrepreneurial women are victims of the same "double day" and concomitant pressures as their North American counterparts, despite the fact that their burdens are partly alleviated by domestic/restaurant employees, who generally work long hours for low wages. Issues of family responsibility still condition and constrain their daily experience.

The wealthier agents in the food-system have options: to relocate, to consult geomancers, to buy condominiums for themselves or their employees, and to drive to work on the new expressway. In the face of rapid socio-economic changes in Bangkok, the manoeuvrability of the middle and upper classes contrasts with the bleak existence and lack of resources of the micro-entrepreneurs selling cooked food.

Chapter 7

Bangkok's Dynamic Foodscape

This chapter knits together the enabling factors that lead to the emergence of Bangkok's dynamic and gendered foodscape as depicted in the case study of the Victory Monument Area. I begin by introducing specific factors conditioning entrance to the occupation of cooked-food seller and, secondly, the use of space in order to carry out business. Topics explored include cooking knowledge and how it is gendered, access to capital, and the importance of mutual aid. The informal and formal mechanisms through which cooked-food sellers directly access a selling space are identified and explained. Selling areas are alternately defined as "public" versus "private" to justify access. The final part of this chapter argues that the individual cooked-food sellers' changing relations with capital and the state have a direct impact on access to public space. Women micro-entrepreneurs are disproportionately affected by these changes. Finally, the blurring of private versus public space in Bangkok's foodscape is summarized and reflected on.

Opening a Food Shop

Various enabling factors condition an individual's ability to open an enterprise selling prepared meals. The critical prerequisites are cooking skills, access to capital, and sufficient labor as well as knowledge of the market. The strategies employed by food-shop owners to attain these enabling conditions are highly varied.

Cooking Knowledge

The ability to cook is a marketable skill and also a gendered one. In Thai society, cooking is primarily a feminine skill. Women are the traditional custodians of Thai food knowledge but men of Chinese background have always been employed as professional cooks. Evidence from this study shows that ethnically Thai and Isaan men are becoming more involved as small food-shop owners and are therefore required to have some cooking knowledge. There is some debate as to the value or complexity of these abilities and how they are obtained. Some authors assert that cooked-food vending is a low-skill occupation typical of the so-called "informal sector." Could this be because it is traditionally defined as women's work?

> The findings of the survey have shown that half of the women in Khlong Toey were not economically active. They were housewives staying home. The remaining half were doing piecemeal work, or were *unskilled laborers in activities such as stall operation, street hawking, vending and small-scale trading* which was the most important aspect of slum life in Bangkok. (Shahand, Tekie, and Weber 1986: 16; emphasis added)

The above passage can be criticized on the grounds that it implies, first, that housewives are economically inactive. I am doubtful that there are many true "housewives" in Khlong Toey to begin with since most individuals would be required to earn revenue. A second weakness is the assertion that operating a street food stall is "unskilled" work.

The findings of my study suggest that most cooking done in Bangkok's food shops requires selecting the best quality food at the market, knowledge of recipes and cooking methods, and the presentation of final meals. Cooked-food sellers therefore exhibit considerable skill and knowledge. Food micro-entrepreneurs are both artists and scientists, particularly those who prepare a complex variety of dishes. It is not only the preparation of individual recipes that requires knowledge, but also the timing required to prepare a series of dishes simultaneously. Operating a micro-enterprise from a financial and managerial standpoint is not simpler.

Samrit reports having worked as an apprentice to learn the art and science of food shop management. Lek claims that she then learned to cook from her husband!

> *Gisèle*: Who taught you how to cook?
> *Lek*: My husband. [Samrit enters the room]
> *K*: He taught you how to make *kwayteow* or ordinary dishes?
> *Samrit*: I used to be an employee.
> *K*: Who taught you how to cook?
> *Samrit*: A friend.

K: Where?
Samrit: In *soi* Thonglor.
Gisèle: You worked there?
Samrit: I wasn't really an employee. I went to do an apprenticeship.

Samrit explains that he worked as an apprentice in a close friend's food shop. Apprenticeships (*feuk ngan* or "practice work") are fairly common in Thailand in both formal and informal enterprises. They are an important means to train workers and future entrepreneurs. Businesses also obtain free or inexpensive labor in the process. Apprentices learn cooking techniques, customer relations, contracting skills, and money management. At the time of the interview, Samrit and Lek had a friend who was an informal part-time apprentice. The friend was still a *tuk-tuk* driver and Samrit was encouraging him to quit and enter a small business so that he would eventually "settle down." The *tuk-tuk* driving lifestyle, according to Samrit, does not encourage good habits. He admitted to drinking alcohol frequently and gambling. Samrit associated his change in occupation with a shift from being irresponsible to looking after his family properly.

Other informants describe having been formally taught how to cook as opposed to girls learning from their mothers as I assumed was typical. Some, like Daeng, had formal training in cooking schools or, like Tip, in small "Chinese" hotels. Ying stated she had learned from a recipe book written by a member of the aristocracy when she worked for a wealthy and powerful family as a cook:

Gisèle: Where did Mother Ying learn to cook?[1]
Ying: I didn't study. I learned by myself. When I worked on *soi* Ratchakruu they wanted me to make *khanom*.[2] I cooked this and that. The employer had a recipe book. I read from that and cooked. The boss told me what ingredients to mix together. At that time I had to plan menus for all the meals. I improved my skills a lot.

Daeng attended cooking school while living with her aunt in Petchabun Province between the ages of 14 to 15. At the time, she also helped care for her younger cousins. She dropped out of the course due to "lack of time and laziness" as she summarizes. At the age 16 she moved to Bangkok and was hired in the cafeteria of a can-making factory in Bang Kae. She worked as an assistant cook:

Daeng: At first, they didn't have a cook, so I went to help. I was called to work in the kitchen. I worked there about two months. I learned to cook there.

The learning of cooking related skills is not confined to the traditional practice of watching mother or grandmother cook at home. Informants perhaps downplay the importance of home-based learning in order to impress a foreign researcher. It is clear that core knowledge learned from parents has been supplemented, at least, by more formalized training.

Formal restaurants, such as Fong Kee and the Professor's Pub, hire "chefs," who have learned from experience but complement their training by teaching them how to prepare and present certain dishes. Fong Kee has two male chefs of Sino-Thai background in their early 40s, grandsons of the restaurant's first chef. They are assisted by four young men aged 25–30 from Isaan. The kitchen is therefore a masculine, bi-cultural space whereby the Chinese tradition of men cooking in restaurant kitchens is reproduced but includes four male members of a subordinated ethnic group:

> *Viwan*: We have assistants who help prepare ingredients. There are several. They cut the vegetables and meat. They are originally from Isaan but have lived here for a long time. We trained them. They came here because someone from their village worked here before. So, after finishing school, they came here to help and learn.

Fong Kee also has eight men who work as waiters and five waitresses. All are in their twenties and from Isaan. Two female cleaning staff are also from Isaan.

Professor Chaichana and his wife diligently train their chefs and six assistant cooks. Though the chefs know how to cook from experience, they are told how to prepare and present dishes according to the owners' specifications. Thai and Chinese cooking are kept separate under the direction of each chef and the chef's assistants.

Important budgeting and management skills are needed to keep an enterprise operating on a daily basis. The smallest-scale entrepreneurs, in particular, are usually responsible from every aspect of the business from shopping through to budgeting. Sidney Mintz, writing in the early 1970s, summarizes the skill levels of women micro-entrepreneurs compared to ostensibly "liberated" educated middle-class North American women:

> Who is more modern, more western, more developed: a barefoot and illiterate Yoruba market woman who daily risks her security and her capital in vigorous individual competition with others like herself; or a Smith College graduate who spends her days ferrying her husband to the Westport railroad station and her children to ballet classes? (1971: 267–68, cited in Tinker 1987: 20)

Although this refers to a now outdated situation in West Africa, as well as the "West," and foodsellers in Bangkok are neither barefoot nor illiterate (for the most part), the risks, skills, astuteness, and vigor necessary to survive as a micro-entrepreneur are undebatable.

Access to Capital

Informants employ a number of methods to obtain the necessary capital to invest in their businesses or to support themselves when sales are poor. Borrowing from friends, moneylenders, or land-owners, going to pawnshops, and participating in rotating credit schemes are all widely-used ways of obtaining cash.

Borrowing

Very few of the informants interviewed have bank accounts, and none has ever borrowed money from a formal lending institution. The most common response to my question "Do you have a bank account?" was to laugh and reply, "I don't have any money to deposit!" It is common, however, to borrow from one of the neighborhood notables or a moneylender:

> *Ying*: At first, I borrowed from one person I know, near Sin's house. I paid it back bit by bit.
> *Morn*: Now, do you still have a debt with someone else or not?
> *Ying*: I still have a debt right now.

Daeng, qualified this during another interview:

> *Morn*: Have you ever borrowed money?
> *Daeng*: Yes, interest is about 5 or 10 % [per month].
> *Morn*: From whom? People from your home province?
> *Daeng*: People around here.
> *Morn*: The money-lender is a relative or the owner of the building?
> *Daeng*: Owner of the property.

Borrowing patterns, part of an established set of patron-client relations, are explored later in this chapter.

167

Gisèle Yasmeen

Pawnshops

Until I learned the word for pawnshop in Thai, *rong rap jam nam*, I was unaware of the critical role these institutions play in Thai society. They are ubiquitous in Bangkok and, having learned the word, I suddenly saw signs for them on nearly every street. Informants reported using pawnshops as a quick source of cash from time to time. The pork noodle seller's father explains: "We have to send money home. I try to keep 50 baht per day in case we get sick. Sometimes I go to the pawnshops and leave some things to get money." Historically, many of these shops were owned by Thai-Chinese. As Skinner explains in his detailed description of occupational groups, pawnbrokers in the 1950s were almost all Teochiu and at the top of the socio-economic hierarchy of Chinese speech groups and remain so today.

Rotating Credit Groups

As noted by Josephine Smart in her study of Hong Kong cooked-food hawkers, rotating credit is a popular way for micro-entrepreneurs to access large amounts of capital on a regular basis (Smart 1989; Chua 1981). The system is known as *tontine* in Singapore and "chit funds" in South Asia. Mitchell (1995) asserts that Chinese rotating credit associations (*hui*) play a role in financing large-scale business ventures of Overseas Chinese capitalists even today. In Thailand, informal rotating credit schemes are known as *len share*, literally to "play a share."[3]

Members of credit groups contribute regularly and can draw from the kitty at varying rates of interest depending on how early they want to access the money. Interest charged, particularly to those who draw first, is very high, and non-borrowing members earn much more interest than they would by depositing in a bank. The system has a few variations but this is its basic structure (see Geertz 1956, 1962).

In an urban milieu, where people are transient and can disappear at a moment's notice, credit circles are risky. Indeed, there have been several high profile scandals involving corrupt fund leaders who moved to other countries after absconding with millions of baht. One of my key informants, Ying, was a fund leader and victim of a cheating member, who disappeared anywhere from 20 to 60,000 baht:[4]

> *Ying*: The cheater got some money, and I could not get it back. I had a headache, couldn't sleep. People were cursing me. I had to take sleeping pills.
> *Morn*: Did the members curse you or not?

Ying: No, not the members. They didn't curse me. I tried to collect the money and give it back to every member.

Daeng added:

> Khun Mae was the leader of the group. She had to reimburse everybody. We had eighteen people in the share, 1,000 baht per person. If we hadn't responded to this cheating, we would not have been able to continue living in this neighborhood. We would have had to move.

Daeng and Ying are experiencing severe financial problems as a result of the cheating in the credit group. They had to pay both principal and interest to the other members. Akin (1978: 30) describes how "Nate," a chit-fund leader in the Bangkok slum of Trok Thai, opted not to pay back members of a failed credit circle that he led and thereby lost his power and prestige in the community. He did not take on the role of a *nakleng* or "big hearted" person:[5]

> In the business of the *chae*,[6] a person with the heart of a *nakleng* would keep the *chae* going to complete the cycle even if by doing so he would himself get so indebted that his own future would be completely ruined. He must dare to take great risks. He must love his *liam* (prestige, honor) more than his property (Akin 1978: 30, cited in Askew 1994: 62).

Daeng explains that she and Ying saw themselves as responsible to the share participants. It was their duty to pay back all group members even if this led to financial ruin. Their honor was at stake. Ying took on the responsibility of *nakleng* even if it worsened her financial situation.

Despite the risks associated with rotating credit and her bad experience, Ying continues to "play" *len share*. She needs to obtain cash for big purchases or to support family members. Even though Daeng's younger brother tends to spend his tuition in snooker halls, living with some of his teenaged friends in a rented room, Ying continues to give him money. Here, nurturing brothers, sisters, nieces, and nephews, even those who take advantage of her, takes precedence over Ying's own individual financial well-being.

Larger enterprises like Fong Kee, the Professor's Pub as well as Wira and Goy who own the Rattana Food Center benefit from generations of family wealth. Their primary advantage over migrants from Isaan is that they own valuable real estate or profitable businesses in Bangkok. Larger tracts of farm land in the provinces are worthless in comparison. Wealth in land has led to capital accumulation and increased opportunities in general. Access to credit and capital is not a cause for concern for owners of formal establishments.

Mutual Aid

In keeping with other research on street foods, the "informal sector" and small food enterprises, mutual aid is a crucial ingredient in providing necessary labor and capital for the functioning of the business. Relatives primarily help one another but help from friends and "patrons," or more powerful "superiors," should be included. Likewise, the withdrawal of support, in terms of labor, financial support, or access to space can also be of detriment to the survival of a food establishment. These factors are now examined in greater detail.

Kinship Networks

The shops studied in the quantitative survey as well as those scrutinized in-depth illustrate the centrality of kinship-based mutual aid. Nearly 60% of respondents in the quantitative survey report having "helpers," while 40% have employees. The great majority of helpers, or volunteers, are nuclear family members or other relatives. They help in their spare time when not studying, working at a job or taking care of family responsibilities. Evidently, small, less formalized establishments rely on this type of support the most. Tip's daughter helps her mother before going to school. Tip's husband is also a principal assistant rather than co-owner:

> *Tip*: He doesn't work now. It's better, isn't it? He used to work, but I told him to quit to come and help me. . .
> *Gisèle*: But who is the owner of the shop?
> *Tip*: I am!

This resembles the findings of Tinker and her team, who report that men often quit their jobs to help their wives when the food business became profitable enough to support the family (Tinker 1987). In The Philippines, "women operate about two-thirds of the firms alone, but when a woman becomes successful she is often joined by her husband who may assist *her* in selling" (Tinker 1987: 16).

Tip's nephew also helps when he has time off from his studies at Ramkamhaeng University.[7] Family assistance is supplemented by the labor of one paid employee.

Spousal aid is the norm. Husbands and wives working together in food shops is the norm in Southeast Asia, as opposed to parts of Africa where women and men keep separate budgets, even within marriage (Tinker 1987). Luung's duck noodle shop depends on his wife's regular assistance. Similarly, Samrit and Lek own and manage their chicken noodle soup stall as a team. These examples from informal enterprises are evidence of gender complementarity in the foodscape. On this micro-scale, women and men in marriage partnerships cooperate for mutual and family benefit.[8]

Noo, the pork noodle vendor, does most of the food preparation and selling, but her father goes to the market and manages the finances. Ying is assisted by adopted daughter, Daeng, who superficially appears to be running the shop most of the time:

> *Daeng*: Really, "Mother" is the owner and started the business, but I am the one who works. Mother is the boss. Mother collects and dispenses the money.

As the senior and maternal figure, Ying controls the enterprise but depends on the full-time help of Daeng and other relatives. Daeng's teenaged niece, Wipa, helps every day during her spare time after school (see Fig. 7.1). A friend named Juk who works full-time at the "7–11" on a nearby street also helps on her time off. Helpers act out of a sense of mutual responsibility. Reciprocity is the basis of the system. Consequently, regular helpers receive meals, information on jobs, and general social and emotional support.

Mutual aid is an important aspect of day-to-day life in larger, more formalized establishments as well. Husbands and wives, as in the case of Professor Chaichana and his wife Vipawan, work as co-managers. Wira and Goy, who own Rattana Food Center, also co-manage Wira's family property, officially owned by his mother. Goy, a business administration graduate, spends most of her time overseeing the operations of their rental shophouses, student residence, and food center. Wira continues to work with an American-owned airline company as a maintenance engineering supervisor. Gender complementarity is therefore not the exclusive domain of lower income groups in Bangkok. Middle-class couples also engage in complementary behavior when it comes to business. This may be a Thai pattern adopted by hybrid Sino-Thai culture. In the Chinese system even today, the man will often work fourteen hours a day to keep the business afloat while his wife works equally long days taking care of family and household chores.[9] The evidence from the Victory Monument Area suggests a more fluid gender division of labor. For the wealthier respondents, though, domestic labor is contracted out to servants.

Figure 7.1 Wipa Helping in Daeng's Shop

At Fong Kee, relatives of the owner have regular salaries and positions. On the surface, the restaurant's organizational structure resembles a highly formal establishment. Family relations, nevertheless, continue to hold sway. Close relatives of the owner have the best jobs. Some come into volunteer but have considerable decision-making power. The elderly mother of the restaurant owner, for example, comes in to help on a regular basis. She sits in the dining-room at lunchtime, assisting with small tasks such as folding napkins. Afterwards, she rests upstairs in one of the rooms available for staff to nap. Although grandmother's contribution appears symbolic and less crucial to the day-to-day operations of Fong Kee, she is in a position of authority and power and helps make major decisions. The decision to shift locations, for example, was hers. Grandmother is a daughter-in-law in this family but, nevertheless, has significant influence in business affairs.

The examples of kinship and neighborhood-based mutual aid suggest a blurring of boundaries between what are often characterized as domestic and private concerns versus the work of business and the public. Patterns of mutual aid not only typify enterprises considered part of the "informal sector" but also larger, more formalized establishments. For micro-enterprises in Bangkok, it is this volunteer labor that keeps the food affordable for the masses in what is becoming a very expensive city. The cost of feeding the city's workers is therefore subsidized by mutual aid practices.

Patron-Client Relations

Patron-client relations are of fundamental importance for explaining the presence of many stalls and restaurants. These relations exhibit both benevolent qualities and traits that work to the detriment of clients with less privilege. Arrangements tend to favour more powerful patrons and uphold the "relations of ruling" that patron-client relations directly reflect. Traditionally, patron-client relations have specific meaning in Thai studies and refer to the feudal *sakdina* system.[10] In this political and economic structure, peasants worked as *corvée* laborers at specific times during the year for their lords and overmasters in return for protection and favours. Akin's (1975) examination of a Bangkok slum advanced the model of "patron-client" roles to depict the ground rules of Thai social organization. This replaced Embree's previously debated description of Thailand as a "loosely structured social system" (1957):

> Akin identifies "reciprocity" between people as the basis of social networks in Trok Thai. Such reciprocity, expressed in patron-client relations, is the basis for the networks

of social ties that knit society in Trok Thai. Leaders are conceived as "nodes" within a network of interaction. (Akin 1975: 293–95, cited in Askew 1994: 60)

Those in positions of power such as landowners, employers, and other influential actors have rights and responsibilities toward their subordinates. Likewise, subordinates extract favours from their patrons but also are required to cater to the needs of their benefactors: "Akin emphasizes the precarious nature of livelihoods and the importance of personal contact and, above all, *patronage from people with greater power and skill*" (Askew 1994: 60 emphasis added). These relationships have direct impact on an individual's life-chances. Patrons, or *luukphi*, garner loyalty from clients (*luuknong*) by bestowing favours. This is an important basis of their power. Those receiving aid are bound to their patrons through debts of gratitude, known as *bunkhun*, a concept difficult to translate (Mills 1990).

What is missing from Askew's discussion of Thai patron-client models is the socio-economic inequality that keeps the system operating. Patron-client relations are far from complementary and are, instead, rife with disparities of power, privilege, and access to resources. Some scholars hesitate to use the term "class" when describing the stratification of Thai society. Nonetheless, the "hierarchical principle," particularly in Bangkok, has been grappled with for many decades (see Evers and Korff 1982; O'Connor 1987).[11] The least economically endowed clients are most vulnerable and must win the favours of their patrons. In the case of cooked-food sellers in Bangkok, clients consist of street foodsellers and micro-entrepreneurs. In Ying's case, landowners and former employers (patrons) have sometimes granted her favours or even direct assistance for starting her business. For this she is very grateful and is bound to those superiors through *bunkhun*:

> *Ying*: The owner took me around to buy many things to open the shop. . . The landlady helped me pay instalments for a "picnic" stove because I didn't have the money. The landlady helped me invest money because she took pity on me.

She continues to keep in touch with her former employers from *soi* Ratchakruu. When a child she had cared for got married, Ying was invited to the reception. They sometimes come to the shop and discretely give her money:

> *Ying*: When they come they buy a little bit of food and give me a lot of money, 500 baht. I don't want the money, but they insist that I take it. They buy a little something

but give more money because they know about my problems. I'm shy with them. They just bought a little something.

These former employers have also asked Ying to suggest other employees for special functions. She sometimes acts as an intermediary between Bangkok's wealthy and impoverished migrants from Isaan. Patrons, like at Fong Kee and the Professor's Pub, prefer to hire employees using a personal network of connections rather than by placing an advertisement or using an agency. This is a way of maintaining and building trust within longstanding relationships thereby enhancing their patron role.

In the case of conflict, patrons are called upon to intervene to settle disputes. When Ying first opened the food shop, another cooked-food seller in the same building tried to prevent her from selling certain types of food:

Ying: That man came to see me and tried to forbid me to sell fried rice and made-to-order food. He told me not to sell soft drinks. I said to him: "That's my decision. That's business. You opened your shop after me. You can't tell me what not to sell." I scolded him. We argued. I told him, "Tell Jae-Noo [the landlady] what you want, and she can tell me directly." I wasn't afraid of him.

This competitor eventually got evicted after two years by Jae-Noo, the landlady. Here, the patron acts as mediator to settle disputes informally. Patrons think of themselves as granting clients "favours" rather than enhancing their own economic and social position.

Ying's case illustrates how clients can be subject to the whims of their patrons. In the case of a micro-entrepreneur, this can involve the granting or removal of one of the key factors of production—the space on which to conduct business. The *soi*, though perceived as such and publicly accessible, is not really public space. It is in many ways privately owned and controlled.

Setting up on the *Soi*

Finding and accessing a suitable selling space is a matter of trial and error. It is risky and many micro-entrepreneurs' life histories are filled with accounts of failed ventures. The people I interviewed are the ones who persisted in the face of failure. A prime example is Samrit, the chicken-noodle vendor who operates a street-stall with his wife, Lek:

Gisèle Yasmeen

Samrit: Prior to this, business wasn't working out. I lost more than 20,000 baht [CDN $1,000].
Lek: Really, we lost money three times.
Samrit: We couldn't sell. . . We were losing money. We changed location until we found this spot.

Location is crucial. Prized selling spots are coveted and disputes often arise as to who has the right to a certain selling space.

The most important aspect of patron-client relations for the well-being of cooked-food sellers operating on the *soi* is the permission to sell on the landowner's property. Noo and Tip both have permission from their respective landladies to sell on their property. When Ying had a pushcart prior to opening her current shop she obtained permission from the landowner to sell in front of the house. This was the same landowner who helped her buy capital equipment. The landlady later withdrew access to this space:

Ying: Then the landlady said that my shop was on her property, and she didn't want me to sell there. The landlady's daughter didn't want me to sell there, in front of her house. Customers could see all her belongings. She told me to find a new location.

The landlady's daughter feared that the boundary between public and private space was being eroded to her family's detriment. Ying's commercial activities were "too close to home" and risked theft of the patron's belongings. Permission to sell was subsequently withdrawn, and a more firm boundary between domestic and commercial space was established. Fortunately, at this very time there was a new building constructed on the site of Ying and Daeng's present shop. Jae-Noo, the owner of the property, gave them access to their present shop space:

Ying: Many people wanted this location but she selected me. This person wanted it, that person wanted it and that one over there!

At the former location, Ying paid the landowner about 350 Bt per month for water and electricity. At the present location her access to the building where her shop and room are located is guaranteed by paying the very expensive rent of 5,000 Bt per month, not including utilities. In some senses she is "lucky" to have found a space so soon after being displaced from her former pushcart location. On the

176

other hand, her ability to make ends meet has been seriously hampered by high overhead costs.

Tip's case demonstrates the beneficial aspects of having a landowner's permission to conduct business:

> *Morn*: Why did you choose to start a food-shop here?
> *Tip*: Because my house is here, and when I asked Auntie [the landlady] she said I could sell but to do it properly. It's a good location.

Tip's selling space is free. She only pays rent for her small inexpensive room and a small amount for utilities. However, when probed deeply, Tip declares the narrow pathway where her shop is located as both a public space and on a second occasion as her own property:

> *Morn*: Did you ask for permission to put the awning here or not?
> *Tip*: I didn't ask permission.
> *Morn*: It's a public place.
> *Tip*: It's a public place. I didn't have to ask.

When asked if the municipal police (*tesakit*) had ever inspected her shop, she stipulated quite clearly that the pathway was part of her house, though she rents this property.

> *Tip*: A municipal inspector came to my house, and I told him that this area is in front of my house. So, if someone comes here, never mind, because this is my own house.

Small food-stall owners justify their use of space in the *soi* in several ways depending on those with whom they are interacting: landowners, or government officials such as the *tesakit*. Definitions of proprietorship shift with the context of the discussion.

Cooked-food sellers who locate on the *soi* acquire the landowner's permission to do so. When questioned about the legitimacy of the BMA's regulation of their access to space they appeal to the "privateness" or "publicness" of the place used for vending. Similar latitude is not granted to those located on the city's major arteries.

Wealthier owners of food establishments have considerably more leeway when accessing and maintaining control of a commercial space. The capital required to rent or buy space within a building is limited to the middle and upper classes. Renting a shop on a long-term lease, like Luung, or even the 8,000 Bt per month required of Rattana Food Center tenants, is a venture that vendors such as Noo, Tip as well as Samrit and Lek cannot possibly fathom. A shophouse selling location is the long-term goal of most small food shop and stall owners. To achieve their objectives, micro-entrepreneurs require a large pool of savings and the wherewithal to deal with the legal and bureaucratic aspects of leasing or, if they are very fortunate, property ownership.

Those in fixed shops as well as stalls on major streets must comply with licensing and health regulations to a greater extent than their counterparts in the lanes. The street-side stalls face the emerging regulations of the BMA, which in the mid 1990s granted greater spatial access to vendors and concurrently seeks further regulation of these activities.

Coming to Terms with the Local State

In January 1993, Bangkok newspapers carried stories about the BMA and, later, the Ministry of the Interior "cracking down" on street vendors. The vendors negotiated with state authorities for the right to use sidewalks contingent upon certain conditions. These conditions revolve around acceptable business hours, the prohibiting of vending one day per week (Wednesdays, for street cleaning) and certain spatial restrictions. Hostile state policy toward street vending is nothing new as McGee has demonstrated for Hong Kong, Singapore, and other Southeast Asian cities (McGee 1971; McGee and Yeung 1977). In the case of the BMA, this hostility has relented in the past few years. Fluctuating policies are another longstanding characteristic of Southeast Asian cities (McGee 1967).

The BMA accused vendors of breaking established rules and proceeded to confiscate the goods of pavement vendors in Khlong Toey Market (*Bangkok Post*, 12 January 1993). Vendors protested vehemently. Further complaints about obstruction of traffic and pavement congestion led the city to relocate some sidewalk food vendors congregated around *pakkhlong talad* to spaces run by the BMA or private markets. The government considered fining patrons of illegal vendors in order to curb the behavior. This tense situation was often assuaged by the payment of bribes to municipal police by illegal vendors, as was reported: "Deputy Interior Minister Chaowas Sudlabha . . . denied charges that the police take bribes, but admitted that officials sometimes neglect their duty (*Bangkok Post*, 19 January 1993).

Several informants report having paid "rent" to the *tesakit* to avoid arrest and the confiscation of their goods and to secure their selling space. Noo used to have a shop on a major street near the Coliseum. She had recently moved to Bangkok from the Northeast when she was nearly arrested and her goods confiscated:

> *Noo*: They took away my chairs. The first time I began my business I had just arrived from the province and I didn't know about the *tesakit*. The *tesakit* normally came on Wednesdays [when vending is prohibited]. That time, they came on a Monday. I couldn't move my things. They took away my tables in a truck. But he was kind, when I asked politely for my belongings, he gave them back.

She then began paying the *tesakit* "rent" of 300 Bt per month for the space. They did not manage the space. "He didn't give a receipt. He would simply take the money and put it in his pocket," she admitted. Selling in a public space, not including a space in front of a shop, is the ideal situation according to Noo:

> *Noo*: If you sell in front of a building, you have to pay. I asked once, and it's expensive. It costs 3,000 baht [per month]. I don't have those means. Selling on the sidewalk is better. You only pay 300 baht per month to the *tesakit*. It's better than paying rent.

Samrit and Lek also used to bribe the municipal police for access to their current location, prior to the introduction of a new municipal policy:

> *Kapuk*: Are you renting the space for your shop?
> *Samrit*: Yes, from the *tesakit*, we used to pay 100 baht per month but not anymore.
> *Kapuk*: And now?
> *Lek*: We don't pay anymore.
> *Kapuk*: Why not?
> *Lek*: *Jut phon pan*. We have the right to conduct business there now.
> *Gisèle*: Did the *tesakit* ever give you a receipt?
> *Lek*: No. . . [Laughter].

The changing policies of the BMA toward street-based hawking are summarized as *jut phon pan*, or "selling tolerated." It is written on signs demarcating spaces that permit vending. Use of the "exempt" space is contingent on the vendors' obtaining identification cards from the district office.

Jut Phon Pan and the BMA's Toleration of Hawking

Since 1992 when I first began fieldwork, the policies of the local state toward street vending have changed. When I returned to Bangkok in 1994, signs demarcating permitted vending areas on major thoroughfares had been established identified by a pictogram of a shoulder pole with hanging baskets and the inscription "*jut phon pan*." This phrase is translated roughly as a space where selling is tolerated. The implication is that some restrictions apply. *Jut* simply means a "point" but the meaning of *phon pan* is less clear. Haas (1964) translates it as "to ease the situation." Following years of harassment by municipal police and related bribery the BMA designated parts of major streets as "vendor friendly" thereby easing tensions.

The director of municipal police (*tesakit*) explained that street vending was primarily viewed as a traffic and health problem (Chalee 1994). The director visited Hong Kong and Singapore in order to compare situations and policies. The *jut phon pan* solution was designed following the explorations of other cities and significantly differs in its view of public space compared to the Draconian measures imposed by Singapore. Singapore's "solution" to the hawking "problem" has been one of the most drastic and comprehensive in the world. All street-food vendors, both mobile and stationary, were forced to relocate according to the government's specifications in typical Singaporean style. The reasons for the relocation were traffic management and public health.

Singapore's Foodscape

"We're not a sandwich culture."
"The only place to get cheap food in Singapore nowadays is in primary school canteens."

Professor Chua Beng Huat

Singapore has a long tradition of "public" eating, albeit one that has slightly different origins from those identified for Bangkok. Lee (1992) interprets the hawker tradition of the Straits of Malacca metropolis as one originating from the city's coolie past; one in which Chinese preferences dominate demographically. The migrant society that took root in Singapore was primarily one of male manual laborers, and their food needs were met by the growth of itinerant and fixed-pitch hawkers selling affordable food. Other factors stimulating the preference for eating in the streets in Old Singapore were the tropical climate making night-stalls particularly popular, and the social role of hawker agglomerations as gathering places primarily for men, but sometimes for families (Lee 1992: 143–48).

The producers of this food have historically been mostly men, in keeping with Chinese tradition. Wives and daughters would occasionally help their husbands with the business. Indians and Malays specialized in the sale of *roti canai/ paratha* and *satay*, respectively, and despite the lack of an urban public eating tradition, particularly for the South Asians, the practice is now very popular (Lee 1992: 153).

As early as the 1930s, the colonial regime in Singapore identified hawking on the streets as a problem and began its attempts to control and redirect, even eliminate, this type of economic and spatial activity (*Report of the Committee Appointed to Investigate the Hawker Question*, 1932).[12] To make thoroughfares available for other types of traffic, the government designed policies to alter the spatial location of food-stalls:

> In 1932 and again in 1950, the colonial government decided to allow for "fixed pitch hawkers," that is, for hawkers to sell from barrows, stalls or baskets, in a place marked out for them in the street. Such pitches were to be made available in any side street designated for such a purpose and itinerant hawkers were to be excluded from such streets. Such streets were often either streets already occupied by groups of hawkers or nearby streets. (Lee 1992: 154–55)

This is essentially the *jut phon pan* system instituted in Bangkok. The designated areas in Bangkok correspond to previous fixed-pitch hawker agglomerations. Lee concludes that this type of policy legitimizes the habit of eating outside the home and was a precursor to the next major shift in Singapore's foodscape: the institution of government food centers and the removal of itinerant hawkers altogether.

As described by Ng (1993) and earlier by Yue-Man Yeung (1990), Singapore's street-food vendors were relocated in the 1970s into government owned and operated "hawker centers" and "market-cum-food centers." Sometimes, old parking lots were used to resettle vendors into covered, controlled environments. The rapid drive to re-settlement is directly related to the development of massive public housing schemes in which 80% of Singaporeans continue to reside (Yeoh 1994). Every Housing Development Board (HDB) estate contains at least one self-serve "hawker center" and usually an "eating house" where customers are served at the table. These government-owned food centers are now being privatized. This is a matter of great controversy in a city where people depend a great deal on meals purchased in these establishments. Concerns revolve primarily around the potential increase in the price of food. The government-owned centers are heavily subsidized, and rents for stall-owners are consequently very low. With the real estate market as it is in Singapore, the privatization of food centers will certainly make food more expensive as rent subsidies are removed.

By the early to mid 1980s, street-food vendors and itinerant hawkers were nearly extinct in Singapore with the exception of sidewalk cafés on Bugis Street and in Chinatown where they are licensed and primarily serve tourists (Chua 1994). Whereas in 1969, the census of hawkers indicated that 84% were mobile and 16% were stationary, the last remaining street vendors of both types in Kreta Ayer (Chinatown) have now been relocated. By 1993 there were only 129 itinerant hawkers left selling ice-cream and bread. No new licenses have been issued since the massive relocation schemes were enacted. Singapore regulates its food vendors even more than Tokyo (Chua 1994). On a trip to Japan in the mid 1990s, mobile roasted yam vendors were seen pushing their carts through the streets of the ultra-modern capital, often accompanied by loud chanting-type music and the smell of hickory smoke. Nothing comparable remains in Singapore.

The newest addition to eating establishments in wealthy Singapore are the food courts located in shopping centers: "In the mid-1980s, another "breed" of cooked-food outlets were added to the cooked-food retail system. This relatively new "genre" of eating place took the cue from the Urban Re-development Authority (URA) after it opened its first air-conditioned food centre in Funan Centre in January 1985" (Ng 1993: 5).

The first privately owned food court was in Scott's Shopping Centre, which opened in 1986. These food courts serve hawker food for the most part but in a more stylish venue. More expensive, full meals are also available and the main cultural groups of the island are always represented. Occasionally, there are outlets selling Western food, but many Singaporean food writers agree that this is not a threat to local foodways. Lee reported that McDonald's has only 5% market-share of the fast food industry in the country, amounting to 6 billion dollars a year. The figures are probably similar for Bangkok.[13]

Today, Singapore is the capital of lavish shopping plaza food courts, many replete with waterfalls, plants, and designer lighting. The popularity of these new eating environments is attributed to the growth of consumerism in Singaporean society. These "value-added neighborhood hawker centers" are considered more fashionable and comfortable, especially by the city's affluent young (Ng 1993: 45–51). They represent a contribution of the Singaporean "new middle-class" to the city's foodscape. Bangkok shows similar trends. Like their counterparts in Western cities, Southeast Asian new middle-classes are redefining their social and spatial environments to accommodate their urbane, sophisticated tastes. In 1996, the traditional working-class foodways in Singapore appeared to have a bleak future with rumours that the famous Newton Circus Hawker Centre would be closed. Indeed, Newton Circus is still thriving and is a glimmer of hope for the future of street foods in Singapore. The "Makansutra" website (www.makansutra.com) shows that Singaporeans are reluctant to let their beloved hawker food disappear, and popular nostalgic interest in "street eats" may result in a revival of the port city's working-class eating traditions.[14]

The Local-Global Dialectic: Food Micro-entrepreneurs and Thai/International Capital

This section shows that Thai food-shop owners are interacting in direct and indirect ways with large Thai and foreign owned food companies and agri-business corporations. The most obvious examples are the food centers that have emerged over the past ten to twenty years. Other, less visible, manifestations of this trend are the employment of (former) food-shop owners and workers in cafeterias and the purchasing of supplies directly from mega-corporations. This represents the blurring of boundaries between the traditional and modern and the local versus global.

The interaction between micro-entrepreneurs and the volatile real estate market as mediated through relations with landowners points to spatial transformations of selling environments vis-à-vis inputs of capital. This results in both opportunities for and marginalization of small-scale cooked-food sellers. Some small food-shop owners have relocated within the growing number of food centers in the city, most situated in department stores and shopping plazas.

Shopping Plazas and Food Centers

Central Plaza (described in the previous chapter) is located in suburban Bangkok serving the middle-class clientele of Ladprao and Bang Kapi. The Plaza has a food-floor in the basement of Central Department Store, which sells take-home food in small plastic bags, and, more recently, styrofoam, which is identical in form and content to that sold in *soi* and street-based food shops. This resembles the type of food retailing prevalent in Japanese department stores (Jadavji 1995; McGee 1995).

Large shopping plazas are becoming ubiquitous in Bangkok, particularly in the suburbs and exurbs, and have their own foodscapes that are spatially distinct from the outside world. Although the Victory Monument Area is in a more central part of the city where densities are higher and large shopping plazas are absent, there exist, nevertheless, miniature versions of "mall foodscapes." Robinson's Department Store, for instance, has its own small, crowded food center on the ground floor. A more pleasant food court is on the air-conditioned mezzanine and contains a full-service sukiyaki restaurant ("Noodle Garden") and five self-serve Thai-owned fast food chains, sharing common seating, that specialize in fresh fruit juice, noodle dishes, fried rice, or other small meals. Again, the coupon system is in use, and individual dishes cost 20–25 Bt. Prices exceed those on the street by about 10 Bt.[15]

The Home Food Center (HFC) is the newest addition to the collection of food centers in the Victory Monument Area. Sor Khon Kaen, HFC's corporate owner, became famous for its fabrication and mass-distribution of a type of cured-pork sausage (*naem*). Fifty percent of Sor Khon Kaen is owned by the family that started the company. The HFC has a branch that opened earlier on Sathorn Road. Prospective tenants were approached and invited to open a branch in the HFC; only businesses that were experiencing successful sales were contacted. This resembles the recruitment process by Central Plaza. HFC similarly uses coupons with a 70/30 split of revenues. Like its counterpart in Robinson's Department Store, however, this food center did not survive the devaluation of the baht in 1997.

Women account for the largest share of workers in food center outlets, as on the street. This shows that traditional gender roles are being superimposed on new spatial forms. The foodscape exhibits "layering" of gender relations that are building on a historically rooted foundation. This does not mean, however, that women workers control individual enterprises. Some of the food center outlets are franchised chains, such as "Five Star Chicken" or "Noodle Duck." These chains are part of Thai corporate structure.

Food sold in food centers, particularly those that are highly formalized such as HFC, tends to be standardized and risks becoming of poorer quality than some of the food sold on the streets (Keyes 1996). Chua Beng Huat (1994) said the same of the comparison of food quality between hawker centres and the former, street-based, eateries in Singapore. Economic development appears to stamp out the diversity of food sold bringing it under more centralized ownership and control. This is a generalized statement, and some food center outlets in highly modern shopping plazas sell excellent food.

McGee (1995) comments that the cost-cutting measures employed by some of these food centers may be a contributing factor to standardization and deterioration of food quality. Some outlets buy poorer quality raw materials (i.e., food) and/or pay their employees very low wages. Poorly paid employees are not motivated to provide good service let alone quality food. Owner-operators are better skilled and motivated (Ley 1996). Further to this, young, inexperienced food center outlet employees lack cooking skills compared to their counterparts in the informal sector.

Independent Food Centers

An example of a less formalized food center is the case of the Rattana Food Center owned and, as explained in the previous chapter, operated by Wira and Goy. Wira's mother, still the official landowner, inherited the property from her mother and developed it into 28 shophouses rented to businesses and residential tenants. One row of shophouses was renovated as a student residence where more than a hundred rooms are rented, and a second row was later gutted and re-developed as a small food center.

At the time of the interview, the food center had existed for a fifteen months. It was opened primarily to serve students in the residence who are prohibited from cooking in their rooms and also serves local residents and workers. Although Wira and Goy own and manage the food center, they do not own the eight food shops within the center:

> *Goy*: We're the property owners here, but we don't own the food shops in the center. We only rent the space. We hire young people to clean up, bus tables, and put things away. We collect the rent from the shops.

The Rattana Food Center charges 8,000 Bt per month, which includes maintenance as well as utilities. Food shops provide their own dishes but utensils belong to the center. In addition, the food center owns a stand where soft drinks and other non-alcoholic beverages are sold.[16] The center is open from 6 a.m. to 11 p.m. The vendors in the center prefer not to use the coupon system:

> *Goy*: The vendors don't like coupons because with coupons they earn less money. They feel that with the coupon "standard" they have to give the proprietor about 30 to 35%.

185

The usual is 30%. With the coupon, they don't pay rent but a share of their income . . . Here, it's a small center. It's not a shopping mall. It's better to charge rent.

Wira explains that this was more satisfactory to the vendors. The result is also less expensive food. Whereas large-scale air-conditioned food centers like the HFC charge 25 Bt for a bowl of noodles, the Rattana Food Center vendor charges only 15 Bt.

The food sold in the food center is normally prepared at home in advance by the shopowners with the obvious exception of noodle soup. The food center owners prefer it this way:

Goy: Really, we don't want them to prepare meals here. They have to do it at home and later bring it here to sell. Our objective is to have them sell it here only, but in the end we can't control it. Sometimes they prepare food here too. . . We encourage them to prepare it at home because the cooking odors disturb the residents who live upstairs.

Businesses are basically home-based since the goods for sale are, for the most part, prepared in the family kitchen. This is another example of the blurring between home and work place. The home kitchen is both a site for household food preparation and commercial production. There is, in addition, continuity between shop and home rather than a sharp division between home and work, or what is ostensibly private versus public. The sharing of Chaichana and Vipawan's domestic employees with their restaurant, The Professor's Pub is another indication of the blurring of private and public.

It is difficult for health inspectors to concern themselves with hygiene at the site of food production. In any case, inspectors do not concern themselves with these issues and grant licenses in terms of the requisite number of toilets and sinks and the clean appearance of the premises rather than food quality or cleanliness of utensils.

Food-shop owners in the Rattana Food Center did not have to bid for their spaces. Most of them operated food shops in the old shophouses prior to renovation and were given priority to relocate in the center by their landlord, the patron:

Goy: The vendors here are former tenants. We proposed to close them down temporarily during renovations and then give them a place in the new food center. If we had just sent them away, they wouldn't have been able to find a place to earn their livings. So, we made it so that they could sell here.

Most of the food-shop owners accepted the offer. The few who declined were, for the most part, male Sino-Thai vendors unaccustomed to the "self-serve" concept:

Goy: Because many Chinese *poh kha* (male vendors) need servers to wait tables. They couldn't accept this self-serve system so they didn't move into the food center.

Only one of the vendors rents a room on the premises. An interesting phenomenon displayed in the center is that of "shop-sharing" whereby two vendors share the same selling space but conduct business at different times. This phenomenon is commonplace (Vespry 1993).

Table 7.1 provides a profile of four shops in the food center as part of the quantitative survey. The remaining four vendors refused to be questioned. Two of the shops specialize in the sale of noodles, both operated by women. One shop, selling chicken rice and pork leg, is operated by a Sino-Thai man of 37. The final shop sells curry and rice and is operated by a single woman of 50. The other shop owners are married. None of the cooked-food sellers has more than a primary education, and all have helpers who come in regularly consisting of family members. These characteristics conform to the data on other food-shop owners.

A difference with other food micro-entrepreneurs is the birthplace of respondents. Three reported being born in Bangkok, and one is originally from Ratburi, a part of the EBMR. This may be an indication of their relative wealth compared to cooked-food sellers from Isaan. The hefty shop rents of 8,000 Bt per month, in

Table 7.1 Characteristics of Food-shop Owners, Rattana Food Center, Victory Monument Area, 1994

Shop	Type of Food Sold	Age	Birth Province	Sex	Marital Status	Address Category[17]	Education Level[18]	Helper (type)[19]
1	Curry and rice	50	Ratburi	F	Single	Same	Primary	Cousins
2	Chicken rice and/or pork	37	Bangkok	M	Married	VMA	Primary	Cousins
3	Noodles	55	Bangkok	F	Married	DD	Primary	Family
4	Noodles	35	Bangkok	F	Married	BKT	Primary	Family

addition to paying rent for one's living quarters, would be beyond the financial abilities of Daeng, Ying, Samrit, and Lek.

Throughout the interview, Wira and Goy used the tone of "patron" to describe relations with their tenants in the food center. Many times, they implied they were doing their "clients" a favour by renting them a selling space or by providing the "youngsters" who cleaned up the center with a job. When I asked them about paying employees minimum wage and following the regulations of the municipal district (*ket*) office I received the following explanation:

> *Wira*: We don't operate like the big centers. We're kind of like a family. If they want a day off they can have a day off anytime they want. We don't make the days up. You come into work, you don't want to work you get someone to replace you. . . We treat them like family. If they're sick, we take care of them. We take them to the doctor.[20]

Clean-up employees, most of whom are related to one another, do not start with minimum wage but work their way up to the legally required 135 Bt per day. A daily wage avoids problems related to "sloughing off," which Wira and Goy complained about when they paid salaries on a monthly basis. Many are teenagers described as irresponsible by management. The employees are no longer allowed to rent rooms in the residence as they were often caught napping during the day! Goy explains that employees also earn "bonuses" such as tips and free meals that justifies the lower wage. "Thais who aren't very well educated don't want to take on responsibilities," I was told. Goy complains that supervision is a problem and that she and Wira plan to hire a manager to supervise the workings of the food center. They see themselves as benefactors for their tenants and employees and, to a certain extent, play such a role.

Wira and his family are pillars of the local community having lived there for several generations. He is critical of large-scale Thai conglomerates, such as CP, which he criticized at length during the interview. The *modus operandi* of the Rattana Food Center is part of a more traditional system of Thai social relations based on patron-client networks and qualitatively different than the more professionalized system in place at HFC, Central Plaza Ladprao, and similar establishments.

Since the opening of the Home Food Center, business at the Rattana Food Center has suffered. Despite renovations, the building is old and dilapidated. Wira and Goy would ideally like to re-develop the property as a high-rise condominium in the next six years depending on their financial situation. They are in the process of preparing a plan and worry that they lack the necessary experience for such a venture.

Small independent food centers like Rattana are less directly a part of national and trans-national corporations but, due to the wealth and power of their proprietors, are inevitably tied into international circuits of capital. When Wira and Goy decide to re-develop the property, the fate of the food vendors will be sealed one way or another. On the one hand, they may be able to cater to more customers in another selling space. On the other hand, they may not be able to compete in the new economic and spatial environment.

Small Food-shop Owners in the New Economy

The cases of two food-shop owners, Daeng and Luung, illustrate the difficulties that some entrepreneurs in the prepared-food system have adjusting to the many changes taking place around them. Daeng has had to resort to working in a cafeteria in order to bring in extra income, and Luung has difficulty finding enough customers.

Daeng and her mother can no longer make ends meet and provide for their family in Isaan with the revenue from the food shop. Daeng found a job as a cook at the cafeteria of the American University Alumnae (AUA) but could not tolerate the exhaustion of having to *arrive* at 5 a.m. The AUA subcontracts the responsibility of the cafeteria to an individual who then pays cooks 6,000 Bt per month to work twelve hour days. Since Daeng continued to help in the food shop after work and would clean up until 10 or 10:30 p.m., the pace at the AUA was exhausting. In addition, the food was of such poor quality at the cafeteria that she resorted to drinking milk or a yoghurt beverage most of the time. She would arrive home hungry and tired. After three weeks on the job, Daeng quit and found more suitable employment at the cafeteria of CP.

Ironically, Luung obtains his ducks from CP and is the next example of a small food-shop owner engaging in direct contact with large corporations: "Before, I was in another trade. I had moved up-country. I sold things from the forest, like corn, to sell in the towns. My first wife worked there with me. After a year, she died. The children were very young so I had to come back to the city."

In his forties, Luung bought his food shop named "Delicious Treat" from someone else and in the first ten years was quite successful. Since then, his duck noodle business has deteriorated. The pictures of his "prime," when he was featured on televized cooking shows, remain faded on the dingy wall. He attributes the decline to the difficulty of finding employees, economic problems, and the growth of shopping centers and night-life. "In the old days, many customers came in the evening. Nowadays, it's very quiet. Before, there weren't places to visit in the evening." He now closes his shop at 5 p.m. "I'm already 60 years old," sighs Luung, "I should be retired, but if I don't work I don't know how I'll survive." Fortunately, Luung has adult children who live at home and contribute to family income.

Vagaries of the Real Estate Market

Discussions with small food-shop owners reveal that they have a fragile relationship to the spaces they occupy for the sale of prepared food. Their access to both public and private space is vulnerable, particularly due to the volatility of the real estate market in the VMA, which is undergoing rapid transformation. This resembles the situation in Jakarta during the 1980s described in detail by Lea Jellinek (1991). Land speculation and re-development have been two of the reasons that enable Bangkok's middle and wealthy classes to accumulate large amounts of capital. The entire local economy is in a state of flux with increasing migration to the city and the growth of a wealthier class of consumers who demand more comfortable living and leisure environments. The case of Ying and Daeng as well as Samrit and Lek provide the most telling examples of potential future displacement due to property development.

Ying and Daeng have been in their present location for five years. The landlady, Jae Noo, has indicated that she is planning a high-rise apartment building for the premises. Their future depends on the wishes of the landowner who will determine whether or not they can operate the food shop in the future apartment:

> *Gisèle*: But there will really be a food shop in the new building?
> *Ying*: There should be. The owner said that they don't want us to move. But, we'll see first. The owner sets the conditions.

Samrit and Lek have finally found a viable selling space on one of the streets in the study area, but the small room where they live with their two children is also owned by Jae-Noo:

> *Gisèle*: I've been told that the landlady will build an apartment here. Where will you go?
> *Samrit*: We've got big problems! We still don't have a place to go to. We're trying to find a place but with no luck. We'd like to find something, but it's hard for vendors to find housing.

Samrit and Lek are not counting on any privileges from their landlady. If they want to retain their prime selling space on the sidewalk, they must live in the vicinity.

As of the mid-1990s, the entire neighborhood was undergoing rapid reconstruction as high-rise apartments and condominiums transformed the cityscape. The onset of the Asian economic crisis after 1997 slowed then temporarily stopped this pace of development.

Spatial Issues and Thai Conceptions of Public and Private

At first glance, Samrit's case provides an example of the "irresponsible" behavior associated with young Thai men; however, to characterize his behavior this way is simplistic. As Sanitsuda (1990) describes, men who come to Bangkok from Isaan to work as *tuk-tuk* drivers often abuse drugs, such as stimulants, to cope with long days in horrible traffic conditions. They then resort to alcohol to "come down" off the stimulants. It becomes a vicious circle, and some have returned to their villages in Northeast Thailand, insane because of the toll the lifestyle has taken on their minds and bodies. Labelling these men as "irresponsible" is blaming the victims of uneven development. Selling noodles on the street with his wife is a healthier and more profitable occupation for Samrit than driving a *tuk-tuk*.

Daeng's younger brother is a more suitable example of the "young irresponsible male" phenomenon. Twice he squandered the college tuition money given to him by his Aunt Ying, hard earned by herself and Daeng. "He's a teenager, do you understand?" Daeng explained to us justifying his behavior. Of course, Daeng, at his age was busy earning money for her family rather than spending time in snooker halls. Like sexual license, "responsibility" carries with it a double standard according to gender. Teenaged boys are expected to be irresponsible; girls are not. Daeng's niece Wipa and Tip's daughter help dutifully in their respective food shops every day. This is certainly related to the construction of femininity as "nurturing." Ying, for example is a *mae liang* for both her extended family and the neighborhood, as are many female micro-entrepreneurs in Bangkok's foodscape.

Some of the factors leading to the opening of a food shop intersect with well-known patterns within Thai society such as patron-client relations and cleavages based on ethnicity or income group. As the case of Fong Kee shows, however, people of different income levels and ethnic backgrounds come together in the foodscape mutually influencing one another.

The discussion also illustrated the complexity of labelling food-related places and activities as "public" versus "private." In the *sois*, for example, selling spaces can be viewed as either public or private depending on circumstances. Legally, however, the space is private, and permission of the land-owner is necessary. Still, as evidenced by Ying's case, permission can be withdrawn unexpectedly, in this particular case when the privacy of the land-owner is perceived as threatened by the "public" nature of cooked-food vending.

On the street, selling space is legally public but, until the introduction of the *jut phon pan* policy some municipal police officers were managing the space as their own fiefdom by charging "rent." Non-payment carried with it the threat of arrest or confiscation of selling equipment. The new policy aims "to ease the situation" and guarantees harassment-free tenure of designated selling spaces on the condition that cooked-food sellers follow a set of rules. This is a step toward making public space truly accessible. However, policies toward street hawking, particular that of food, are known to fluctuate as evidence from Singapore suggests.

Food shops located in fixed buildings face a vastly different set of circumstances. For the most part, these entrepreneurs are wealthier and able to sign long-term leases guaranteeing access to their selling spaces. They are protected from the local state's fluctuating policies. Restaurant owners such as Professor Chaichana and Vipawan own their property outright and have increased options. Their peers, Wira and Goy, are considering re-developing their property into a high-rise apartment complex thereby increasing revenues considerably. For these agents in the food-system, access to public space is not an immediate concern though they may generate revenue from the rental of spaces in "public" food centers.

The practices associated with cooked-food vending and the restaurant industry indicate that there is a blurring between the activities and spaces commonly thought of as public and private. Food being prepared at home and later sold in a food center, and expensive restaurants purchasing condominiums to house employees are examples of this as is the Professor's sharing of domestic and restaurant employees. The "family" discourse propagated by Wira and Goy is yet another instance of this blurring that ties in with the system of patron-client relations. These systems of interaction are far from being equal and complementary but are rather part of Thai society's "relations of ruling" (Smith 1987) that help maintain the superior position of the more powerful patrons. Individuals studied do not interpret events in this manner, and patrons rather see themselves as altruistically bestowing favours with clients showing gratitude for the gift.

Given the quickly changing real estate environment, the less resource-endowed "clients" are constrained in their choices and vulnerable to the whims of their land-owners, the market, and changing state policies. Even though they may eventually find niches in the new economy, such as in privately-owned and indoor food centers, the medium-term future appears uncertain for the micro-entrepreneurs in the VMA.

Most micro-entrepreneurs who occupy sidewalks and lanes to sell food are female. Women are therefore disproportionately affected by re-development. Most are also subordinated with respect to their rural status, as migrants from the provinces.

The following excerpt from my field notes illustrates some of the issues involved when discussing "public" space in Bangkok:

Field Notes 7.1: Taxes, Utilities, and Interim Land-Use Restaurants

8 September 1994: K bought *luukcin nua* brochettes. On the way back K said "You know, these people (meaning the street vendors) make a lot of money, but they pay no tax." I asked him to estimate how much they make. . . He said he figures about 1,000 baht per day. He said that they don't have to pay rent because the street is public space, but I suspect differently. Ironically, as we arrived at the travel agency, I noticed a hose going to the restaurant on the corner. . . I indicated what I noticed and he said that he supplies that food shop with water and electricity. I said, "Oh you sell that person utilities! Is that a fairly common arrangement between shopkeepers and food-shop owners? K became rather defensive. . . He said, "Oh, that food-shop owner asked me to help him because he doesn't really have a 'proper place' so I said 'yes.'" As though the food shop isn't paying for the services! Yet another income-generating strategy. Another apartment consisting of rooms (*hoh pak*) is going up on the lane where the food shop in question is located. The restaurant that K supplies with utilities appears to be an "interim land-use" restaurant.

"K" is an acquaintance who owns a travel agency and student residence. He assumes that access to "public" space is unproblematic. This is a fairly typical response to the "street foods" question by the general public.[21] Those who accuse vendors of earning too much disregard the high cost of food, which offsets much income, and it seems to be forgotten that those who use public space for business purposes sometimes have (or had) to pay bribes to the *tesakit*. These vendors also support family members in the provinces, filling the void of an ineffective social welfare system and a development agenda focused on cities at the expense of rural areas.

In the above vignette, K exonerates his own behavior of collecting undeclared money from a food-shop owner on the grounds that he is "helping" a person who does not have a "proper place." Not surprisingly, the small student residence that K owns and operates is also undeclared and therefore untaxed. Ironically, K and his family agree that food sold in small shops on the street is of good quality for the most part, and they frequent street restaurants.

Chapter 8

Bangkok's Post-crisis Foodscape

Food is one of the many lenses through which to view place. Likewise, gender relations can be illustrated and understood better through examining foodways. I have braided three different strands of empirical information to portray public eating in Thai urban society. Gender relations, food-systems, and questions of urban change have been pieced together to construct a foodscape of Bangkok. The foodscape presented is a *bricolage*. A range of improvised techniques were used and adapted to the subject under study depending on the tools and materials available. Methods were contingent upon the circumstances encountered. As much as possible, comments were framed by the moment of contact where observations and discussions took place. I attempted to keep the reader close to the "ground" by incorporating excerpts from my field notes and lengthy quotations from informants. This resulted in the creation of a "blurred genre" between conventional scholarly tome, field diary, and interview transcripts.

My first research question was "How can one represent Bangkok's foodscape?" The heuristic value of the foodscape approach is the recognition that it is a construction of the viewer, like landscape, and that the criteria selected (such as gender relations and urban change) are potentially unlimited. A more thorough consideration of ethnicity, age, income group, or time of day, for example, would have produced a different piece of research. A single study cannot address the entirety of Bangkok's complex food-system. This chapter will summarize the findings presented as well as provide a brief *quo vadis* pertaining to Bangkok's foodscape following the impact of the Asian economic crisis of 1997–98.[1]

Gisèle Yasmeen

The Gendering of Bangkok's Foodscape

Informal food shops are a life-support system for urbanites, providing affordable food for all income groups. The predominance of women as small-scale entrepreneurs in the prepared-food sector is the result of many factors, not least of which are Thai constructions and practices of gender. Foreign observers have interpreted women's presence in public space and control of small businesses, such as food shops, as indications of their "high status." An added complication is the fact that Thailand, like neighboring societies, does not emphasize gender differences linguistically or engage in obviously brutal treatment of women such as clitoridectomy or foot-binding "which scream out for ethnographic investigation" (Errington 1990: 4, citing Atkinson 1982: 257):

> Because feminist theories about gender tend to be formulated for and from societies where male-female difference is highly marked, we may be missing issues germane to the topic when we glance casually at the "high status of women" in an area where the treatment of women seems *relatively* benign. Actually, it could be that differences between men and women are not socially visible to us because they are not marked in ways we easily recognized. (Errington 1990: 4–5; emphasis added)

Bangkok's foodscape is a superb venue in which to explore complex gender ideologies not immediately understood by an outside observer. A contributing stereotype leading to women's dominance of food micro-enterprises is the view that women are better money-managers than men. Thai women are trusted with the family purse and are considered more responsible than males for "getting things done," qualities associated with powerful persons in a Western context (Errington 1990: 4). Related factors are the structure of the rural Thai household as a "corporation of kinswomen" giving females access to relatives for support in the running of a small enterprise.

Micro-entrepreneurs must be seen as skilled agents rather than simply part of the "informal sector" or "household economy." They engage in a high risk occupation in terms of the fickle tastes of customers, changing state policies, and the vagaries of the real estate market. Food-vending micro-entrepreneurs are having an ever more difficult time earning livings in the rapidly changing and deteriorating urban environments of mega-cities such as Bangkok.

The second two sets of factors, access to capital and labor/help, depend on kinship networks, neighborhood organizations (such as informal credit groups) and patron-client relations. For micro-entrepreneurs, access to capital is difficult and, when available, often insecure as they are relegated to borrowing from money-lenders, pawning belongings or engaging in high-risk informal rotating credit groups. Fortunes have been lost to these funds but many participants have no other means of obtaining large amounts of capital.

Mutual aid is an important outcome of interactions between kin, neighbors, patrons and clients. These social relations are absolutely necessary for the commercial viability of the establishment since keeping food affordable for consumers gives a food shop its competitive edge. Free family labor therefore subsidizes the costs of social reproduction by feeding workers at a low cost.

Landowners who play the role of patron can either be of assistance to their food-selling tenants/clients or can jeopardize the latter's ability to earn a living by withdrawing access to space on their property to food-shop owners. Some micro-entrepreneurs are forced to abandon their selling spaces as a result. Patron-client relations in Bangkok's foodscape are clearly part of the Thai "relations of ruling" (Smith 1987) where, ultimately, interactions are structured in the patron's favour because of a significant power imbalance. When the economy is booming, landowners in central Bangkok choose to re-develop their property to increase profitability. This has a contradictory effect. On the one hand, several small food-shop owners in the Victory Monument Area are forced to relocate due to re-development of their living and/or work spaces as high-density apartments and condominiums. On the other hand, higher population densities bring more customers to the area resulting in the creation of many more small food shops. Since it is mostly poor women who engage in small-scale cooked-food vending they and their families are most affected by these socio-economic and spatial changes.

The spatial and economic positions of the smallest, most vulnerable cooked-food sellers are unsure in the volatile environment of Bangkok. Public space, such as the sidewalk, is the cheapest place to conduct business but is less secure because of fluctuating municipal policies. With the deteriorating environmental situation, a street-front location may eventually become a liability. For those who can access public contracts or else a place within a food center, economic conditions improve, but individual control over work and the flexible informality of the enterprise is compromised.

Blurred Vision

It is striking how at every point of entry into Bangkok's foodscape, boundaries between what are conventionally thought of as discrete theoretical and empirical categories are blurred. What would have been framed as "traditional" vs. "modern," "informal" vs. "formal" or "public" vs. "private" ten or twenty years ago can no longer be viewed in this way. This is both an analytical problem, related to the binary concepts inherent in much Western theory and one related to the rapidity with which Bangkok society is changing making it difficult to anchor down and use particular concepts. Teleological approaches popular in the 1970s and even the 1980s that would have attempted to depict Bangkok's foodscape as undergoing a straightforward process of "modernization" are today unthinkable.

A taken-for-granted daily activity, eating, is shown in its cross-cultural complexity in the portrait of Bangkok's foodscape. The discussion has helped us interrogate whether some of the core aspects of Western social theory, such as private/public sphere models, are appropriate to such a context. Their relevance, or lack of relevance, has a direct impact on feminist post-colonial conceptualizations of gender relations.

Non-Western Sphere Models?

Thai definitions of something resembling "public" and "private" spheres are difficult to ascertain. Certainly with respect to gender, femininity, and masculinity are uniquely marked and spatialized, particularly in relation to food and the taking of meals. Differences are very stark compared to the foodscape painted by Conlon in "Dining Out in Bombay" (1995) where public eating has been a poorly serviced domain due to the plain lack of eating establishments because people without question prefer to eat at home. Secondly, the presence of South Asian women customers in stalls and restaurants is a fairly recent and still under-represented phenomenon because of the shame associated with being seen as a "public woman." In comparison to East or South Asia, Thai restrictions on feminine mobility are practically absent.

Impact of the Asian Economic Crisis

This concluding section of the final chapter examines self-employment in the food sector in light of the economic crisis that ravaged Southeast Asia following the devaluation of the Thai baht in July 1997. First, it highlights the crisis of development in the region and globally; and, secondly, opens up the discussion on the role of the misnamed "informal" sector in assuring the economic security of the victims of the crisis. The worst effects of the crisis were felt in the few years following the devaluation of the baht, and many parts of the economy have to a certain extent recovered. Nevertheless it is still worth examining the dramatic impacts of the crisis because of the sharp contrast it poses with the "boom period" described in Chapters 1–7. In addition, the critical role of the prepared-food delivery system as a type of "social safety" net became extremely evident from 1997 to 1999, and its importance is still highly visible today.

Sandwiches, Security, and Social Capital

Thailand's Sirivat Voravetvuthikun . . . [t]he bankrupt stockbroker, who is "hundreds of millions" in debt because of a 28-unit condominium project, now peddles sandwiches. "I'm still trying to sell the condo units," he says, "I can't give up, especially since I've had so much support from the media and the Thai people who buy my sandwiches. I was very depressed, but my morale is up now." Sirivat, 48, has given about 40 TV and print interviews. To outsiders, he personifies Thailand's rise and fall—and possible redemption.

Bacani 1997: 52

Sirivat's story made the cover of numerous magazines and was the subject of television news reports around the world in late 1997 and early 1998 and continues to draw attention as a symbol of the financial crisis and gradual recovery in the region (*Bangkok Post* 1998; CBC Television 1997, 1998; McDowell 1998; Yasmeen 2001a–b). The media focused on this vignette for its shock value, forcing the public to scrutinise the "Asian Miracle" discourse that permeated depictions of East and Southeast Asian booming economies in the 1980s and early 1990s (Pasuk and Baker 1998). In a very Southeast Asian and particularly Thai fashion, it also points to the creativity associated with micro-entrepreneurialism and the fact that food, specifically, is a sector of economic strength and resilience.[2] The "sandwich man" vignette, however, contains three ironies in terms of its depiction of small-scale food retailing in the region.

First, as has been demonstrated here, most food vendors in Southeast Asia, particularly in Thailand, are women. This gendering of the food-system is a distinctive feature of the region and has implications for intra-household resource allocation and the economic security of families (see Yasmeen 1992, 1996a–d). Secondly, most of the lore about vendors vis-à-vis the corporate world are rags-to-riches stories rather than this tale of riches to rags. There are sagas of both women and men, particularly the Overseas Chinese, starting out in life thirty years ago as vendors and ending up at the helm of conglomerates such as Central Pattana group and Charoen Pokhpand (CP). Lastly, most Southeast Asian street foods, despite outside influences, are local or Chinese specialities rather than an obviously Western food item such as the sandwich.[3] Locally available ingredients still overwhelmingly dominate local diets with rice as a staple. The devaluation of local currencies makes the importing of wheat flour and other foodstuffs used to make food items such as sandwiches out of reach for the masses and middle-class.

A more appropriate vignette for the region might have been the depiction of an impoverished migrant woman in her forties selling noodle soup on the streets of Bangkok or Manila. Nevertheless, there is a reason for this inversion of imagery and representation that emphasises the way in which the economic crisis has turned thinking about Southeast Asia upside down questioning the conventional paradigm of development. Sirivat's tale also draws attention to human security issues, particularly the role played by micro-entrepreneurship in keeping people afloat financially. Beyond the obvious reference to food and income security, the widespread availability of prepared food is another distinguishing feature of the region. The turn of events has pointed to consumer trend of purchasing traditional fast foods to the detriment of Western-owned chains and restaurants formerly catering to the middle-class and elite (Kwanchai 1997; Marshall 1998). Laid-off employees are opening eateries and vending operations to earn needed cash on a daily basis (Busaba and Busrin 1998). Policymakers and scholars need to take small-scale food retailing seriously as an important component of economic security of the under- and unemployed. The simple act of selling food is, in the end, of far more basic value to the consumer than engaging in activities that cater to desires for conspicuous consumption alone, such as buying or selling a Mercedes-Benz.

Coping with the Crisis

In Thailand the economic downturn since 1997 has made a huge impact on the small-scale food retailing system. Whereas a few years ago, some vendors were threatened with relocation due to the imminent construction of condominiums and office towers, the halt on construction post-crisis initially left many of their selling spaces intact.[4] However, the relatively positive impact of selling spaces being less threatened was quickly offset by the decline in revenues for all prepared-food business across the board. There have been ups and downs for many of the food-shop owners profiled in this book over the past few years.

Daeng, for example, thought she and her Aunt Ying would be forced to vacate their selling space when she was interviewed in late 1994. In 1999, her business was doing well. Customers at that time were regular, and there were no threats of re-development. In September 1999, Daeng had even acquired a cellular phone, and her "mother," Aunt Ying, had retired to the Isaan countryside. However, Daeng's business began to suffer in early 2001 when she borrowed 100,000 Bt to lease a shophouse on Rajavitee Road for her restaurant and as a place of residence. The risk and debt was too great for her to bear and, after less than a year she had to sell the business and, having already relinquished her former selling space, had to resort to renting a house from her former land owner, Jae Jiu. As of June 2002, Daeng had a makeshift and run-down looking eatery set up in front of the house she was renting along with her brother, his wife, and baby. Given the much greater number of food shops on the same *soi* and fewer customers available generally, Daeng's revenues are a third of what they were in the mid-1990s. She is tired and discouraged.

Middle-class families such as the Chanprasets, for example, experienced some downward mobility from 1997 to 1999. Their travel agency rarely gets business any more, and the informal residence for university students in their two shophouses is shabby and run down compared to 1994. Fortunately, Mrs Chanprasert still has her job as a secretary for a government agency. In April 1999, Mr Chanprasert opened a food shop in order to earn extra income for the household. There are several similar examples throughout the Victory Monument Area. The presence of new eateries in nearly all parts of the city is overwhelming. Mr Chanprasert's food shop income-generating strategy also points to the accelerated involvement of men in food vending following the crisis.

The most vulnerable victims of the downturn, however, initially left Bangkok to return to their impoverished rural areas:

> Nouphen Chartsri is no poster child for the Asian crisis, no high-flying stockbroker who lost his Mercedes-Benz and is now selling sandwiches to survive. . . She's a far more average Asian, a farmwoman with a few years of education who had found a measure of the good life in Thailand's booming economy. The tropical sun has aged her beyond her 30 years. (McDowell 1998)

Nouphen, from Isaan, worked in a factory on the outskirts of Bangkok where she earned twice her previous income from farming. When the financial crisis hit she, like many migrants, went back to her village, resorting to cutting sugarcane for free to work off a family debt. Articles in the *Far Eastern Economic Review* in the late 1990s suggested that migrants were slowly trickling back to Bangkok as the economy started to recover (Crispin 1999). Many of these returnees are living in slums and doing odd jobs to survive. They borrow from moneylenders and pay exorbitant interest to make ends meet from day-to-day.

Though the information on the social impacts of economic crisis is somewhat anecdotal, the general observations and countless similar stories of individuals together paint a portrait of the emerging living and working conditions: "The indications of mounting social problems are seen in growing unemployment and the need to turn to the informal sector for a living, as well as increased migration of displaced workers" (Woo 1998: 3).

In the few years immediately following the crisis, Thai urbanites "downshifted" their consumption habits away from places formerly patronized exclusively by the well-heeled classes to inexpensive eateries catering to the masses. Street restaurants, food-stalls, and home-based businesses, therefore, have a much larger pool of customers from which to draw. The prepared-food system has gone from "servicing" the formal economy to replacing it. The loss of paid employment, particularly in construction, resulted in more constricted incomes and, hence, restriction in the number and types of eating places that could be patronized.[5]

To redress the information gap on the "informal sector" but more importantly identify policy solutions, organizations such as the International Labor Office and the UNDP through UNIFEM (the UN agency for women) are beginning to examine ways in which to enhance coping strategies for micro-entrepreneurs, particularly women.

Post McDonaldization: Fast Foods and the Economic Downturn

Several middle-class restaurants in Bangkok closed following the devaluation of the baht including the former world's largest restaurant, Tom Nuk Thai. Immediately following the crisis, Western fast food chains struggled to keep afloat and compete with the resurgent street-food sector. Thai agri-food conglomerates such as Central Pattana Group (CP) license most of the large chains such as McDonald's and KFC. Though a number of KFCs in the region resorted to laying off staff or even closed due to reduced sales, spokespersons for these establishments insisted in 1997 that they still had a future in the region. Suwanna Usanachitt, Marketing Manager of KFC International Thailand, explained:

> We have not positioned KFC as a luxury restaurant but as a fast-food outlet affordable to middle to lower income earners . . . the parent company is still confident in Thailand's

economic situation and is providing strong marketing and investment support . . . Fast-food chains that offer good products at reasonable and fair prices and benefit customers will survive. (Kwanchai 1997: B3)

Indeed, Bangkok as of 2002 was still replete with several branches of KFC. Fast food chains like McDonald's coped during the most difficult post-crisis chaos by introducing new products to compete with traditional fast foods such as those sold by small vendors. In Indonesia, McDonald's introduced the "RiceEgg" sold for 2,000 Rp (24 cents) as opposed to the burger, which jumped to 10,400 Rp ($1.20), representing two days wages for most workers. Still, on the street in 1997, one could purchase a dish made of rice, meat, and eggs for 2,000 Rp, or even less if one was not insistent about having a place to sit down: "In Jakarta, the price of a Big Mac can buy you an 8-km cab ride, two cans of locally-produced Bintang beer, a big bag of good-quality rice, or a ticket for the 112-km ride to the hill retreat of Bandung" (Marshall Ibid: F3).

One is tempted to applaud the tarnishing of the Golden Arches, which are symbols of food imperialism and the converging of consumer tastes.[6] Whatever one's stand is on international fast food chains, there are serious consequences for employment when these large, normally stable establishments decline or go out of business:

Coca Holding International Co., Ltd., operator of the Coco sukiyaki restaurant chain, is suffering badly in cash-strapped Indonesia, Malaysia, and Thailand, where a heavy drop in spending power is keeping clients away. . . "[Richard] Loo (executive director of Coca Restaurant Takashimaya) said the company has targeted a 10 percent reduction in staff this year by putting a freeze on hiring to fill vacancies. Pitaya [Phanphensophon, managing director of Coca Holding International Co., Ltd.] said the company is considering shutting down poorly performing branches in Thailand and overseas, such as in Surabaya in Indonesia (Kwanchai 1997).

Some of those laid off from formal employment, such as a fast food chain or a factory, cope by opening their own micro-enterprises (Busaba and Busrin 1998). Those who turn to the food business appear to be the vast majority. Customers are assured, as we all need to eat. Lack of kitchen space, the high price of cooking fuel, and complexity of Thai food preparation guarantees customers for small places offering good value for money. Table 8.1 indicates approximate investment costs and profit margins for micro-entrepreneurs in the foodscapes of urban Thailand, particularly Bangkok. However, the "sandwich strategy," which requires less

Table 8.1 What to Sell (Food)

Business	Investment (baht)	Working Capital	Profit	Margin Rate
Sandwich franchise	10,000	500–800 bt/day	400–600 bt/day	30–40%
Sandwich non-franchise	n.a.	n.a.	400–500 bt/day	n.a.
Rice soup stall	200,000	4–5,000 bt/day	n.a.	n.a.
Grilled seafood	70,000– 300,000	1–5,000 bt/day	n.a.	n.a.
Mobile noodle stall	15,000	500–600 bt/day	500–800 bt/day	100%
Juice	2,500	1,000–1,500 bt/day	n.a.	15–20%

Source: "Retailers press government for more relief to ensure survival," *Bangkok Post* 3 August 1998: 8 (from the Thai Farmers Research Center)

equipment and cooking experience/knowledge, spawned new post-crisis micro-enterprises in the new economy.

By August 1998, less than a year after making international news reports, Khun Sirivat was already seeing changes in his life:

Siriwat Voravetvuthikhun, the former high-flying businessmen [sic] who set up a sandwich-making venture to keep staff a year ago is now finding lean pickings as rising costs have eaten into profits. . . His new line of business reflects trends toward natural products. "Sandwiches do not make much profit any more. My staff and I are now offering fruit and vegetable juice, such as aloe juice. We also sell vegetable products from Doi Kham," he says. (Bangkok Post 1998)

As of 2000, Sirivat had added gourmet coffee and his unique brown rice sushi to his many kiosks found throughout the city. He had also published two books on his experience (Sirivat 1999, 2002) and launched an impressive website in Thai and in English (www.sirivatsandwich.com). Sirivat's shift in business strategy may have more to do with the particular type of food he sells, his notoriety, spending habits, and general lifestyle than indicating a serious change in coping strategies for Thailand's urban poor and middle-class.

Although Thailand felt the Asian economic crisis more deeply than The Philippines, it still appears as though well entrenched patterns of micro-entrepreneurship, particularly in the prepared-food sector, have helped Thais to survive and ride out economic uncertainties. Less economically successful than Thailand before 1997,

The Philippines had less far to "crash" (Glassman 1999). In addition, the impact of the crisis on The Philippines has been somewhat cushioned by OCW remittances, and economic survival has been enhanced by a strong civil society consisting of NGOs and People's Organizations. This social fabric contributes to the growth of social capital by strengthening community networks, organizing citizens and sub-groups such as vendors, and providing services such as micro-credit.

Building the Social Capital of Food Micro-entrepreneurs

In Thailand, local strengths are in the field of food retailing and a general preponderance of entrepreneurship, especially of women. There are, however, serious lacunae when it comes to protecting these workers and the existence of schemes to increase access to credit and federate them as a group: "The 7th Development Plan was more specific toward target groups in the informal sector by including plans for employment opportunities and welfare for the urban poor and underprivileged groups" (Napat 1994: 33). Micro-enterprises have been targeted by the latest national development plan, but there is no inclusion of welfare and social protection, notes Napat. Instead, supporting these enterprises is seen as a way to ease the financial burden on government and social tensions surrounding unemployment. The notion of entitlements and the concept of social capital are not built into the plan and should be, particularly in light of the devastation of the recent financial crisis.

At present, unlike The Philippines, only a small number of NGOs in Thailand provide financial support such as credit and revolving funds to their beneficiaries according to Napat (1994: 41–43). Though agricultural cooperatives are strong, there is no indication that the cooperative movement is alive and well in urban areas. Similarly, the well-known Assembly of the Poor is famous for its ability to organise and mobilize villages with respect to land rights—the protest against the Pak Mool Dam being an example. There is the potential, however, for the Assembly to become more active in urban areas.

Thailand is sorely lacking in the area of community-building activities and can learn from some of the practices emerging in the neighboring Philippines. Due to many similarities in terms of social structure and some cultural overlaps, The Philippines and Thailand are in a good position to engage in the types of "South-South" exchanges and partnerships being fostered by groups such as "Focus on the Global South" (Annual Report 1997). Thailand's more well-developed indigenous food-retailing system and creative entrepreneurship would benefit from experiences in The Philippines that aim to strengthen civil society through public policy and the work of community-based organizations. The policies of development agencies in the North should concentrate on fostering these types of horizontal linkages and using their vast networks in the South to facilitate the process.

Self-help Groups and Services for Food Vendors

Vendors' organizations do exist in Bangkok, as is evidenced by the ability to organize protests and demonstrations when there are attempts to introduce municipal policies. The best organized vendors are located in the vicinity of the wholesale market, Pak-khlong Talad, and there are also associations of vendors selling a variety of goods, including food, on busy thoroughfares such as Silom Road (Rakawin 2000). The food vendors interviewed in the VMA, however, are not involved in any association. In December 2000, informal discussions about the possible establishment of a "self-help group" among women food vendors were held with Thai anthropologist, Kamonrat Sa-Ngeam and myself. There was serious interest in forming a local group to engage in micro-finance schemes, and in obtaining training on how to negotiate access to vending spaces. Some of the food vendors in the VMA were forced to relocate in February 2001 following the demolition of their low-rise place of residence/business to make way for a high-rise building. As such, they can be viewed as casualties of Thailand's recovery from the economic crisis.

A number of occupational health and safety issues related to food-vending would be more adequately addressed if vendors in the VMA were organized and therefore in a more economically and spatially secure position. The interest in organizing such a group makes clear that exchanges among developing countries to diffuse the experiences of SEWA, CCUVA, and other groups are needed to facilitate the creation of similar food vendors' organizations where they are needed. It is also essential that IFS workers in the VMA become more aware of and ensconced in Thai civil society organizations, such as the internationally recognized Assembly of the Poor, on condition that they have the necessary time and resources to do so.

In late June 2001, newly elected Prime Minister Thaksin Shinawatra announced the nationwide launch of the "People's Bank," also known as "Bank for the Poor" (*krongkarn thanakarn phu prachachon*). This scheme, to be operated by the Savings Bank of Thailand, provides micro-financing for people wanting to start a small enterprise such as a food-vending establishment. Low interest loans of up to 15,000 Bt are available to micro-entrepreneurs on condition that they seek a government or private sector official as guarantor. Thaksin's new micro-finance policy is also accompanied by a micro-insurance scheme (Kamol 2001;

S. N. Kamonrat 2001, personal communication). For Thai urban food vendors, this project is a first step toward improving their living and working conditions and social capital.

To summarize, then, micro-entrepreneurs in the food sector, if organized, can and should be:

- valued by society at large for their economic, social, and cultural roles
- recognized legally and on a wider political scale by the state at various levels
- supported through micro-financing and social protection such as micro-insurance
- involved in making decisions that affect their lives through a democratic, accountable, multi-stakeholder framework.

Finally, there is a need for conceptually innovative participatory action research, with an emphasis on the policies and programs needed at the neighborhood, city, regional, national, and international scales. Such research and praxis can facilitate diffusing strategic information and result in creating transparent, accountable, and democratic membership-based organizations that represent the interests of the urban IFS.

Bangkok's Foodscape: *Quo Vadis?*

The Asian economic crisis hit Thailand particularly hard following the baht's devaluation July 1997. At the time, the initial impacts on the food-system were dramatic and highly visible, including the closing of various "formal sector" eating establishments, the explosion in the number of "informal" stalls and street food eateries as well as a rise in preparing food at home. One would have thought, in the years following the upheaval, that the crisis had launched a whole new set of imperatives with respect to the question of Bangkok's foodscape. In fact, however, by the year 2001 the country's economy had recovered sufficiently that the city's food-system began to feature some of the trends noticed during the Southeast Asian boom period of the 1990s.

By the year 2000, a number of new hypermarkets and "big box stores" such as Carrefour and Big-C, to add to the well-established Makro stores, had made their way into the city, partly at the expense of small, traditional family-owned shops such as the *cho hway*, small Chinese shops selling various "dry goods" (rice, oil, and so on) both on the wholesale and retail levels (Kamolrat 2000, personal communication).

Thai government statistics collected since the crisis point in a few interesting directions. The results shown in Table 8.2 of average monthly expenditures per household by type of food consumed for 2002 can be interestingly compared to Table 4.6 indicating the same figures for 1990. Here, one sees a dramatic decrease in the extent to which prepared food is made at home for the whole country with a drop from 76% to 50% of expenditures. This result, collected five years after the baht's devaluation, indicates the recovery of the Thai economy as households are now prepared to contract out food preparation once again. As reported in Table 8.3, the report of the 1998 Socio-Economic Survey indicated an increase in the patronizing of noodle shops from 14.3% of weekly expenditures in 1990 (see Table 4.7) to 16.45% in 1998.

As mentioned, in December 2000, we held an informal meeting with a group of vendors in the Victory Monument Area. This enabled us to get a sense of how some of the micro-entrepreneurs Kamolrat and I had interviewed in 1994 were doing after the crisis. Samrit—of the husband/wife chicken noodle vending team—was away from Bangkok, and, for the first time, his wife Lek was able to speak somewhat freely. She explained that the last few years had been turbulent, not only because of the economic problems but also because Samrit had had a serious drinking and gambling problem up until a few years before. "We have many debts," she explained. "He borrowed money from everyone in the neighborhood resulting in a sum total of baht 300,000." Samrit and Lek were forced to open a new stall at the nearby school to make ends meet. They withdrew their two children from a private school and put them into the public system. Their financial problems, therefore, were mostly due to Samrit's vices, which, apparently, were now somewhat under control. In fact, "We've fared a bit better than other food vendors over the last two to three years in terms of sales," she reported. If there were to be a women's micro-finance initiative in the district, Lek enthusiastically stated that she would be the first to join.

As for Daeng's situation, as documented earlier, her business initially boomed in the years immediately following the crisis with the threat of relocation due to property re-development put on hold. By early 2001, she was feeling confident enough to put out 100,000 Bt to lease a shophouse for her food shop as well as for her housing needs. Unfortunately, a year later, she was forced to approach her former landlady once again to ask for a selling space as the business venture failed miserably. She is now in a worse situation than she was before in terms of sales.

Table 8.2 Average Monthly Expenditures per Household
by Type of Food Consumed, 2002

Type of food consumed	All-Thailand	Greater Bangkok
Food prepared at home	1,269 Bt (50 %)	3,263 Bt (49.9%)
Prepared food taken home	506 Bt (19.9%)	1,112 Bt (17.03%)
Food eaten away from home.[1]	763 Bt (30.06%)	2,152 Bt (32.9%)

Source: National Statistical Office, Office of the Prime Minister: Preliminary Report of the 2002 Household Socio-Economic Survey
[1] Excludes alcoholic drinks away from home

Table 8.3 Average Weekly Expenditures for Prepared Food Taken Home,
Greater Bangkok, 1998

Type of Food	Expenditure (baht)	Percentage of total
Rice and curry	152.00	69.70%
Noodles	35.88	16.45%
Fried rice	12.78	5.86%
Meals (pinto food)	3.95	1.81%
Snacks	11.65	5.34%
Other Prep. Food	1.79	0.84%
Total	218.05	100.00%

Source: National Statistical Office, Office of the Prime Minister: Report of the 1998 Socio-Economic Survey: Bangkok Metropolis, Nonthaburi, Pathum Thani and Samut Prakan (1998: 24)

The Professor's Pub is still in the neighborhood, and, as of 2000, similar to the small food shops on the soi, reported a third fewer sales since the onset of the crisis. The restaurant continues to attract many foreign customers, particularly workers who visit at lunchtime from Nokia and guests staying at a nearby four-star hotel. In 1995, Professor Chaichana and his wife Vipawan had even opened a second location in a large shopping center in 1995 but had to close it in 1998 because it was running at a loss. Their other two businesses have suffered to an even greater extent since 1997. The furniture factory was being rented out as of December 2000, and the interior decorating business was flailing. When asked about their plans to move their family out of the shophouse and into a condominium, Professor Chaichana

209

and Vipawan reported having bought an apartment a few years ago but decided to rent it out to generate extra income.

In June 2002, I finally had the opportunity to meet "Sirivat the Sandwich Man" in Bangkok. His business was booming. He had expanded into several lines of products in addition to sandwiches, including brown rice sushi and pita wraps. He continues to receive much media attention. We kept in touch by e-mail and by post. On learning that Sirivat was due to visit Vancouver, where I then resided, in March 2003, to accompany his two daughters then about to undertake student exchange programs, I made arrangements for him to make a presentation at the University of British Columbia, attempted to set up media interviews, and arranged a visit with representatives of a very successful Canadian coffee and sandwich chain, Tim Horton's (www.timhortons.com) due to Sirivat's growing involvement and interest in the coffee business. Sirivat's visit to my home brought my past decade of research on Bangkok's foodscape full circle. The global-local dialectic combined with the ease of information and communication technologies in the twenty-first century had resulted in the phenomenon I had studied on the opposite side of the planet coming back to visit me.

Glossary

ahaan: food

ahaan tam sang: "made to order" dishes whereby the customer chooses a dish from a "short-order" menu rather from already prepared food (e.g., fried rice, fried noodles)

baht: Thailand's unit of currency (abbreviated Bt)

bunkhun: a debt of gratitude

café: a lounge serving alcohol and featuring live music, primarily provided by young female singers

Chao Mae Guan Im: "Holy Mother Guan Im," the Thai name for the Chinese "Goddess of Mercy" (*Guan Yin*)

cho hway: small Chinese shops selling various "dry goods" (rice, oil, etc.) both wholesale and retail

dek: child

deuk taew: shophouse

Doi Moi (Vietnamese): "renovation," the Communist government's endorsement of free enterprise

farang: foreigner

feng shui (Mandarin): geomancy

feuk ngan: literally, "practice work"; an apprenticeship

gaeng som: a mild stew

gai yang: fried chicken

hab re: a vendor who sells using a shoulder pole and two baskets
halal (Arabic): food permitted to Muslims and/or prepared according to Koranic custom
hoh pak: dormitory, residence rooms for students
hong taew: a term for shophouse (see *deuk taew*)
hui (Mandarin): mutual aid and rotating credit groups

Isaan: Northeastern Thailand, an ethnically Lao region

jai ron: literally, "hot hearted," an impatient and emotional person (not well viewed in Thai society)
jok: rice porridge, also known as *khao tom*
jut phon pan: literally, "a point (*jut*) to ease the situation (*phon pan*)"; spaces where vending is tolerated by the Bangkok Municipal Administration

kampung or *kampong* (Malay): village, but in an urban neighborhood sometimes taken to mean a "slum district"
ket: municipal district
kaow niew: "sticky" or glutinous rice
kaow tom: rice porridge, also known as *jok*
kaow phad: fried rice
kaow gaeng: literally, "curry and rice"; refers both to "pre-prepared" curries, soups, and vegetable dishes eaten with rice and the food shops or restaurants where they are sold
kaow man gai: known in Malaysia and Singapore in English as "chicken rice," a Hainanese dish featuring boiled chicken, rice cooked in chicken broth and soup usually served with several condiments
kha moo: pork leg
khanom: a dessert or sweet
khanom jeep: Chinese steamed dumplings
kha po paa: fish stomach
khay dao: fried egg
khay jieaw: Thai omelette often prepared with onion and tomato
khlong: a canal, Central Thailand's dominant mode of transportation until the 1960s

khon Isaan: people from Northeastern Thailand, ethnically Lao

khwan: vital essence, associated with rice. "If the *khwan* becomes detached or if it wanders, their person will be left vulnerable to illness and eventually to death" (Keyes 1987: 224). Many agricultural and social rituals involve securing or beckoning vital essence.

kin khao rue yang?: "Have you eaten yet?", a common greeting in Thailand

kwayteow: generally, rice noodles of any thickness but can also include egg noodles depending on the dish

kwayteow latna: broad noodles, pan fried in a thick vegetable sauce

kwayteow reua: literally, "boat noodles"; usually beef noodle soup served in a small boat on dry land and nostalgic of an earlier era

lap gai: a "chicken salad" from Northeastern Thailand marinated in garlic, lime juice, herbs, and spices; also made with pork or beef; traditionally served raw in Isaan and marinated in bile and blood (Van Esterik 1992)

len share: to participate in a rotating credit association; members each contribute monthly to the pot and withdraw the sum one at a time while paying interest to the other members

liam: prestige; honor

liang: to nurture; can mean to "feed" or to tend; to invite someone out and pay the bill (i.e., to treat)

luuk: child or offspring

luuk chin ping: barbecued meatball brochettes of a slightly rubbery quality; made of fish or meat

luuk kreung: literally, "half offspring"; a thing or person of mixed ancestry

luuknong: subordinate

luukphi: elders, superiors, patrons

mae: mother; also a common prefix

mae baan tung plastic: literally, "plastic bag housewife"; a colloquial term for women who purchase take-out food for their families on their way home from work

mae kha: a female vendor or shopkeeper

mae nam: literally, "mother of waters"; a river

Mae Posop: the Rice Goddess

maeng da: giant water beetle; its essence (extracted by pounding pregnant female with a mortar and pestle) used to flavour numerous Thai dishes *mia noi*: a "minor wife" or mistress

moo daeng: Chinese red pork

naem: Chinese-style cured pork sausage

nakleng: rogue, rascal, gambler; bold person; sporting type; big-hearted person; person who is an authority on something (Haas 1964: 261)

nam phrik: a liquid condiment made of fermented fish or shrimp, to which is added chillies, and other herbs and spices; a distinguishing feature of Thai cuisine; eaten with any number of dishes or even plain rice

nam tok: literally, "waterfall"; a dish consisting of spiced slices of roast beef

pad si ieuw: pan-fried noodles, vegetables, pork, and red soy sauce

paeng: a selling platform

paeng loy: a street-stall

Pakklong Talad: Bangkok's central wholesale fruit, vegetable, and flower market

pattakarn: an elegant expression for restaurant; used in formal literature or to refer
to a sophisticated dining establishment

pau liang: a stepfather; however, the term can also describe a man who takes care of others

pau to lo min (Mandarin): literally, "to uncover your head and show your face"; idiomatic Confucian expression alluding to the seclusion of women in the home

Peranakan (Malay): Chinese whose families immigrated to the Straits of Malacca several generations ago and mixed in with Malay culture. Peranakans developed a unique culture including distinctive food, dress, and language.

pheung: a stall covered by an awning

phuying dii: literally, "good woman", that is a woman who is chaste

phuying mai dii: "bad woman"; refers to women who do not adhere to Thai ideals of chastity

ping mun ye jung wooi (Cantonese): literally, "poor man's night club"; colloquial expression referring to street-food stalls in Hong Kong (Smart 1989)

pinto: a "tiffin" box or tiered lunch-kit that comes apart into three or four bowl-shaped sections

pla ré: "ready to eat fish"

plaa tod mamuang: fried fish with green mango chutney

purdah (Persian and Urdu): the seclusion of women from men both in the home and public places

raan ahaan: literally, "food shop"; a restaurant or eating establishment, large or small

rai: Thai unit of measurement equalling 1,600 square meters

rong rap jam nam: pawnshop

rot khen: pushcart

roti canai: (Malay) (*roti paratha* south of Kuala Lumpur) Indian flatbread made of white flour and fried in clarified butter (ghee), served with a curry sauce

ruen taew: a wooden one-storey building

rupiah: the unit of currency of the Republic of Indonesia (abbreviated Rp)

sakdina: literally, "power over the fields"; Thai feudalism. "During Ayutthayan times and the first half of the Bangkok era, every person in the realm was accorded a status associated with a specific acreage of rice land; the greater the acreage, the higher a person's position in a social hierarchy headed by the monarch. This hierarchy constituted the *sakdina* system. Despite the association of a status with an area of cultivated land, a particular status did not indicate control over a specified amount of land" (Keyes 1987: 225).

sala thai: a traditional open pavilion, usually with a sloping roof

salapao: Chinese steamed buns

Sampeng: a narrow lane in Chinatown known for its good prices for merchandise

Sangha: the order of Buddhist monks

sari-sari (Tagalog): a "mixed store" selling sundry goods and prepared foods

satay (Malay): barbecued brochettes, usually served with peanut sauce

say foam: "put it in a foam take-out box"

Shell chuan chim: "'Shell' invites you to taste. . ." Restaurant endorsement campaign sponsored by Shell Oil

Siam: name of the Kingdom of Thailand prior to 1932

soi: lane

som tam: spicy, shredded, green papaya salad, made in the Northeastern way, with tiny raw crabs, or the Central way, with dried shrimp

suan ahaan: open air "garden" restaurants, often quite large, some decorated in a style reminiscent of Thai traditional architecture

sukiyaki (Japanese): a boiling pot of broth into which egg, vegetables, rice vermicelli, and meat are mixed and cooked

talad: market

talad din: land-based market

talad nam: "floating" market taking place on canals in the early morning

tam sang: "made to order"

talad to rung: night-market

tesakit: municipal police inspectors concerned with obstructions to roads and sidewalks, building permits, and public hygiene

tom yum plaa/guung: hot-and-sour fish/prawn soup

tuk-tuk: motorized trishaw

warteg (Tegal): a restaurant (Klopfer 1993)

warung (Malay: Indonesian dialect): a stall; some also define it as a store that also sells prepared food (see McGee and Yeung 1977)

Wirtschaft (German): economics; pub or restaurant

yam: any type of soup

Yaowaraj: Bangkok's Chinatown

yong tao-foo or *niang tofu* (Mandarin): literally, "stuffed tofu"; an assortment of tit-bits (mostly tofu-based but also including fish balls, vegetables, etc.) that one can choose from and from which the seller will chop up and combine with noodles of one's choice. Ingredients are placed in a clear soup or served "dry" with soup on the side (Woo 1996).

Appendices

The following five appendices are English versions of the research instruments used to complete this study as well as supplementary information not in the main text. Appendices 1–3 are the guides used for in-depth qualitative interviews. Appendix 4 is the questionnaire used to conduct the short quantitative survey. Appendix 5 includes three monthly budgets of small food-shops not included in the main text.

Three qualitative interview guides were designed due to the vastly different circumstances of small versus large food establishments as well as the distinctive nature of chains and food centers. The same questions were not appropriate for each category. The guides included here were often modified depending on the individual being questioned and the appropriateness or inappropriateness of the guide contents. They are therefore included as indicators of themes discussed as well as specific questions asked.

The quantitative survey was administered by five contractual research assistants under my supervision. Individual assistants sometimes skipped over questions that sometimes make the data difficult to compare. This is particularly true for information concerning helpers and employees, a subject not thoroughly probed by some assistants. The basic data, however, concerns age of the enterprise, owner/manager characteristics, and number of customers and can be considered quite complete, reliable, and comparable.

Finally, the extra expense reports are included since only two were presented and discussed in detail in the main text. Again, some responses were incomplete depending on what informants were willing to offer. As explained above, larger establishments were not questioned in such detail about their expenditures because the owners/managers were not as certain about spending patterns and it was not seen as an appropriate subject for discussion. Generally, the wealthier the informant, the less willing the individual to discuss budgetary matters.

Appendix 1

Interview Guide A:
For Stalls and Small Food Shops

Food Shops in Bangkok:
Eating Habits of Urban Dwellers

Gisèle Yasmeen, PhD candidate
University of British Columbia
Vancouver, Canada

Questions will be asked in three categories:
  a. Shop's history and day-to-day activities
  b. Relations between your business and government and other businesses.
  c. Your personal background and relations in the neighborhood

A. History and Day-to-Day Activities

1. How long have you owned your shop? Did you buy it from someone else, or did you start this business yourself? If the latter, what type of changes did you make? How much money did you have to invest to start the business / buy the shop, and where did you obtain this money (i.e., for equipment, etc.)?
2. What types of food do you sell? Do you always obtain food from the same suppliers? Approximately how much do you spend on food every day? Please help me to fill out Table 1.
3. Are there any other activities (paid or unpaid) that take place in your shop besides selling food (e.g., babysitting, selling non-food items, etc.)? Which activities are remunerated, and who performs them?
4. Do you have assistants or employees? What is the difference between a "helper" and an employee? Do your helpers or employees get room and board

instead of or in addition to wages? If not, where do these various people sleep? How did you meet them? Do they have any other jobs/money-making activities? Please help me to fill out Table 2.

5. Describe a typical day (what time you wake up; who does what and goes where; when do you make what type of food; busy periods of the day, week, and month; slow periods, etc). Are your activities affected by change of seasons (flooding, etc.)?

6. Approximately how many customers come to your shop per day? What do they usually buy and / or how much to they usually spend? What percentage eat in the shop, and how many take home the food (estimate)? Are most of your customers "regulars"?

7. Can you describe your typical customer or name different types (social or occupational groups) of customers? E.g., ages, men or women, where they live, what type of work they do . . .

8. Do you extend credit? If yes, to whom? Have you ever borrowed money? If yes, from whom? If no, would you be interested in borrowing money? Preferably from what source (e.g., bank, informal credit organization)?

9. Why or how did you choose/learn this occupation?

B. Relations with Government and Other Businesses

1. How much does it cost to rent your premises? How does this compare with the rent paid by neighboring shopkeepers? How did you find out about this space? How is this type of information usually obtained, and what types of arrangements are usually made? For example, is there a lease and how are rent increases negotiated? Who is your landlord/lady?

2. Do you have a licence or permit from the government to operate your shop? Have you ever been contacted by city officials about this matter or related issues such as health and cleanliness standards and adherence to the labor code? Have you ever been harassed by police or government officials? How were disputes (if any) resolved? Do you know about any of these regulations? Tell me what you know.

3. Is your shop independent, or is it linked / federated with other food shops or restaurants? Are you a member of any vendors or business organization? Would you like to be a member of such an organization in order to receive information about issues of concern to your occupation or further training (for example)?

4. Have you ever been offered a public contract to provide food (e.g., to a school, hospital, or university)? Would you be interested in having such a contract? Would you consider relocating in a food center in a shopping center or other privately owned and regulated space?

5. Do you have a bank account? Have you ever dealt with a bank? Do you participate in informal credit schemes like *len share*? Please tell me about how you organize your finances, and if you save money, how.

6. Life in Bangkok is becoming very difficult. What issues concern you most (e.g., cost of living increases, crime, pollution, traffic problems)? Is this a dangerous part of the city? Are there any changes taking place in the neighborhood that may affect your ability to conduct business? Would you like to have more information about these issues?

C. Life History / Personal Information

1. Where are you from originally (where were you born and raised)?

2. What educational level have you achieved? Can you read and write? Do you read the newspaper regularly? If so, which? Do you listen to the radio and/or watch television?

3. What jobs have you had in the past? Did you receive training for these?

4. Are you married, divorced, or separated? Do you have children? Tell me about your family. Where are your parents and your brothers and sisters? What do they do? Do you support your family economically? Do you spend time helping them?

5. When did you move to Bangkok? Why? Did you ever live elsewhere in the city? If so, where?

6. Where do you live now? Describe your accommodations. Who lives with you?

7. What are your future goals? How do you plan to reach these? Do you enjoy working in the food industry? What are your other employment or money-earning options?

Appendix 1

Table 1
Monthly Expenses

Item	Price	Times/Month	From Where
Rent			
Utilities			
water			
electricity			
telephone			
garbage			
Fuel			
gas			
charcoal			
Rice			
Noodles			
Oil / fat			
Meat / fish			
Spices/seasoning/			
curry paste			
Vegetables			
papaya (*som tam*)			
Ice			
Drinks (water)			
soft drinks			
Other?			

Table 2
Restaurant Staff Characteristics

Occupation	Number	Age	Salary
Chefs			
Cooks			
Waiters (male)			
Waitresses (female)			
Cleaners			
Other? (Specify)			

Appendix 2

Interview Guide B:
For Larger, Formalized Restaurants

Food Shops in Bangkok:
Eating Habits of Urban Dwellers

General

1. Why did you choose to become involved in the restaurant business? How long have you been in this business? Is this your first restaurant? Do you own other restaurants in the city at this time? Are you the sole owner of this establishment? If not, please explain who the co-owners are.
2. Do you hold any other occupation? Please explain the nature of any other money-earning, professional, and voluntary activities? What kind of professional training did you receive for these occupations?
3. Did you purchase the restaurant from someone else, or did you first open the establishment? If you purchased it from another person, please explain changes to the menu, décor, and management style. Please explain in what ways the restaurant has evolved over the years.
4. How many staff do you have? Please help fill out the attached chart that summarizes characteristics about your staff. What are the wages for the various occupations? Are tips a significant part of staff income? Are employees provided with meals and lodgings instead of a portion of their wages or in addition to what they earn? Do you have any volunteer help (such as family and friends)?
5. Where does the restaurant obtain its supplies? For example, explain where you purchased your furnishings and equipment along with estimated costs involved. Also, explain where day to day supplies are obtained such as perishable food, dry goods, fuel, ice, and the estimated costs associated with these items.

6. How many customers do you receive per day (on average)? Can you provide me with a socio-economic profile of your clientele? Where do they live, how did they find out about your restaurant (e.g., how do you advertise), what are their occupations and income-levels, what percentage are men versus women, ages, etc.? How much do they usually spend per person?

7. What are your busiest periods of the day, month, year? Why is this so? Do you hire extra staff for these periods? What are your slowest periods of the day, month, year?

8. Are you federated or linked with any other restaurants? (Is this a chain or a franchise)? Are you a member of any professional organizations related to the restaurant business or business in general?

9. What type of contact have you had with the Ket Ratchathewi office or BMA? Do government bodies provide you with regular information as well as inspections regarding health standards, taxes, etc.? What specific contacts have you had with government officials?

10. Do you rent this building, or are you the owner? If you rent, what type of leasing arrangements do you have? Do you rent space to other businesses, organizations, or individuals?

11. Do you know many people in this neighborhood? Do you know other restaurant or small food-shop owners? What local restaurants do you patronize yourself? In what way has this area changed since you first moved here? Do you like your present location? Why or why not?

12. Many people think that life in Bangkok is becoming very difficult. What are the issues that concern you most (e.g., cost of living increases, crime, pollution, traffic problems)? Is this a dangerous part of the city? Are there any changes taking place in the neighborhood that may affect your ability to conduct business? Would you like to have more information about these issues?

Life History / Personal Information

1. Where are you from originally (where were you born and raised)?
2. What educational level have you achieved?
3. What jobs have you had in the past? Did you receive any training for these?
4. How old are you? Are you married, divorced, or separated? Do you have children? Tell me about your family. Where are your parents and your broth-

ers and sisters? What do they do? Do you support your family economically?
Do you spend time helping them?

5. When did you move to Bangkok? Why? Did you ever live elsewhere in the
city? Where?

6. Where do you live now? Describe your accommodations. Do you live alone?
Who lives with you?

7. What are your future goals in terms of your career and this business? Do
you enjoy being involved in the food industry? Is there any chance that this
business may change significantly or close in the near future?

Restaurant Staff Characteristics

Occupation	Number	Age	Home province
Chefs			
Cooks			
Male serving staff			
Female serving staff			
Cleaners			
Other? (Specify)			

Appendix 3

Interview Guide C:
For Fast Food Outlets and Food Centers

Food Shops in Bangkok:
Eating Habits of Urban Dwellers

General

1. Who is the proprietor of this restaurant/food center? Is it a "chain" or a franchise?
2. How long has this restaurant been here?
3. What are the hours of operation?

Location

1. Why did you choose this location for your business? Has the restaurant/food center changed its site, design, or decor?
2. Do you rent this space, or are you the owner? Do you have a lease? How much is the rent?
3. How many square meters is the restaurant/center? Seating capacity, number of tables? Do you have a floor plan of the premises?
4. Who are your competitors? Did you do market research to ascertain your share of the market?
5. Would it be possible for us to obtain a copy of your company's annual report? Do you have information about your monthly budget?

Customers

1. Customer profile:
   Age, sex, occupations?

How much does each person spend on average?

How long do customers stay on average?

Do the customers live/work in the neighborhood?

2. What type of advertising do you do? Where do you advertise (print, radio, television)?

Employees

1. How many? How many men/women? Educational levels? Birthplace or place orignally from? Salaries?

2. How many hours per day do the employees work? Do they work shifts or the entire day?

3. Please explain the hierarchy of employees, for example:

manager

cooks

serving staff

Operations

1. Where is the food prepared? How and where do you buy raw ingredients? Is there a central kitchen?

2. Where did you obtain your license/permit to conduct business and sell food (i.e., district office, etc.)?

3. Have sanitary inspectors ever come to your premises? How regularly?

4. What are your peak hours/busy periods?

Personal Questions for the Manager

1. How long have you been the manager here?

2. How old are you? Please tell us about your training and educational background.

3. What are your future prospects/goals? Are there possibilities for advancement in this company?

Employee Characteristics

Occupation	Number	Age	Birthplace
Chef(s)			
Cooks			
Male serving staff			
Female serving staff			
Cleaners			
Other? (Specify)			

Appendix 4

Questionnaire Quantitative Survey

Food Shops in Bangkok:
Eating Habits of Urban Dwellers
October 1994

Researcher: Gisèle Yasmeen, PhD candidate
University of British Columbia
Vancouver, Canada
(Associated with CUSRI)

To be filled out by research assistant/interviewer

Name of interviewer _____
Date (day, month, year) _____
Time _____
Location (street or neighborhood, name of shop) _____
Type of food sold _____

1. General Information

1.1 Occupation of interviewee:
   a. Owner
   b. Manager
   c. Other _____
1.2 Type of business:
   1. *Hab re*
   2. *Paeng loy*
   3. *Rot khen*
   4. *Pheung*

     5. *Hong thaew*
     6. Air-conditioned food shop ($)
     7. School cafeteria shop
     8. Hotel food shop
     9. Food center
    10. *Pattakarn* ($$$)
    11. Fast-food chain (e.g., M-K Suki)
    12. Other (specify) _____

2. Personal Characteristics of Respondent

2.1 Age _____
2.2 Birthplace _____
2.3 Sex a. M b. F
2.4 Marital status _____
    a. Singleb. Married
    c. Divorced / separatedd. Other
2.5 Home address _____ (street, soi, neighborhood)
2.6 Educational level attained _____
2.7 Do you have another occupation? a. Yes b. No
    If yes, specify _____

3. Business

3.1 How many years old is this business? _____
3.2 Does the proprietor own other restaurants?
    a. Yes
    b. No
    If yes, where are the other restaurants? _____
    What type of food do they sell? _____

4. Customers

4.1 Approximately how many customers per day do you receive?
    a. Fewer than 50
    b. Between 50–100
    c. More than 100

4.2 Peak hours are normally between:
   a. 6–9 a.m.
   b. 11 a.m–2 p.m.
   c. 5–7 p.m.
   d. 7–11 p.m.
   e. After 11 p.m.

4.3 What percentage of your customers live in the neighborhood?
   a. Less than 30%
   b. About 50%
   c. More than 70%
   d. Other (explain)_____

4.4 What percentage of your customers work in the neighborhood?
   a. Less than 30%
   b. About 50%
   c. More than 70%
   d. Other (explain) _____

5. Employees

5.1 Do you have any employees?
   a. Yes
   b. No

5.2 Employee Characteristics

Occupation	Number	Age	Province of origin
Chef			
Cooks			
Male serving staff			
Female serving staff			

Cleaning staff			
Other? (Specify)			

5.3 Do you have any unpaid assistants (*phu chuay*)?
    a. Yes
    b. No

    If yes, who are they?
    a. Family members
    b. Friends
    c. Relatives
    d. Other (explain) _____

5.4 Are employees provided with lodging and meals?
    a. Lodging and meals
    b. Meals only
    c. Neither lodging nor meals
    d. Other (explain) _____

Appendix 5

BUDGETS FOR SMALL FOOD SHOPS

Samrit's and Lek's Chicken Noodle Soup Shop
EXPENSES

Item	Price (baht)	Times/ Month	From Where
Rent*	100 /wk**	4	*Tesakit*
Utilities			
water	350	1	Store next
electricity	–	–	door
telephone	–	–	
garbage	–	–	
Fuel			
gas	60 /day	30	Delivery
charcoal	–	–	
Rice	–	–	
Noodles	10 kg/day @ 10 bt/kg	30	Say Yut Market
oil/fat	–	–	
Meat/fish	22 kg/day @ 28 bt/kg	30	Khlong Tan Market
Spices/seasoning/ curry paste	–	–	(*roong gai*)
Vegetables	30 Bt/day 15 bags	30	Say Yut Market
	6 salung (1.5b)	30	Say Yut Market
Ice	30 /day	30	Delivery
Drinks (water)			
soft drinks	1 case @ 92 Bt/every 3 days	10	Delivery

* This is rent for their selling space. The cost of their rented room where they live is 1,850 Bt per month.

** They no longer pay rent to the *tesakit* because of *jut phon pan*, in other words, vending is tolerated in that specific space.

Luung's Duck Noodles and Red Pork Shop
EXPENSES

Item	Price (baht)	Times/Month	From Where
Lease	300,000	1 / 3 years	–
Utilities			
water			(city)
electricity	300–400	1	(city)
telephone	1,000+		(city)
garbage	500	1	
Fuel		1	
gas	500 per barrel	30	Delivery
charcoal	20–30 /day	4	?
Rice	2 kg /day	30	Say Yut Market
Noodles	10 kg (30 Bt/kg)		Older brother
oil/fat	–		
Meat/fish	1 duck/day (?)		CP delivers
Spices/seasoning/	–		
curry paste		30	
Vegetables	1 kg (?)		Say Yut Market
		30	
Ice	8/ day	–	?
Drinks (water)	"Not much"	–	?
soft drinks	"Not much"		Delivery

Some categories are incomplete because Luung was reticent to divulge information. He also frequently changed the subject and did not think certain questions were relevant. We were therefore unable to complete the table.

Noo's Pork Noodle Shop
EXPENSES

Item	Price (baht)	Times/Month	From Where
Rent (room)	2,500	1	
Utilities			
water	100	1	
electricity	100	1	
telephone	–	–	
garbage		–	
Fuel			
gas	161 Bt/4 days	7.5	Delivery
charcoal	–	–	
Rice		–	
Noodles	–	30	Say Yut Market
"Mama" variety	5.5 kg / day @ 10 Bt/kg	30	"
oil/fat	18 pkg @ 4 Bt/ ea	-	"
Meat/fish	-	30	"
abat	2 kg 65 Bt/kg	30	"
Luuk chin	2.5k 75 Bt/kg	30	"
Spices / seasoning /	2 kg. (4 bags)	–	–
curry paste	–	–	–
Vegetables		30	Say Yut Market
Green papaya	100 /day	–	–
Ice		30	Delivery
Drinks (water)	24 Bt/day	30	Delivery
soft drinks	24 bottles/day		Delivery
	92 Bt/case		

Notes

Preface

[1] Foodways refers to the gamut of ideologies and practices, which are both constitutive, and the outcome of the set of activities related to all aspects of human nourishment (Wagner 1994).

Chapter 1
Public Eating and Bangkok's Foodscape

[1] See also Chiong-Javier (1989).

[2] The term Siamese will sometimes be used interchangeably with Thai although, as Benedict Anderson explains, Siam was never as much of an ethnic designation as Thai. "Siam," used to refer to the Kingdom before 1949, was more all encompassing and is sometimes preferred as a less nationalistic designation for the nation's citizens (1985: 25–26).

[3] This has been informed by discussions with Charles Keyes who argues that middle-class Thai culture is very Sino-Thai (see note below). *Luuk kreung*, literally "half breed" can refer to anyone or anything of mixed heritage but the term *luuk ciin* is preferred to identify descendants of Chinese immigrants, whether of mixed ancestry or not.

[4] Sino-Thai is an ambiguous term mainly because it is a self-identification. Keyes defines Sino-Thai as those who identify mostly with Thai culture, practicing Theravada Buddhism and speaking standard Thai, but who continue to keep some

Chinese customs (1987: 20). I use it to refer to persons of Thai nationality who are partly or mostly of Chinese ancestry.

[5] I place the term "developing" in quotation marks because it, and the related term Third World is rife with implications of colonial discourses as Escobar has argued so eloquently (1995). This book is not situated within mainstream views of "development," or even the popular "gender and development" framework, although it engages these discourses. I would prefer to see this work situated within the discourse of sustainable community development. The book ultimately remains an academic piece rather than a concrete set of policy recommendations.

[6] There is some dispute in the literature about the extent to which Thai men cook. In the case of Central Thailand, the classic Cornell studies of Bang Chan Village argue that men and women participate quite equally in food-related work (Hauck, Saovanee, and Hanks 1958). A Master's thesis on the "culture of food" in Bangkok, written by a young urban Thai woman, argues that cooking is considered women's work (Bhavivarn 1993).

[7] The Greater Bangkok Metropolitan Area (GBMA) is defined by the National Statistical Office as the Bangkok Metropolitan Area plus the provinces of Nonthaburi, Pathum Thani, and Samut Prakan (see Fig. 1.2).

[8] For the case of Indonesia, see Klopfer (1993) and Jellinek (1991).

[9] For no apparent reason, this passage is written in the past tense. The descriptions are all valid today and explored in detail in Chapter 4.

[10] The nature of food centers in Singapore will be introduced in the following chapter and discussed in detail in Chapter 7.

[11] For example, in Pakistan where notions of *purdah* result in the spatial and social segregation of the sexes, women have one of the lowest labor force participation rates in the world at 15% (Donnan 1988).

[12] See particularly Chapter 7: "Gentrification, Cuisine, and the Critical Infrastructure: Power and Centrality Downtown."

[13] The term "Western" is used throughout to refer loosely to North American and Western European societies. I am aware of the critique of this terminology and the reification of the so-called Occident as opposed to the Orient. The term is used for the sake of simplicity and to compare Southeast Asia, itself a questionable construction, with another part of the world.

[14] Dolores Hayden chronologizes the development of household "labor saving devices" that actually increase the burdens on women by exacting higher cleaning standards and the maintenance requirements of appliances.

Chapter 2
Public/Private Spheres and Thai Food-systems

[1]   The very definition of a restaurant in the Thai context is difficult and is discussed in Chapter 5. The Thai terms, which are many, help distinguish types of "indigenous" eating establishments although the introduction of Western style (as well as Japanese and "new style" Chinese) restaurants complicates this process. However, the very idea of searching for "indigenous" or vernacular culture implies that Thai culture was somehow pristine or devoid of foreign contact, which is not the case.

[2]   Westerners tend to exaggerate the effect of Islamic revival on women's status in the Malay world. Perhaps it is due to the stark visible difference presented by the adoption of *hijab* (veiling) by Muslim women in Malaysia, which has come into fashion in the last twenty years. In a number of Muslim regions of Southeast Asia, such as Kelantan, Minangkabau, and Southern Thailand, women dominate as food vendors in markets, on the streets, and even in small restaurants (Chavivun 1985; Jamilah 1994; Klopfer 1993).

[3]   Tai is a linguistic term. Over 80% of Thailand's citizens speak a Tai language. The Tai (or Daic) category also includes Lao, Shan (from Burma), and certain dialects of northern Vietnam and South China. "Standard Thai," the national language taught in the schools, used on all official occasions and employed in almost all printed materials is based on only one of the Tai languages spoken in the country, namely that of the Siamese or Central Thai. People who speak Siamese as their domestic language, that is, the language of the home, constitute only about a quarter of the total population or 30% of all Tai speakers in Thailand (Keyes 1987: 15).

[4]   Sino-Thai, more influenced by local kinship practices, tend to opt for neo-local residence after marriage (Skinner 1957; Keyes 1996).

[5]   In a discussion with a historian of China, essentializing representations of ostensibly Confucian Chinese society are empirical overgeneralizations (Lary 1996). There are many Chinese women, both within and outside mainland China, who do not and have never subscribed to the "three obediences."

[6]   This phrase could also be transliterated with the Mandarin pronunciation as *pau tuo lo mie.*

[7]   There are exceptions to and variations of this tendency in South Asia. For example, Kerala is known to be matrilineal and a state where women have a great deal of financial independence and mobility. One explanation for this vastly different state of affairs is that Keralan men traditionally spent much time away from home

sailing and conducting business leaving women in charge of agriculture and local business.

[8] La Loubère presents contradictory information indicating that noble women went out in public quite freely then stating that some were required to venture forth into the city with an entourage and seat themselves in a sedan. Both practices must, in fact, have been common.

[9] As Keyes (1996) informed me, *mae* does not always refer to feminine occupations or things female. An example is *mae thap* (a general).

[10] The play on Brillat-Savarin's (1970) often quoted "you are what you eat" is borrowed from Lantos (1987).

[11] The article attributes the decline of the café to five factors: (1) high taxes; (2) expensive food and beverage prices; (3) competition from fast food outlets and street vendors; (4) the crusade against smoking and alcohol; and (5) American-style "cocooning" (staying home and watching television).

[12] I first heard the term "freelance" applied to prostitution in Bangkok. It refers to sex workers not bonded to a brothel or massage parlour and consequently having greater control over their incomes. Pimps, sometimes bar owners or even family members, often collect a portion of revenues.

[13] To provide another example, evidence from China's T'ang Dynasty points to the availability of "exotic" female prostitutes for transient male customers on many Eurasian trade routes. Many had light hair and blue eyes and were referred to as Western courtesans (Chang 1977: 137). Hattox (1985) describes the construction of masculinity within Turkish coffee-houses where men in the Ottoman Empire gathered for leisure. Geisha and Kota houses have historically been institutions catering to men in Japan and South Asia, respectively staffed largely by women and usually serving food and drink and, of course, providing various forms of "entertainment."

[14] See also Dyson-Hudson 1970; Pimentel and Pimentel 1979; Goody 1982; McGee 1971; McGee and Yeung 1977; MacLeod 1989, 1990. The food-systems concept may be part of a Western discourse (Ley 1993b). I argue that the food-system concept is simply a tool of value in many socio-cultural contexts. It enables the researcher to piece together disparate parts of the food puzzle.

[15] This term is not used for the first time here. A thesis completed in the Department of Geography of the National University of Singapore (Lee 1992) has a chapter title using the word "foodscape," but the author left the concept undeveloped.

[16] See in particular Porteous' chapter on "smellscape," an interesting concept that unfortunately is not thoroughly explored.

[17] The suffix "scape" comes from the Old Dutch *skip* meaning "to cut" (Hoad 1986; Shipley 1984). It therefore implies taking a "slice" of reality. Viewing should be seen as an active, not a passive process. Research in optics and human vision indicates that this is indeed the case (Sacks 1995).

[18] See, for example, their journal *Public Culture*, where Appadurai's aforementioned essay first appeared. Breckenridge edited a collection of papers on "public culture" in South Asia (1995). One of the most interesting essays in the book, Frank Conlon's chapter "Dining Out in Bombay," paints a foodscape of that city from a historian's perspective.

[19] Gayatri Chakvrorty Spivak's "Can the Subaltern Speak?" (1988) may be one of the most widely misinterpreted pieces of the 1980s. Spivak was advancing that non-representation of the research object was impossible. She was not arguing for the researcher/critic to be "transparent" and to allow the "voices" of the oppressed speak for themselves. The essay has, ironically, been taken to mean just that, leading to scholars denying that they create representations when "allowing others to speak" thereby absolving themselves of responsibility.

[20] An earlier edition of this volume was translated into English as *The Practice of Everyday Life* (1984).

[21] *"Mais la recherche s'est surtout consacrée aux pratiques de l'espace, aux manières de fréquenter un lieu, aux procès complexes de l'art culinaire."*

[22] *"S'il est vrai que partout s'étend et se précise le quadrillage de la «surveillance,» il est d'autant plus urgent de déceler comment une société entière ne s'y réduit pas. . . Ces «manières de faire» constituent les mille pratiques par lesquelles des utilisateurs se réapproprient l'espace organisé par les techniques de la production socioculturelle. . . Ces procédures et ruses de consommateurs composent à la limite, le réseau d'une antidiscipline."*

[23] The process of observation is problematized by both de Certeau and Smith. Some of these issues are addressed in Chapter 3.

[24] By public and private space I refer not to the public versus private ownership of land (i.e., state versus private property) but rather questions of access to various urban places. Access is defined as ability or permission to use and approach certain spaces. For example, a privately owned shopping center may be accessible to the public, within limits, and is therefore a public place.

[25] Gatens traces the public/private question in relation to gender to the debates between Rousseau, Wollstonecraft, and others (Gatens 1991).

[26] The most pertinent member of the Frankfurt School for the purpose of this project is Plessner, who concentrated on the changing weight of public and private

and its relation to the character of the city (Sennett 1974: 32).

[27] I am grateful to Charles Keyes for indicating to me that Thai women now serve in the higher ranks of the military and that some are even generals.

Chapter 3
Feminist Ethnography and Field Research

[1] I conducted research from September 1992 to February 1993 while affiliated with the Asian Institute of Technology on a Canadian University Consortium travel grant. The second period of field work which began in July 1993 was truncated due to illness so I returned the following year in August and completed my work in December 1994. The second period of work was sponsored by the International Development Research Center, and I was hosted by Chulalongkorn University's Social Research Institute.

[2] Even though Escobar's purpose is to attack and deconstruct the creation of the Third World as a category of Western thought and discourse, he continues to use the term throughout his work.

[3] Post-structuralist approaches trace their genealogy to a number of French social theorists such as Foucault and Lacan with their feminist counterparts (or critics), Cixous, Irigaray, and Kristeva. Ironically, there is no term used in French for "post-structuralism" except in works translated from English.

[4] *Khaek* is a term that has many meanings. It literally means "guest" and historically refers to some of the first foreigners in the Kingdom, namely, missionaries and emissaries from India as well as Arab merchants on Muslim trade routes. It is therefore used to refer to people who trace their origins as far away as Palestine and Lebanon (*khaek khaaw* or "white khaeks") and as close as Bangladesh. I have even heard the term applied to Malays and sub-Saharan Africans. The appellation is slightly archaic though still widely used. In polite educated society, it is considered somewhat derogatory.

[5] Daeng and I continue to correspond by mail. Contact with people in Thailand through letters, including the Internet, has been a way to continue with fieldwork at a distance.

[6] The expression *jai ron* is one of the many words using the root, *jai* or heart, which are difficult to translate. It literally means "hot hearted" and is taken to mean impatient or one who has difficulty controlling his or her emotional outbursts. Thais consider this behavior rude and embarrassing. The ideal Thai state of mind is *jai yen* or "cool hearted."

[7] Daeng, who had never been to a floating market, was quite thrilled at the prospect

of participating in this formerly traditional activity, today almost entirely staged for tourists.

[8] Walker (1991, 1996) defines the Thai concept of *pantree* as a room adjacent to the kitchen where food is sometimes prepared and dishes kept. It is not a storage space like a Western pantry. She defines the *pantree* as a transitional space between the traditional Thai kitchen and a modern Western kitchen.

[9] *Shell Chuan Chim* literally means "Shell invites you to taste" and is a system of restaurant endorsements sponsored by Shell Corporation. A guide, similar to the Michelin Guide is also published as a guide to the city's best eating spots.

[10] While conducting the final phase of fieldwork, I employed two assistants and a small group of casual assistants for help with the more labor intensive quantitative survey. For the first half of this period, I employed Kamolrat Sa-Ngeam (known as Morn), an anthropologist by training. After this time, Kamolrat was no longer available, and I was fortunate to meet a nurse/dietician by the name of Arporn Somjit (known as Kapook) who assisted me full time from October until mid-December, 1994. They will be referred to by the first initials of their nicknames in the interview transcripts (M and K respectively). The assistants hired on a casual basis were already employed as research assistants at CUSRI or were students at a local teacher's college and helped conduct surveys on weekends.

[11] General information on Bangkok's foodscape was provided by hundreds of Bangkok residents (neighbors, students, academics, government officials, etc.) that I talked to over the course of 1992–94.

[12] The discrepancy between number of individuals questioned and total number of food shops is because both members of a married couple were questioned in one case (Samrit and Lek) and both mother and daughter in another case were interviewed (Daeng and Ying). Informants' names have been changed to protect privacy.

[13] My first assistant, Kamolrat Sa-Ngeam, spoke English, whereas the second, Arporn Somjit, was fluent in French. At the time of the interview I did not yet have the software enabling me to write Thai on my computer. I therefore wrote in phonetics, which, in any case, was more expedient.

[14] Wira reports that his maternal grandmother, who is now well into her 90s, had initially bought the property, totalling three *rai* (approximately 0.5 hectares) when it was still agricultural land for a very low price (3,000 baht). Wira described his grandmother as traditional by referring that, to this day, she refuses to wear shoes. She was clearly from a Thai farming background. She divided her property evenly among her three children, one of them being Wira's mother.

[15] When colleagues asked me where I was doing my research and I answered

Thailand, the most common query was "Are you studying prostitution?" Though I recognize that it is of utmost importance to understand this industry, which is exploiting, and now killing, women and children (Foundation for Women 1995), I feel as though some of this work by foreign scholars is slightly voyeuristic (see Cohen 1982). It also has the unfortunate effect of stereotyping Thai culture as being somehow uniquely associated with the sex industry. The problem is universal. I wanted to draw attention to another, perhaps more positive, aspect of the Thai urban way of life.

Chapter 4
Thai and Southeast Asian Food-systems

[1] In Thai, *khao* means rice but also means "to eat" when combined with *kin* (*kin khao*, literally, "eat rice").

[2] Others have referred to this regional characteristic as the "rice soul."

[3] In Malay, this pounded mixture is known as *sambal* or *belachan* (McGee 1995). Fermented fish paste has a few basic ingredients but prepared differently by every cook.

[4] Until the early 1970s, part of the area now under the jurisdiction of the Bangkok Metropolitan Administration (BMA) was known as Bangkok-Thonburi. Thonburi is the community facing Bangkok on the Chao Phraya River's west bank.

[5] Crawfurd did not consider the sale of flowers, cooked foods, desserts and sweets, restaurants and "others" (1977a: 25).

[6] Some items on the list did not specify quantity. Daeng knew through experience how much to buy for the day.

[7] Convergence refers to the "apparent gradual unification of global consumption norms toward an evolving global standard" (MacLeod 1989: 3).

[8] I was told by one of my informants of an incident concerning a "7–11" in the Victory Monument Area. Apparently, CP had threatened an entrepreneur in the neighborhood who wanted to open up rival convenience store, "AM/PM," which has a less expensive franchise and is cheaper to operate depending on the licensing agreements negotiated. The family in question was strong-armed into opening a "7–11" because otherwise CP would have opened in close proximity at its own expense to drive the competition out of business.

[9] Malaysia, however, has preserved and enhanced its street foods.

[10] See Glossary.

[11] For *pinto*, see Glossary. The item has an agricultural origin and is referred to

by Hauck et al. (1958) who describe how lunch was often transported to the fields in this three- or four-tiered metal container.

[12] "Uncle" and "Aunt" are polite terms of address to an older person in an informal context.

[13] Thai kitchens are traditionally located outdoors for precisely this reason (Walker 1991).

[14] Cafés and other eating venues are typologized in Chapter 5.

[15] A German woman I met in Bangkok complained that her Thai maids fed her two-year old "constantly," which irritated her and her Swiss husband. She insisted that they stop this in order to retain the discipline of three meals per day.

[16] I should like to thank Associate Professor Narumol Nirathron of Thammasat University (Social Work) for reminding me of the other meaning of this phase, which is that "Thai people eat rice all the time." In other words, rice is the staple food.

[17] Another factor sometimes mentioned by informants was the question of traffic jams. Since people no longer know how long it will take to get home, it seems as though they often eat immediately after leaving work in the evening.

[18] Wang, a Chinese student at AIT, had been eating with the others in the cafeteria every day. He spoke some Thai and was known to eat many types of food. When he no longer joined us, I inquired as to his whereabouts. "Wang joined a Chinese mess," lamented an Indian student. When I asked why she sounded disappointed, my acquaintance responded: "He was becoming very Thai."

[19] This passage is not from my field notes.

[20] It is difficult to ascertain how economically viable this system of "contracting out" is at the household budget level. Certainly, it is clear that individuals are trading potential monetary savings for convenience and time (which can presumably be used to earn extra income).

[21] The distinction between children/young people "helping" and the delicate issue of child labor is often hard to distinguish.

[22] The area being referred to is the zone of demolished housing. At the time of this journal entry in 1992 the houses were not yet torn down.

[23] Bangkok's name in Thai (in shortened form) is *Krungthepmahanakorn*, "The Great City of Angels." Most Thais refer to the capital simply as *Krungthep*.

[24] This was initially for population control and more recently in response to the AIDS pandemic.

[25] The article states that the female waitresses are scantily clad and that more than just food may be "served." This is certainly not the way "Cabbages and Condoms"

operates in Bangkok where a pleasant family-friendly atmosphere is promoted.

[26] Somboon Pattakarn is a famous Chinese restaurant near Lumphini Boxing Stadium. *See Faa* (meaning "light blue") is now a chain with outlets all over the city. It is famous for its *bami*, "a thick Chinese noodle" (Van Esterik 1992). These restaurants are popular with university professors.

Chapter 5
Food Micro-entrepreneurs and Eating Establishments

[1] In Malay as spoken in Indonesia, small food-stalls are normally known as *warung* (street-stall). A *warteg* (a Tegal expression) is slightly larger than a *warung* and involves renting a room and employees (Murray 1991, 58). McGee and Yeung (1977: 23) define a *warung* as "more like a store" and argue that, at least hawker stalls, were referred to as "kiosks." This is similar to the Filipino *sari-sari* or "mixed" store (Laquian 1993).

[2] *"L'alimentation vietnamienne, qu'elle soit à l'intérieur du pays ou à l'extérieur, servie au sein de la famille ou dans un lieu public comme le restaurant, ne peut se faire qu'avec les femmes, détentrices de tout le patrimoine gastronomique traditionnel."*

[3] Prabuddha-bath municipality is a town in Central Thailand north of Bangkok. The study had shocking conclusions. Water and ice showed high bacterial contamination levels of 80% of the time. Nearly all utensils were similarly contaminated (99%). 96.2% of vendor's hands were contaminated with a hundred bacterial colonies per square centimeter. In a Bangkok study conducted by the Medical Science Department and the Ministry of Public Health, unacceptably high incidences of E-coli and salmonella were found in food containing raw fish or seafood such as *som tam lao*, a salad made of green papaya, vegetables, and small raw crabs, as well as other fresh and cooked foods (*Bangkok Post* 1994).

[4] Chonburi is a town on the rapidly developing (or developed?) eastern seaboard, which is certainly part of the extended Bangkok Metropolitan Region described by Greenberg (1994). At the time of the CUSRI study, however, it still had a provincial character. I suspect that the food-system found there now resembles the situation described for Bangkok.

[5] *"Cependant, chez les Isaan ce type d'activités ne relève pas exclusivement de la sphère féminine et il est admis que les hommes prennent en charge dans la vie courante la cuisson du riz ou la confection de plats d'accompagnement, dès lors que la main d'oeuvre féminine est insufflsaante ou temporairement absente."*

⁶ Indeed, Tha Prachan is known as an area where authentically prepared traditional foods that have largely disappeared in mainstream Thai society are available.

⁷ Restaurants were defined as places preparing full meals. The nature of the "informality" of establishments surveyed was based on the non-registration of activities, the use (but not exclusive) of unpaid (usually family) labor. The study focused on small-scale enterprises (fewer than twenty employees) for all three sectors surveyed (garments, metal work, and restaurants).

⁸ A question that needs addressed is the reliability of Thai government statistics, particularly those collected by the Department of Labor. First, the household surveys I believe are quite reliable as they are based on a weighted sample of a cross-section of the population. The Labor Force Survey, however, suffers from under-enumeration. I suspect that surveyors did not count the stalls and shops in the *sois* and/or, neglected to account for stalls that open only in the evening.

⁹ Bussaracum markets itself as a venue serving authentic Thai food prepared in the royal style. Marilyn Walker's 1991 thesis outlines the debates surrounding this claim. She concludes that the restaurant is primarily geared toward a Western clientele because the menu breaks with the conventions of Thai gastronomy.

¹⁰ The restaurant operated until some time in late 1993 or early 1994 at which point it was converted into a bookstore cafe. Comparative photos of the site are found in Figure 3.4.

¹¹ A series of debates ensued after Embree published this article on Thai society as a "loosely structured social system." The debates either refuted or asserted Embree's thesis of Thai society being "loosely structured." What critics sometimes failed to note was that Embree was making his comments about Thailand in contrast to Japanese society.

¹² "Johnny Walker Black Label" is the drink of choice among wealthy Thai men, or those who want to appear so. Second choice is "Johnny Walker Red Label" and the masses drink Mekong or another brand of Thai "whisky" (so called, as this is technically a rum).

¹³ A feature article from *The Nation* (Bangkok) describes this cabaret culture where male cross-dressers, or "women of the second type" (*phuying praphet song,* more often referred to as *kathoey*) perform.

¹⁴ One of the problems with Thai data is that women often refer to themselves as housewives even though they may own a small business such as a food shop. This is particularly true in rural areas where, in addition, women are highly active in farming.

¹⁵ Due to the overlapping of practices, totals do not add up to 100%.

[16] Four respondents (7%) told us that they worked at other jobs. There was one housekeeper, a company employee, one worker for an electrical company and a civil servant. For this minority, selling prepared food was a part-time occupation.

[17] We attempted to collect data on as many family/household members as possible. Unfortunately, some of my assistants did not pursue this line of questioning thoroughly enough. Hence, the only reliable information concerns the occupation of the other main adult in the family/household.

[18] The primary level is known as *prathom* and is composed today of Levels 1–6, Level 7 having been phased out. The secondary level (*mathayom*) also has six levels.

[19] The remaining 5% of respondents did not declare their place of birth. Some interviewees simply stated they were from Isaan rather than name their specific home province.

[20] Like most parts of Asia, Africa, and the world in general, Thailand is a racist and color-conscious society. Dark skin is considered unattractive, especially for women.

[21] The categories used were borrowed for the most part by those employed in the Chonburi study of street foods (Napat and Szanton 1986) with the addition of the following categories: shophouses, expensive restaurants, hotel food shops, franchises, and establishments located in apartments and food centers.

[22] Only one food center in the area agreed to be studied and its name, like that of individual informants, shall remain anonymous. Another new center owned by a large Thai company did not grant me permission to interview vendors. I did, however, sketch map the premises and counted the number of employees and customers. The manager was briefly and informally interviewed. These results will be discussed in the next two chapters.

[23] The number of cases is abbreviated as "n."

[24] Among the Chinese in Malaysia and Singapore this is known as "hot pot."

[25] With the exception of *tom yam gung* (a hot-and-sour prawn soup), most Thai food can and often is served at room temperature. Foreign food is also commonly served lukewarm if it has not been prepared immediately beforehand.

[26] Commensality promotes community and kinship bonds but also leads to the frustration of many women who are responsible for rounding up family members in addition to food preparation (cf. Charles and Kerr 1988; Giard and Mayol 1980).

[27] "Chicken rice," as it is known in Malaysia and Singapore, is a Hainanese specialty in which boiled chicken is served with rice cooked in chicken broth. Chicken

bouillon is usually served as well. Condiments such as ginger sauce, thick soya sauce, and chili dip are included.

Chapter 6
Lives and Voices of Food-shop Owners

[1] Other factors listed by the International Labor Organization (ILO) include: (1) family ownership; (2) reliance on indigenous resources; (3) labor intensive and adapted technology; (4) skills acquired outside formal system; and (5) unregulated competitive markets (McGee and Yeung 1977: 21).

[2] These profiles are for 1996. As of 2003, Daeng was 36 going on 37 as her birthday is in November.

[3] MBK is a seven-storey labyrinth filled mostly with small shops and vendors but also including the giant Tokyu Department Store. It is truly a sight to behold, a rather daunting labyrinth, and I have never come across anything like it elsewhere.

[4] Many food centers in Kuala Lumpur continue to have service at the table and have avoided or else abandoned the use of coupons.

[5] For a discussion of the importance of food appearances and display, see Walker 1991.

[6] A contrasting example was provided by 30-year old Lamun from Isaan who formerly operated a pushcart selling *luuk chin* (a type of meatball brochette). She gave up this work because it was so physically demanding. Lamun was presented with an opportunity to work for a foreign professional who lived alone in a large comfortable home and took it up immediately.

[7] Our interview took place while the store was under renovation.

[8] Here, Viwan misunderstood my question which was not very well phrased to begin with. In other restaurants, such as the Professor's Pub, there is a chef who looks after the Chinese food—usually a man of Chinese background—and a chef who is responsible for Thai dishes—often a woman who is ethnically Thai. At Fong Kee, the two Sino-Thai male chefs are responsible for all types of food prepared.

[9] For example, a number of serial dramas on Thai television have begun to explore the Sino-Thai heritage. One program was written up as a three or four volume set of books that are best-sellers. My assistant, Arporn Somjit, explained that many Thais believed that the books contain an esoteric message that, if discovered and understood, leads the reader to greater material prosperity. Another example of the Sino-Thai renaissance is the exponential growth of the annual Chinese New Year parade, a low-key event several years ago but now one of the city's biggest events.

[10] Vipawan and her husband were interviewed together. This was the only interview conducted in English. All citations from these two informants are direct quotations.

[11] Her employee, Phi Oy, contradicted this and said that set-down begins at 6 p.m and sometimes did not finish until 9 p.m.

[12] At Mister Donut for example, janitors received the first delivery of doughnuts at 4:45 a.m. The shop closes at midnight. Cashing out in the evening, however, is a crucial function, requiring management supervision.

[13] Tip worked in a hotel that is in walking distance from her present home and business. It is a traditional Chinese hotel catering mostly to a local clientele. The hotel is also a "temporary" hotel associated with Thai-oriented prostitution. These establishments can be identified by the draped car-parks that protect the identity of customers by shielding their license plates. Like the hotel rooms, these sheltered parking spaces can also be rented on a short time basis.

[14] The Guan Im cult is becoming very popular in Southeast Asia even among non-Chinese. This may be due to the fact that she is associated with prosperity. It may also be an indication of the feminization of Buddhist icons. Keyes (1996) explains that Guan Yin was a male Boddhisattva named Prajunaparamita, who through the course of history became a female deity.

[15] A "picnic stove" is a wok on a gas source. I am told its use is illegal in Bangkok, but it is nevertheless ubiquitous in the city's food shops.

[16] The fact that they and their children eat the restaurant food every day is one of the factors they identified explaining the high quality of the food served and cleanliness surrounding its preparation.

[17] This is the actual name of the center. The identity was impossible to conceal because it is the only one of its kind in the area. I did not have permission to interview food shopowners or employees in the center but did speak with the manager. All information provided here is therefore public.

[18] Askew embarked on a project to study the historical evolution of a *soi* in Bangkok as part of an urban sociology undertaking (Kamolrat 1994).

[19] As explained in the Chapter 8, the Home Food Center in the Victory Monument Area went out of business shortly after the onset of the Asian economic crisis.

Chapter 7
Bangkok's Dynamic Foodscape

[1] In some instances, it is a form of respect to address an older woman as "Mother" or "Auntie." "Mother" is the more respectful of the two.

[2] *Khanom* is a general expression for sweets.

[3] Askew has transliterated this as *chae* and calls them "credit circles" so my information about the word's derivation from the English "share" may be wrong. While in Malaysia and Singapore, I brought up the topic of chit funds, to hear typically that this is a Chinese concept (*hui*; see Chua 1981). On further consideration, rotating credit appears to be indigenous to many societies.

[4] The amount lost due to cheating is not clear as there are discrepancies in the amounts reported by Daeng and her Aunt Ying, who was the share leader. Amounts may have been confused due to other losses that were the result of a member dying unexpectedly.

[5] *Nakleng* is a term with several contradictory meanings. In Haas' dictionary, it has four distinct definitions: (1) rogue, rascal, gambler; (2) bold person, sporting person; (3) big-hearted person; and (4) person who is an authority on something (1964: 261). For a discussion of the relationship with masculinity, especially with regard to definition one of rogue, rascal or gambler, see Keyes 1986: 87–88.

[6] Here, Akin is transliterating "share" as *chae* in keeping with Thai pronunciation of an English loan word.

[7] An open university, Ramkamhaeng permits students to study through correspondence and part-time. It is one of the most accessible post-secondary institutions for low-income students who need to work or for those who cannot pass the difficult entrance exams at top universities.

[8] Certainly, I was not privy to marital disputes during my fieldwork because I did not get to know the informants as close friends (with the exception of Daeng, who was unmarried).

[9] In a discussion with Tanya Lary, an MA student in Urban Planning at the University of British Columbia, street vendors in Beijing are 70% male. Their wives were reported to be at home full-time. In a study conducted by Roslyn Kunin and Diana Lary for the Asia Pacific Foundation on Chinese-Canadian entrepreneurs, this firm gender division of labor was also evident among entrepreneurs.

[10] See the Glossary for a full definition of *sakdina*. Feudalism is shorthand for this historical period but not altogether accurate.

[11] Blanchard argued that "class" in the traditional sense, could not be applied to Thai society. He did, however, roughly sketch five major status and occupational groups ranging from the aristocracy to the lowest rung of "unskilled" laborers and hawkers. O'Connor provides a more developed and subtle schema of "hierarchy and community" thereby sketching a theory of indigenous Thai urbanism.

[12] As described by Lee 1992 (157–59), attempts to regulate hawkers began much earlier, with licensing regulations in 1913 and the construction of the first hawker shelters in 1923. Most were simple covered places without sanitation facilities.

[13] Dr Napasri Maneewong informed me of a television documentary on the subject of adolescent behavior in Bangkok. One segment reported that teenagers typically go as a group to fast food restaurants such as McDonald's where they linger for hours with a very small order of soft drinks or food.

[14] I should like to thank Terry McGee for alerting me to the existence of Makan Sutra.

[15] This "mini-food center" closed immediately following the onset of the Asian economic crisis in 1997.

[16] Goy explained that alcohol was deliberately not sold to avoid problems, such as violence.

[17] "Same" refers to those who reporting their address as the same as their food shop. In this case, it refers to a vendor renting a room in the residence adjacent to the Rattana Food Center. "VMA" refers to the Victory Monument Area; "DD" is the Asoke-Din Daeng-Huay Kwang neighbourhood; "BKT" refers to "Bang Khun Thian" on Bangkok's outskirts.

[18] "Primary" refers to Prathom 1–7, the equivalent of Grades 1–6 of primary school in Canada and the United States. By law, all Thai citizens must attend school until Prathom 6 or the age of 12, whichever comes first.

[19] The category "cousins" refers to all blood relatives outside the nuclear family (parents, spouses, and children). The latter are included in the category "Family."

[20] This part of the interview took place in English. When I found out that Wira spent most of his adult life studying in the United States, we switched from Thai to English, but his wife continued in Thai.

[21] For an interesting group of articles advocating different positions on the issue see *Good Life Magazine* 3(32), August 1994 [in Thai]. It contains three articles written by three Thai academics in the nutrition field.

Chapter 8
Bangkok's Post-crisis Foodscape

[1] Readers interested in greater detail about the impacts of the economic crisis on the Bangkok system of public eating are invited to consult Yasmeen 2001a.

[2] I should like to thank Jim Glassman for underlining the link between the growth of food vending post-crisis and the link with the continued relationship between

Thais and the agricultural sphere.

[3] There are, of course, many exceptions to this generalization, particularly because of colonial influences.

[4] The halt on construction, however, also dampened prospects for some food vendors, as construction workers are a good revenue source.

[5] Glassman (1999), based on the Thai Labor Force Survey, reports that between February 1996 and 1999 approximately 1.5 million construction jobs were lost.

[6] Although *Golden Arches East* (Watson et al. 1997) argues that McDonald's has become culturally entrenched in the localities in which it is based in East Asia, taking on a distinct cultural meaning in those places rather than resulting in a standardization imposed on the periphery by the center.

Works Cited

Note: Following Thai practice, Thai names are listed under first name with the surname spelled out in full. Malay names (e.g., Jamilah) listed also listed by first name. Chinese Japanese, and Vietnamese authors are listed by surname (e.g., Ng, Yoshihara, Trinh), followed by the given name without a comma according to their referencing systems. When an individual has a "combination" name, such as Brenda Yeoh, it is referenced with the surname first.

Articles and Books

Afshar, Haleh and Bina Agarwal, eds. 1989. *Women, Poverty, and Ideology in Asia.* London: Macmillan.

Amara Pongsapich 1988. *Occasional Papers on Women in Thailand.* Women's Studies Program Publication No. 3. Bangkok: Social Research Institute, Chulalongkorn University.

Amdur, Louis et al. The Bubbling Cauldron: Global and Local Interactions in New York City Restaurants. In *After Modernism: Global Restructuring and the Changing Boundaries of City Life*, ed. M. Smith. 105-32. London: Transaction Publishers.

Amin, Nurul 1991. *A Policy Agenda for the Informal Sector in Thailand.* A Report for Submission to the National Economic and Social Development Board, Royal Government of Thailand. New Delhi: International Labor Organization, Asian Employment Program.

Anderson, E. N. 1988. *The Food of China.* New Haven: Yale University Press.

Appadurai, Arjun 1986. Theory in Anthropology: Center and Periphery. *Comparative Studies in Society and History* 28: 356-61.

Appadurai, Arjun 1990. Disjuncture and Difference in the Global Cultural Economy. *Theory, Culture, and Society* 7: 295-310.

Ardener, Shirley 1986. The Representation of Women in Academic Models. In *Visibility and Power: Essays on Women in Society and Development.* L. Dube and E. Leacock, eds. p. 3-14. Delhi: Oxford University Press.

Ardener, Shirley 1993. Introduction. In *Women and Space: Ground Rules and Social Maps*, ed. S. Ardener. 2nd rev. edn. Oxford: Berg.

Arendt, Hannah 1957. *The Human Condition.* Garden City, NY: Doubleday.

Arendt, Hannah 1960. *Vita Activa.* Stuttgart: W. Kohlhammer Verlag.

Argenti, Olivio 2000. *Food for the Cities: Food Supply and Distribution Policies to Reduce Urban Food Insecurity.* "Food into Cities Collection, DT/43-00E. Rome: FAO. Available at: www.fao.org/ag/ags/ AGSM/SADA/SADAE-5_.htm

Arnott, M., ed. 1976. *Gastronomy: The Anthropology of Food and Food Habits.* The Hague: Mouton.

Aron, J-P. 1989. *Le Mangeur du XIXe siècle.* Paris: Payot.

Asia Magazine. Store Wars. 20-22 November 1992:10-17.

Askew, Marc 1994. *Interpreting Bangkok: The Urban Question in Thai Studies.* Bangkok: Chulalongkorn University Press.

Askew, Marc, and Paritta Chalermpow Koanantakul 1992. Bangkok: The Evolving Urban Landscape. In *Regional Development and Change in Southeast Asia in the 1990s.* Amara Pongsapich et al., eds. 163-72. Bangkok: Chulalongkorn University Social Research Institute.

Atkinson, J. M. 1982. Anthropology: Review Essay. *Signs* 8: 236-58.

Atkinson, J. M., and S. Errington, eds. 1990. *Power and Difference.* Palo Alto: Stanford University Press.

Bacani, C. Surviving the Slump. *Asiaweek* 28 November 1997: 52-55.

Bangkok Post 1992. At Thanying there's always something to delight you. 8 December: "Holiday Time" Insert: 3.

Bangkok Post 1993a. BMA launches crackdown on city vendors. 12 January: 3.

Bangkok Post 1993b. Vendors at Pak Klong Talad to face crackdown. 19 January: 2.

Bangkok Post 1998. Retailers press government for more relief to ensure survival. 3 August: 8.

Barrau, J. 1983. *Les Hommes et leurs aliments.* Paris: Temps Actuels.

Baudrillard, Jean 1981. *Simulacres et simulation.* Paris: Editions Galilée.

Belasco, Warren 1989. *Appetite for Change: How the Counterculture took on the Food Industry, 1966-88.* New York: Pantheon Books.

Bell, David and Gill Valentine 1997. *Consuming Geographies: We are Where We eat.* London: Routledge.

Bell, Peter 1992. Gender and Economic Development in Thailand. In *Gender and Development in Southeast Asia*, ed. P. Van Esterik and J. Van Esterik. Vol. 2: 61-82. Proceedings of the 20th Meeting of the Canadian Council for Southeast Asian Studies (CCSEAS), York University, 18-21 October 1991. Montreal: CCSEAS.

Bencha Yoddumnern-Attig 1992. Thai Family Structure and Organization: Changing Roles and Duties in Historical Perspective. In *Changing Roles and Statuses of Women in Thailand: A Documentary Assessment*, ed. Bencha Yoddumnern-Attig, et al. 8-24. Nakhon Pathom: Institute for Population and Social Research, Mahidol University.

Benhabib, S. 1992. Models of Public Space: Hannah Arendt, the Liberal Tradition, and Jürgen Habermas. In *Habermas and the Public Sphere*, ed. Craig Calhoun. Cambridge, MA: MIT Press.

Berson, G. 1974. Slumming it in the Middle-class. In *Class and Feminism: A Collection of Essays from THE FURIES*, ed. C. Brunch and N. Myron. 56-62. Baltimore: Diana Press.

Better Meals 1995. Welcome to the Better Meals Progam. Advertising Brochure.

Bhavivarn Noraphallop, 1993. *Thai Food Culture: A Study of the Food- System in Tha Prachan.* Unpublished MA thesis. Department of Anthropology, Thammasat University, Bangkok. [In Thai.]

Bourdieu, Pierre 1979. *La Distinction: Critique social du jugement.* Paris: Minuit.

Bowlby, Sophia 1988. From Corner Shop to Hypermarket: Women and Food Retailing. In *Women in Cities: Gender and the Urban Environment*, ed. J. Little, L. Peake, and P. Richardson. 61-83. New York: New York University Press.

Bray, Francesca 1986. *The Rice Economies: Technology and Development in Asian Societies.* Oxford; New York: Blackwell.

Bryson, V. 1992. *Feminist Political Theory: An Introduction.* New York: Paragon House.

Busaba Sivasomboon and Busrin Treerapongpichit 1998. "Laid off workers turn to small businesses." *Bangkok Post* 23 March: 10.

Camporesi, P., 1993. *The Magic Harvest: Food, Folklore and Society.* Trans. Joan Krakover Hall. Cambridge: Polity Press.

Caplan, Karen 1994. The Politics of Location as Transnational Feminist Critical Practice. In *Scattered Hegemonies*, ed. I. Grewal and C. Kaplan. 137-52. Minneapolis: University of Minnesota Press.

CBC Television, November 1997 and June 1998. "Pacific Rim Report: Report on effects of Asian financial crisis."

Chai-anan Samudavanija 1991. State-Identity Creation, State-Building, and Civil Society. In *National Identity and its Defenders, Thailand, 1939-1989*, ed. C. J. Reynolds. 59-86. Monash Papers on Southeast Asia No. 25. Melbourne: Centre of Southeast Asian Studies, Monash University.

Chan Kwok Bun and Tong Chee Kiong 1995. The Ethnic Chinese of Thailand. Special Issue of the *Southeast Asian Journal of Social Science*. 23(1).

Charles, N., and Kerr, M. 1988. *Women, Food, and Families*. Manchester: New York: Manchester University Press.

Chiong-Xavier, M. 1989. Women Vendors in Metro Manila Markets. In *Manila: History, People and Culture. The Proceedings of the Manila Studies Conference (1986)*, ed. W. Villacorta, I. Cruz, and M. Brillantes. 167-74. Manila: De La Salle University Press.

Cohen, Erik 1982. Thai Girls and Foreign Men. *Annals of Tourism Research* 9: 403-28.

Conlon, Frank 1995. Dining Out in Bombay. In *Consuming Modernity: Public Culture in a South Asian World*, ed. C. Breckenridge. 90-127. Minneapolis: University of Minnesota.

Cook, Ian 1995. Constructing the Exotic: The Case of Tropical Fruit. In *The Shape of the World*, ed. J. Allen and D. Massey. 137-42. Oxford: Oxford University Press.

Cook, Ian, and Philip Crang 1996. The world on a plate: culinary culture, displacement, and geographical knowledges. *Journal of Material Culture* 1: 131-54.

Crang, Philip 1994. It's showtime: On the workplace geographies of display in a restaurant in Southeast England, *Environment and Planning D: Society and Space* 12: 675-704.

Crawfurd, John (1820) 1987. *Journal of an Embassy to the Courts of Siam and Cochin China*. Singapore: Oxford University Press.

Crawfurd, Margaret 1977. *Urban Food Supply and Distribution: Supply Linkages of Bangkok and Thonburi Fresh-Food Markets*. Southeast Asian Development Series No. 6. Ann Arbor: Center of South and Southeast Asian Studies, University of Michigan.

Crawfurd, Margaret et al. 1977. *Urban Food Supply and Distribution: Characteristics and Utilization of Fresh Food Markets in Bangkok and Thonburi*. Transportation Series No. 5. Ann Arbor: Center of South and Southeast Asian Studies, University of Michigan.

Crispin, Shawn W. "Cycle of Despair." *Far Eastern Economic Review* 23 September 1999: 22. http://www.feer.com/9909_23/p22thailand.html

Curtin, D., and L. Heldke, eds. 1992. *Cooking, Eating, Thinking: Transformative Philosophies of Food*. Bloomington: Indiana University Press.

Cwiertka, K., and B. Walraven, eds. 2001. *Asian Food: The Global and the Local*. Honolulu: University of Hawaii Press.

Daniels, Stephen, and Dennis Cosgrove. 1993. Spectacle and Text: Landscape

Metaphors in Cultural Geography. In *Place/ Culture/Representation*, ed. J. Duncan and D. Ley. 57-77. London: Routledge.

Darunee Tantiwiramanond and S. R. Pandey. 1991. *By Women, For Women: A Study of Women's Organizations in Thailand*. Research Notes and Discussion Paper No. 72. Singapore: Institute of Southeast Asian Studies.

Davidoff, L. 1995. *Worlds Between: Historical Perspectives on Gender and Class*. London: Routledge.

Dear, Michael 1994. Post-modern Human Geography: A Preliminary Assessment. *Erdkunde* 48: 2-13.

de Certeau, Michel 1984. *The Practice of Everyday Life*. Berkeley: University of California Press.

de Certeau, Michel 1990. *L'Invention du quotidien. Tome I: Arts de faire*. 2nd edn. Paris: Gallimard.

de La Loubère, Simon (1693) 1986. *The Kingdom of Siam*. Introduction by David K. Wyatt. Singapore: Oxford University Press.

Denzin, N.K. 1978. *The Research Act: A Theoretical Introduction to Sociological Methods*. New York: McGraw-Hill.

Desai, Inderjit and Prapimporn Somnasang 1996. Indigenous Food Habits and Nutritional Status of Rural Isaan People in North-eastern Thailand. In *Contemporary Perspectives on Thai Foodways*, ed. M. Walker and G. Yasmeen. Centre for Southeast Asian Research Research Monograph No. 11. 44-53. Vancouver: Center for Southeast Asian Research, University of British Columbia.

de Wandeler, Koen 1990. Food Consumption and Dwelling Environment: A Comparison of an Urban and a Rural Case-study in Thailand. Unpublished paper.

de Young, J. 1955. *Village Life in Modern Thailand*. Berkeley: University of California Press.

Djamour, Judith 1959. *Malay Kinship and Marriage in Singapore*. New York: Humanities Press.

Douglas, Mary (ed.) 1984. *Food in the Social Order: Studies of Food and Festivities in Three American Communities*. New York: Russell Sage Foundation.

Drakakis-Smith, David 1990. Food for Thought or Thought about Food: Urban Food Distribution Systems in the Third World. In *Cities and Development in the Third World*, ed. R. Potter and A. Salau. 100-20. London: Mansell Publishing.

Drummond, Lisa 1993. Women, the Household Economy, and the Informal Sector in Hanoi. MA Thesis. Department of Geography, University of British Columbia, Vancouver.

Duncan, Jim and David Ley, eds. 1993. *Place / Culture / Representation*. London: Routledge.

Elshtain, J. 1981. *Public Man, Private Woman: Women in Social and Political Thought*. Princeton: Princeton University Press.

Embree, John 1950. Thailand: A Loosely Structured Social System. *American Anthropologist* 52: 181-93.

Employment and Immigration Canada 1990. *Canadian Foodservices Industry: A Human Resource Study*. Report prepared by Ernst & Young for the Steering Committee of the Canadian Foodservices Industry, Fall 1990. Ottawa: Employment and Immigration Canada.

Engels, Freidrich 1972. *The Origin of the Family, Private Property, and the State*. New York: Pathfinder.

Enloe, Cynthia 1989. *Bananas, Beaches, and Bases*. Berkeley: University of California Press.

Errington, S. 1990. Recasting Sex, Gender, and Power: A Theoretical and Regional Overview. In *Power and Difference*, ed. J. M. Atkinson and and S. Errington. 1-58. Stanford: Stanford University Press.

Escobar, Arturo 1995. *Encountering Development: The Making and Unmaking of the Third World*. Princeton: Princeton University Press.

Everett, Joanna and Mira Savara 1991. Institutional Credit as a Strategy Toward Self-reliance for Petty Commodity Producers in India: A Critical Evaluation. In *Women, Development and Survival in the Third World*, ed. H. Afshar. 239-59. London: Longman.

Evers, Hans-Dieter and Korff, Rüdiger 1982. Subsistence Production in Bangkok, in Comparison with other Southeast Asian Cities. *Second Thai-European Research Seminar, 14-18 June 1982, University of Bielefeld*.

Eyles, John D. 1988. Interpreting the Geographical World: Qualitative Approaches in Geographical Research. In *Qualitative Methods in Human Geography*, ed. J. D. Eyles and D. M. Smith. 1-15. Cambridge: Polity Press.

Farm Folk/City Folk 1995. *Newsletter* Various Issues.

Fenton, A., and T. Owen, eds. 1981. *Food in Perspective*. [Proceedings of the Third International Conference on Ethnological Food Research, Cardiff, Wales, 1977] Edinburgh: John Donald Publishers.

Finkelstein, J. 1989. *Dining Out: A Sociology of Modern Manners*. New York: New York University Press.

Firth, Rosemary 1966. *Housekeeping among the Malay Peasants*. 2nd edn. London: Athlone Press.

Focus on the Global South 1998. *Annual Report 1997.* Bangkok: Focus on the Global South.

Food and Agriculture Organization (FAO) 1988. *A Summary of FAO Studies and Other Activities Relating to Street Foods.* Rome: Food and Agriculture Organization.

Food and Agriculture Organization (FAO) 1989. *Street Foods: Report of an FAO Expert Consultation, Yogjakarta, Indonesia, 5-9 December 1988.* Rome: Food and Agriculture Organization.

Formoso, Bernard 1989. Influence du milieu et des activités de production sur le régime alimentaire de deux villages du Nord-Est de la Thaïlande. In *Alimentation et région,* ed. C. Thouvenot and J. Peltre. 210-23. Nancy: Presses Universitaires de Nancy.

Formoso, Bernard 1993. Les Repas de fête des paysans Isaan du Nord-Est de la Thaïlande. In *Autour du riz: Le repas chez quelques populations d'Asie du Sud-Est,* ed. N. Krowolski and I. Simon-Barouh. 83-118. Paris: L'Harmattan.

Forster, R., and O. Ranum, eds. 1979. *Food and Drink in History: Annales, économies, sociétés, civilisations.* Trans. E. Forster and P. M. Ranum. Baltimore: Johns Hopkins University Press.

Furnivall, John S. 1939. *Netherlands India: A Study of the Plural Economy.* Cambridge: Cambridge University Press.

Fuss, Diana 1992. *Essentially Speaking: Feminism, Nature, and Difference.* London: Routledge.

Gatens, M. 1991. *Feminism and Philosophy: Perspectives on Difference and Equality.* Bloomington: Indiana University Press.

Geertz, Clifford 1956. *The Rotating Credit Association: An Instrument for Development.* Cambridge, MA: MIT Press.

Geertz, Clifford 1961. *The Javanese Family: A Study of Kinship and Socialization.* New York: Free Press of Glencoe.

Geertz, Clifford 1962. The Rotating Credit Association: A Middle Rung in Development. *Economic Development and Cultural Change* 10: 421-63.

Geertz, Clifford 1963. *Agricultural Involution.* Berkeley: University of California Press.

Geertz, Clifford 1983. *Local Knowledge: Further Essays in Interpretive Anthropology.* New York: Basic Books.

Giard, Luce and Pierre Mayol. 1980. *L'Invention du quotidien. Tome 2: Habiter, cuisiner.* Paris: Union Général des Editions.

Glaser, B. G., and A. S. Strauss. 1967. *The Discovery of Grounded Theory.* Chicago:

Aldine.

Goodman, David and Michael Redclift 1991. *Refashioning Nature: Food, Ecology, and Culture*. London: Routledge.

Goody, Jack 1982. *Cooking, Cuisine, and Class*. Cambridge: Cambridge University Press.

Greenberg, Charles 1994. Region-based Urbanization in Bangkok's Extended Periphery. Unpublished PhD Thesis. Department of Geography, University of British Columbia, Vancouver.

Gregory, Derek 1990. Chinatown, part three? Soja and the missing spaces of social theory. *Strategies* 3: 40-104.

Gregory, Derek 1994. *Geographical Imaginations*. Oxford: Blackwell.

Guerrero, Sylvia H. 1975. *Hawkers and Vendors in Manila and Baguio: Final Country Report*. Ottawa: International Development Research Centre.

Gumperz, John 1981. Conversational Inference and Classroom Learning. In *Ethnography and Language in Educational Settings*, ed. J. L. Green and C. Wallat. Norwood, NJ: Ablex.

Gurstein, Penny 1995. *Planning for Telework and Home-based Employment: A Canadian Survey on Integrating Work into Residential Environments*. Report for the Canadian Mortgage and Housing Corporation] Vancouver: Centre for Human Settlements, University of British Columbia.

Haas, Margaret R. 1964. *Thai-English Student's Dictionary*. Stanford: Stanford University Press.

Habermas, Jürgen 1989. *The Structural Transformations of the Public Sphere*. Cambridge, MA: MIT Press.

Hammersley, M., and P. Atkinson 1983. *Ethnography: Principles in Practice*. London: Routledge.

Hanks, Jane R. 1960. "Reflections on the Ontology of Rice." In *Culture in History: Essays in Honor of Paul Radin*, ed. Stanley Diamond. 298-301. New York: Columbia University Press.

Haraway, Donna 1988. Situated Knowledges: The Science Question in Feminism as a Site of Discourse on the Privilege of Partial Perspective. *Feminist Studies* 14(3): 575-99.

Haraway, Donna 1991. *Simians, Cyborgs, and Women: The Reinvention of Nature*. London: Routledge.

Harding, Sandra 1986. *The Science Question in Feminism*. Ithaca: Cornell University Press.

Hartmann, Heidi 1986. The Unhappy Marriage of Marxism and Feminism: Toward a

More Progressive Union. In *The Unhappy Marriage of Marxism and Feminism: A Debate on Class and Patriarchy*, ed. L. Sargent. London: Pluto Press.

Hattox, R., 1985. *Coffee and Coffee Houses: The Origins of a Social Beverage in the Medieval Near East*. Seattle: University of Washington Press.

Hauck, H. M., S. Sudsaneh, and J. Hanks 1958. *Food Habits and Nutrient Intakes in a Siamese Rice Village: Studies in Bang Chan, 1952-54*. Ithaca: Southeast Asia Program, Cornell University.

Hayden, D. 1981. *The Grand Domestic Revolution: A History of Feminist Designs for American Homes, Neighbourhoods and Cities*. Cambridge, MA: MIT Press.

Hayden, Dolores 1984. *Redesigning the American Dream: The Future of Housing, Work, and Family Life*. New York: W. W. Norton.

Hellwig, Tineke 1994. *Adjustment and Discontent: Representations of Women in the Dutch East Indies*. Windsor, ON: Netherlandic Press.

Heyzer, Noeleen 1986. *Working Women in Southeast Asia: Development, Subordination, Emancipation*. Milton Keynes: Open University Press.

hooks, bell 1984. *Feminist Theory: From Margin to Centre*. Boston: South End Press.

hooks, bell 1990. *Yearning: Race, Gender and Cultural Politics*. Boston: South End Press.

Hopkins, Jeff 1990. West Edmonton Mall: Landscape of Myths and Elsewhereness. *The Canadian Geographer* 34: 2-17.

Hopkins, Jeff 1991a. West Edmonton Mall as a Center for Social Interaction. *The Canadian Geographer* 35: 268-79.

Howell, P. 1993. Public Space and the Public Sphere: Political Theory and the Historical Geography of Modernity. *Environment and Planning D: Society and Space* 11: 303-22.

ILO (International Labor Organization) 2000a. Training in the informal sector. *World Employment Report 1998-99*. Available at www.ilo.org/public/english/bureau/inf/pkits/wer98/wer98ch5.htm

ILO (International Labor Organization) 2000b. *Yearbook of Labor Force Statistics*. Geneva.

Jacobs, Jane 1961. *The Death and Life of Great American Cities*. New York: Modern Library.

Jameson, Frederick 1983. Post-modernism and Consumer Society. In *The Anti-Aesthetic: Essays on Post-modern Culture*, ed. H. Foster. Port Townsend: Bay Press.

Jay, M. 1992. Scopic Regimes of Modernity. In *Modernity and Identity*, ed. S. Lash and J. Friedman. 178-95. Oxford: Blackwell.

Jellinek, Lea 1977. The Life of a Jakarta Street Trader. In *Third World Urbanization*, ed. J. Abu-Lughod and R. Hay. 244-56. London: Methuen.

Jellinek, Lea 1991. *The Wheel of Fortune: The History of a Poor Community in Jakarta*. Sydney: Allen & Unwin.

Jones, Gavin ed. 1984. *Women in the Urban and Industrial Workforce: Southeast and East Asia*. Canberra: Australian National University in collaboration with University of Hawaii Press.

Keller, S. ed. 1981. *Building for Women*. Lexington, MA: Lexington Books.

Keyes, Charles F. 1977. *The Golden Peninsula: Culture and Adaptation in Mainland Southeast Asia*. London: Macmillan-Collier.

Keyes, Charles F. 1984. Mother or Mistress But Never a Monk: Buddhist Notions of Female Gender in Rural Thailand. *American Ethnologist* 11: 223-41.

Keyes, Charles F. 1986. Ambiguous Gender: Male Initiation in a Northern Thai Buddhist Society. In *Gender and Religion: On the Complexity of Symbols*, ed. C. Bynum, S. Harrell, and P. Richman. 66-96. Boston: Beacon Press.

Keyes, Charles F. 1987. *Thailand: Buddhist Kingdom as Modern Nation-State*. Boulder, CO: Westview Press.

Khin Thitsa. 1980. *Providence and Prostitution: Women in Thailand*. London: Change International Reports.

Kirsch, A. Thomas 1982. Buddhism, Sex-Roles and Thai Society. In *Women of Southeast Asia*, ed. P. Van Esterik. 16-41. Northern Illinois University Series on Southeast Asia, Occasional Paper No. 9. De Kalb: Northern Illinois University.

Kirsch, A. Thomas 1985. Text and Context: Buddhist Sex Roles/Culture of Gender Revisited. *American Ethnologist* 12: 302-20.

Klodawksy, Fran and Aaron Spector 1988. New Families, New Housing Needs, New Urban Environments: The Case of Single-Parent Families. In *Life Spaces: Gender, Households, Employment*. ed. C. Andrew and B. Moore-Milroy. 141-58. Vancouver: University of British Columbia Press.

Klopfer, Lisa 1993. Padang Restaurants: Creating "Ethnic" Cuisine in Indonesia. *Food and Foodways* 5: 293-304.

Konvitz, Josef 1987. Gastronomy and Urbanization. *South Atlantic Quarterly* 86: 44-56.

Korea Newsreview. 1996. Foodservice Industry Hits W20 Trillion in '95. 2 February 1996: 16-21.

Korff, Rüdiger 1989. *Bangkok and Modernity*. Bangkok: Social Research Institute, Chulalongkorn University.

Krowolski, N. 1993. Autour du riz. In *Autour du riz: Le repas chez quelques populations d'Asie du Sud-Est*, ed. N. Krowolski and I. Simon-Barouh. 7-13. Paris: L'Harmattan.

Kwanchai Rungfapaisarn. "KFC plans big expansion in local market: Fast food chain still confident." *The Nation* 11 November 1997: B3

La Bianca, O. 1991. Food-systems Research: An Overview and Case Study from Madaba Plains, Jordan. *Food and Foodways* 4(3-4): 221-35.

Lagopoulos, A.P. 1993. Postmodernism, Geography and the Social Semiotics of Space. *Environment and Planning D: Society and Space* 11: 255-78.

Lam, T. 1982. Food for the City: The Role of the Informal Sector. *GeoJournal* (Supplementary Issue) 4: 49-59.

Lansing, J. Stephen, 1991. *Priests and Programmers: Technologies of Power in the Engineered Landscapes of Bali*. Princeton: Princeton University Press.

Law, Lisa 2001. Home cooking: Filipino women and geographies of the senses in Hong Kong. *Ecumene* 8 (3): 264-83.

Leclant, J. 1979. Coffee and Cafes in Paris, 1644-93. In *Food and Drink in History*, ed. R. Forster and O. Ranum. 86-91. Baltimore: Johns Hopkins University Press.

Lefebvre, Henri 1991. *The Production of Space*. Trans. Donald Nicholson-Smith. Oxford: Blackwell.

Lessinger, Joanna 1989. Petty Trading and the Ideology of Gender Segregation in Urban South India. In *Women, Poverty, and Ideology in Asia*, ed. H. Afshar and B. Agarwal. 99-127. London: Macmillan.

Ley, David 1993. Cooperative Housing as a Moral Landscape: Re-Examining "The Post-modern City." In *Place/Culture/Representation*, ed. J. Duncan and D. Ley. 128-48. London: Routledge.

Ley, David and M. Samuels, eds. 1978. *Humanistic Geography*. Chicago: Maaroufa.

Licuanan, Victoria 1992. *Women Entrepreneurs in Southeast Asia*. Manila: Asian Institute of Management with the assistance of the Canadian International Development Agency.

Licuanan, Victoria 1995. *Breaking Barriers. Businesswomen of Southeast Asia*. Manila: Women Managers Program, Asian Institute of Management with the assistance of the Canadian International Development Agency.

Lim, L. 1982. *Women in the Singapore Economy*. Singapore: Chopmen.

Lyotard, Jean-François 1989. Scapeland. In *The Lyotard Reader*, ed. A. Benjamin. 212-19. Oxford: Basil Blackwell.

MacClancy, Jeremy 1992. *Consuming Culture*. London: Chapmans.

McDowell, P. 1998. Crisis drives migrants back to villages. *Vancouver Sun*, 16 July: F3.

McGee, Terry G. 1967. *The Southeast Asian City*. New York: Frederick A. Praeger.

McGee, Terry G. 1971. *The Urbanization Process in the Third World: Explorations in Search of a Theory*. London: G. Bell & Sons.

McGee, Terry G. 1973. Peasants in the Cities: A Paradox, a Paradox, a Most Ingenious Paradox. *Human Organization* 32: 135-42.

McGee, Terry G. 1992. The Geography of Southeast Asia. Course Notes. Department of Geography, University of British Columbia.

McGee, Terry G., and Ira Robinson, eds. 1995. *The Mega-Urban Regions of Southeast Asia*. Vancouver: University of British Columbia Press.

McGee, Terry G., and Yue-Man Yeung. 1977. *Hawkers in Southeast Asian cities: planning for the bazaar economy*. Ottawa: International Development Research Centre.

McKay, Deirdre 1994. Engendering Ecologies: Interpretations from the Uplands of The Philippines. Unpublished paper. Annual Meeting of the Canadian Asian Studies Association, Calgary.

McKay, Deirdre 1995. Figuring the Filipina Subaltern: Globalization, Postcolonialism, and Femininity. Unpublished paper. Anual meeting of the Canadian Council for Southeast Asian Studies, Quebec City.

MacLeod, G. 1986. *New Age Business: Community Corporations that Work*. Ottawa: Canadian Council on Social Development.

MacLeod, Scott 1989a. *A Fortune in Cookies?: Changing Contexts of Consumption and the Emergence of the Industrial Palate in Hong Kong*. Vancouver: Institute of Asian Research, University of British Columbia.

MacLeod, Scott 1989b. *Food Systems in Asia: A Select Bibliography on Changing Food Habits in Asia*. Working Paper No. 1. Vancouver: Institute of Asian Research, University of British Columbia.

Manderson, Lenore ed. 1983. *Women's Work and Women's Roles: Economics and Everyday Life in Indonesia, Malaysia and Singapore*. Canberra: Development Studies Center, Australian National University.

Marshall, A. "Indonesians toil 2 days for a Big Mac." *Vancouver Sun* 16 July 1998: F3.

Massey, Doreen 1994. *Space, Place, and Gender*. Cambridge: Polity Press.

Matichon 1994. Hazards related to supermarket food. 7 October: 25. [In Thai.]

Mead, Margaret 1964. *Food Habits Research: Problems of the 1960s*. Washington, DC: National Academy of Sciences.

Mennel, Stephen 1985. *All Manners of Food*. Oxford: Basil Blackwell.

Menzies, Heather 1981. *Women and the Chip: Case Studies of the Effects of Informatics on Employment in Canada*. Montreal: Institute for Research on Public Policy.

Mies, Maria 1986. *Patriarchy and Accumulation on a World Scale*. London: Zed Books.

Mills, Caroline A. 1989. Interpreting Gentrification: Post-industrial, Post-patriarchal, Post-modern? Unpublished PhD Dissertation. Department of Geography, University of British Columbia, Vancouver.

Mills, Mary Elizabeth 1990. "We are not like our mothers": Migrants, Modernity and Identity in Northwest Thailand. Unpublished PhD Dissertation. Department of Anthropology, University of California at Berkeley.

Mintz, Sydney 1971. Men, Women, and Trade. *Comparative Studies in Society and History* 13: 249-69.

Mohanty, C., A. Russo, and L. Torres, eds. 1991. *Third World Women and the Politics of Feminism*. Bloomington: Indiana University Press.

Montanari, Maria 1994. *The Culture of Food*. Translated by Carl Ipsen. Oxford: Blackwell Publishers.

Moore-Milroy, B. and S. Wismer. 1994. Communities, Work and Public/Private Sphere Models. *Gender, Place, and Culture* 1: 71-90.

Muecke, Marjorie 1992. Mother Sold Food, Daughter Sells Her Body: The Cultural Continuity of Prostitution. *Social Science and Medicine* 35: 891-901.

Mumford, Lewis 1961. *The City in History*. New York: Harcourt, Brace, and World.

Murray, J. 1991. *No Money, No Honey: A Study of Street Traders and Prostitutes in Jakarta*. Singapore: Oxford University Press.

Napat Sirisambhand and Christina Szanton 1986. *Thailand's Street Food Vending: The Sellers and Consumers of "Traditional Fast Foods."* Publication No. 5/1990. Bangkok: Social Research Institute, Chulalongkorn University.

Naruemol Bunjongjit and Xavier Oudin 1992. *Small Scale Industries and Institutional Framework in Thailand*. Technical Papers Nos. 81 and 81a. Paris: Organization for Economic Cooperation and Development, Development Center.

National Economic and Social Development Board 1992. *The Seventh National Economic and Social Development Plan, 1992-96.* Bangkok: Office of the Prime Minister, Royal Thai Government.

National Statistical Office (NSO) 1963. *Household Expenditure Survey, 1962-63.* Bangkok: Office of the Prime Minister, Royal Thai Government.

National Statistical Office (NSO) 1991a. *Preliminary Report of the 1990 Socio-Economic Survey: Bangkok Metropolis, Nonthaburi, Pathum Thani and Samut Prakan.* Bangkok: Office of the Prime Minister, Royal Thai Government.

National Statistical Office (NSO) 1991b. *Preliminary Report of the 1990 Household Socio-Economic Survey.* Bangkok: Office of the Prime Minister, Royal Thai Government.

National Statistical Office (NSO) 1994. *Report of the 1990 Socio-Economic Survey: Bangkok Metropolis, Nonthaburi, Pathum Thani and Samut Prakan.* Bangkok: Office of the Prime Minister, Royal Thai Government.

National Statistical Office (NSO) 2003. *Preliminary Report of the 2002 Household Socio-Economic Survey.* Bangkok: Office of the Prime Minister, Royal Thai Government.

Nguyen Xuan Linh 1993. Le Riz est plus parfumé: L'Alimentation des Vietnamiens en France. In *Autour du riz: Le repas chez quelques population d'Asie du Sud-Est*, ed. N. Krowolski and I. Simon-Barouh. 165-96. Paris: L'Harmattan.

Nicholson, L., ed. 1990. *Feminism/Post-modernism.* London: Routledge.

O'Connor, Richard 1987. Mechanical and Organic Solidarity in Bangkok. *Contributions to Southeast Asian Ethnography* 6: 13-26.

Ong, Aihwa 1987. *Spirits of Resistance and Capitalist Discipline: Factory women in Malaysia.* Albany: State University of New York Press.

Ong, Aihwa 1989. Center, Periphery and Hierarchy: Gender in Southeast Asia. In *Gender and Anthropology*, ed. S. Morgan. 294-312. Washington, DC: American Anthropological Association.

Pannee Auansakul 1995. Chinese Traders and Thai Groups in the Rice Business. *Southeast Asian Journal of Social Science* 23: 29-42. Special Issue on the "The Ethnic Chinese of Thailand" edited by Chan Kwok Bun and Tong Chee Kiong.

Papanek, H., and G. Minault 1982. *Separate Worlds: Studies of Purdah in South Asia.* Delhi: Chanakya Publications.

Peake, Linda and Caroline O. Moser. 1987. *Women, Human Settlements, and Housing.* London: Tavistock.

Peltre, Jean and Claude Thouvenot 1989. *Alimentation et region.* Nancy: Presses

Universitaires de Nancy.

Pimentel, D., and M. Pimintel 1979. *Food, Energy, and Society*. New York: John Wiley & Sons.

Pitch Pongsawat 1994. *Shopping Life in Bangkok: Progress Report*. Unpublished paper. "Thai Society in Transition: Presentation of Theses in Progress," 12 September, Thai Studies Program, Chulalongkorn University.

Pollock, G. 1988. *Vision and Difference: Femininity, Feminism, and Histories of Art*. London: Routledge.

Porteous, John D. 1990. *Landscapes of the Mind*. Toronto: University of Toronto Press.

Potter, S. H. 1977. *Family Life in a Northern Thai Village: A Study in the Structural Significance of Women*. Berkeley: University of California Press.

Pranom Supavimolpun [publisher] 1993. *Thai Hawker Food*. Bangkok: Book Promotion and Service.

Reddy, Geeta 1994. Hyderabad-Secunderabad: A Profile of Slums. Unpublished Paper. Third International Conference on the Geography of the ASEAN Region, Kuala Lumpur, 25-29 October.

Reiter, E. 1991. *Making Fast Food: From the Frying Pan into the Fryer*. Montreal: McGill-Queen's University Press.

Renu Sangktongjin 1994. Women workers earning a living in Bangkok: Case Study of Vendors in Food Stalls. *Weekend* 24-25 September: 18-19.

Report of the Committee Appointed to Investigate the Hawker Question in Singapore, 1932. Straits Settlements.

Rosaldo, Michelle and Louise Lamphère, eds. 1974. *Woman, Culture, and Society*. Palo Alto: Stanford University Press.

Rose, Gillian 1990. The Struggle for Political Democracy: Emancipation, Gender, and Geography. *Environment and Planning D: Society and Space* 8: 395-408.

Rose, Gillian 1993. *Feminism and Geography: The Limits of Geographical Knowledge*. Cambridge: Polity Press.

Rouffignat, Joël 1989. Convivialité et nutrition: Des lieux et des espaces de la restauration dans le champ urbain de Québec. In *Alimentation et région*, ed. J. Peltre and C. Thouvenot. 497-515. Nancy: Presses Universitaires de Nancy.

Ryan, M. P. 1990. *Women in Public: Between Banners and Ballots, 1825-1880*. Baltimore: Johns Hopkins University Press.

Salaff, Janet W. 1984. Wage Earners in Hong Kong. In *Chinese Working Women*, ed. M. Sheridan and J. Salaff. 146-71. Bloomington: Indiana University Press.

Salih, D., et al. 1988. *A Preliminary Review of Changes in the Malaysian Food System*. Vancouver: Institute of Asian Research, University of British Columbia.

Sanitsuda Ekachai 1990. *Behind the Smile: Voices of Thailand*. Bangkok: Post Publishing.

Sargeant, S. 1985. *The Foodmakers*. Sydney: Penguin Books.

Sauer, Carl O. 1963. *Agricultural Origins and Dispersals*. Berkeley: University of California Press.

Schlosser, Eric 2001. *Fast Food Nation: The Dark Side of the All-American Meal*. Boston: Houghton Mifflin.

Sennett, Richard 1974. *The Fall of Public Man: On the Social Psychology of Capitalism*. New York: Vintage Books.

Sethuraman, S. V. 1981. *The Urban Informal Sector in Developing Countries*. Geneva: International Labor Organization.

Shahand, A., M. A. Tekie, and K. E. Weber 1986. *The Role of Women in Slum Improvement: A Comparative Study of the Squatter Settlements at Klong Toey and Wat Yai Sri Suphan in Bangkok, Thailand*. Bangkok: Division of Human Settlements Development, Asian Institute of Technology.

Shankar, M. K. 1992. Sweet danger rears its head: Study discovers pesticide residue on some tangerines sold in mart. *The Nation* 22 December: B10.

Sharp, Laurence and Lucien Hanks 1978. *Bang Chan: Social History of a Rural Community in Thailand*. Ithaca: Cornell University Press.

Shelton, Anthony 1990. A Theater for Eating, Looking, and Thinking: The Restaurant as Symbolic Space. *Sociological Spectrum* 10: 507-26.

Simoons, Frederick J. 1961. *Eat Not This Flesh: Food Avoidances in the Old World*. Madison: University of Wisconsin Press.

Simoons, Frederick J. 1991. *Food in China: A Cultural and Historical Inquiry*. Boca Raton, FL: CRC Press.

Simple Salmon 1995. Publicity Brochure for Home Catering Service.

Sirivat Voravethvutikhun 1999. *May yom phae* [Never give up]. Based on an interview recorded with Mana Sumthong. 1st edn. Bangkok: Thai-Euro Project Press.

Sirivat Voravethvutikhun. 2002. *Nab neung may* [Starting over]. Bangkok: Duang Kamol Books and Readers' Digest.

Skinner, G. William 1957. *Chinese Society in Thailand: An Analytical History*. Ithaca: Cornell University Press.

Smart, Josephine 1989. *The Political Economy of Street Hawkers in Hong Kong*. Center of Asian Studies Occasional Paper No. 81. Hong Kong: Centre of Asian

Studies, University of Hong Kong.

Smith, Dorothy 1987. *The Everyday World as Problematic: A Feminist Sociology.* Boston: Northeastern University Press.

Smith, Dorothy M. 1988. Toward an Interpretative Human Geography. In *Qualitative Methods in Human Geography*, ed. J. D. Eyles and D. M. Smith. 255-67. Cambridge: Polity Press.

Sorre, Max 1952. La géographie de l'alimentation. *Annales de Géographie* 61: 184-99.

Spiro, M. E. 1977. *Kinship and Marriage in Burma: A Cultural and Psychodynamic Analysis.* Berkeley: University of California Press.

Spivak, Gayatri Chakravorty 1988. Can the Sub-Altern Speak? In *Marxism and the Interpretation of Culture*, ed. L. Grossberg and C. Nelson. 271-312. Urbana: University of Illinois Press.

Spradley, J. P. 1980. *Participant Observation.* New York: Holt, Rinehart, and Winston.

Staeheli, Lynn 1996. Publicity, Privacy, and Women's Political Action. In *Environment and Planning D: Society and Space* 24: 601-19.

Sunanthana Saenprasert and Sriprat Boonnamma 1993. *The Sanitation Conditions of Street Foods in Prabudda-bath Municipality.* Saraburi Province: Sanitation Division. [In Thai.]

Suntaree Komin 1989. *Social Dimensions of Industrialization in Thailand.* Bangkok: National Institute of Development Administration.

Szanton, Christina B. 1983. People in Movement: Social Mobility and Leadership in a Central Thai Town. Unpublished PhD Dissertation. Columbia University, New York.

The Economist 1993. A Survey of the Food Industry: Indigestion. 4 December. Special insert.

(FEER) Far Eastern Economic Review 1993. Full Speed Ahead. 21 October: 66-70.

(FEER) Far Eastern Economic Review 1995. Review 2000 Thailand. 29 December 1994: 70-71.

The Nation 1993. Retailing boom. February 16: B16.

Tinker, I. 1987. Street Foods: Testing Assumptions about Informal Sector Activity by Women and Men. *Current Sociology* 35:1-110.

Trinh T. Minh-Ha 1989. *Woman/Native/Other.* Bloomington: Indiana University Press.

Turner, Sarah 2002. *Indonesia's Small Entrepreneurs: Trading on the Margins.*

London: Routledge.

Van Esterik, Penny ed. 1982. *Women of Southeast Asia*. Northern Illinois University Series on Southeast Asia Occasional Paper No. 9. De Kalb: Northern Illinois University.

Van Esterik, Penny ed. 1986. Feeding Their Faith: Recipe Knowledge Among Thai Buddhist Women. *Food and Foodways* 1: 197-215.

Van Esterik, Penny ed. 1992a. From Marco Polo to McDonald's: Thai Cuisine in Transition. *Food and Foodways* 5: 177-93.

Visser, Margaret 1991. *The Rituals of Dinner*. Toronto: HarperCollins.

Visweswaran, Kamala 1994. *Fictions of Feminist Ethnography*. Minneapolis: University of Minnesota Press.

Vitit Muntarbhorn 1985. *Women's Development in Thailand*. Published by the National Comittee for International Cooperation under the Thailand National Commission on Women's Affairs, for the World Conference of the United Nations Decade for Women, Nairobi, 15-26 July 1985.

Walker, Marilyn 1990. *Food Consumption Survey*. (Thailand). Conducted by Frank Small and Associates (unpublished).

Walker, Marilyn 1991. Thai Elites and the Construction of Socio-Cultural Identity. Unpublished PhD Dissertation. Department of Social Anthropology,York University, Toronto.

Walker, R. 1981. On the Uses of Fiction in Educational Research. In *Practising Evaluation*, ed. D. Smetherham. Driffield: Nafferton.

Walton, John K. 1989. Fish and Chips and the British Working-class, 1870-1930. *Journal of Sociological History* 23: 243-66.

Warde, A. and L. Martens. *Eating Out: Social Differentiation, Consumption, and Pleasure*. Cambridge: Cambridge University Press.

Warren, Stacey 1994. "This Heaven Gives Me Migraines": The Problems and Promise of Landscapes of Leisure. In *Place/Culture/Representation*, ed. J. Duncan and D. Ley. 173-186. London: Routledge.

Warren, W., and R. I. Lloyd. 1989. *Bangkok's Waterways: An Explorer's Handbook*. Bangkok: Asia Books.

Watts, Michael 1983. *Silent Violence: Food, Famine, and Peasantry in Northern Nigeria*. Berkeley: University of California Press.

Wekerle, Gerda 1988. *Women's Housing Projects in Eight Canadian Cities*. Ottawa: Canada Mortgage and Housing Corporation.

Wekerle, Gerda et al., eds. 1980. *New Space for Women*. Boulder, CO: Westview Press.

Winzeler, R. 1982. Sexual Status in Southeast Asia: Comparative Perspectives on Women, Agriculture and Political Organization. In *Women of Southeast Asia*, ed. P. Van Esterik. 176-213. Northern Illinois University Series on Southeast Asia Occasional Paper No. 9. De Kalb: Northern Illinois University.

Wolf, Diane 1990. Linking Women's Labor with the Global Economy: Factory Workers and their Families in Rural Java. In *Women Workers and Global Restructuring*, ed. K. Ward. Ithaca: Cornell University Press.

Wolf, Diane 1992. *Factory Daughters: Gender, Household Dynamics, and Rural Industrialization in Java*. Berkeley: University of California Press.

Wong, Chan. 1995. Eat Food, Drink Tea, Do Business: The Zen of Chinese Business Dining. *Pacific Business* 1: 2.

Yasmeen, Gisèle 1992a. Bangkok's Restaurant Sector: Gender, Employment, and Consumption. *Journal of Social Research* (Chulalongkorn University, Bangkok) 15: 69-81.

Yasmeen, Gisèle 1992b. Women's Autonomy and Power in Southeast Asia: The Case of Thailand. Unpublished paper.

Yasmeen, Gisèle 2001a. Stockbrokers turned sandwich vendors: The economic crisis and food-retailing in The Philippines and Thailand. 32(1): 91-102.

Yasmeen, Gisèle 2001b. *Feeding Asian Cities*. Proceedings of a Regional Seminar convened by CityNet, The Association of Food Marketing Agencies in Asia and the Pacific with technical support from the FAO, November 2000, Bangkok. Rome: FAO ("Food into Cities" Collection AC/37-01E).

Yeoh, Brenda and Lily Kong 1994. Reading Landscape Meanings: State Constructions and Lived Experiences in Singapore's Chinatown. *Habitat International* 18: 1-19.

Zukin, Sharon 1991. *Landscapes of Power: From Detroit to Disneyworld*. Berkeley: University of California Press.

Personal Communications
(*Location Bangkok unless otherwise specified*)

Archer, Ray 1992.

Chalee Sintunava Municipal Police Department. 1994.

Chongrak Tripakvasin, Property and Building Manager, Central Pattana Company. 1993

Chua Beng-Huat 1994. Singapore.

Demeritt, David 1995. Vancouver.

Dubuis, Claudia 1995. Vancouver.

Fauza Abdul Ghaffar 1994. Universiti Malaya, Kuala Lumpur.

Greenberg, Charles 1993. Bangkok and Vancouver.

Jadavji, Altaf 1995. Various locations.

Jamilah Mohamed. 1994. Kuala Lumpur.

Kamolrat Sa-Ngeam. 1994 and 2000.

Kelly, Philip 1995. Vancouver.

Keyes, Charles F. 1995. Seattle.

Laquian, Aprodicio 1993.

Lary, Diana 1996. Vancouver.

Ley, David 1993 and 1996. Vancouver.

Lin, George Chu-Sheng 1995. Vancouver.

McGee, Terry G. 1995. Vancouver.

Pasuk Pongpaichit. 1993.

Pendakur, Setty 1992.

Rakawin Leechanavanichpan, Coordinator, HomeNet Thailand. 2000.

Reese, M. 1996. Vancouver.

Robinson, Ira 1992.

Vespry, Arthur. 1993 and 1994.

Vespry, Marianne. 1994.

Woo Yuen-Pau 1996. Vancouver.

Index

Nonthaburi Mall, 61–62
Northeastern Thailand (Isaan)
  cultural attitudes of, 87, 97–98, 104
  ethnographic encounters, 37, 70, 106
  foodways, 53, 78
  kinship patterns, 5
  mainstream attitudes towards, 109, 117
  migrants, 5, 67, 78, 94, 116–17, 118, 123, 126–27, 128, 129, 131, 132, 134,
    161, 169, 179, 191, 201–02

Pawnshops (*rong rap jam nam*), 168
Phetchaburi Road, 129, 130
Philippines, The, 20, 170, 200, 204–06
Police (*tekasit*), 83, 129, 146, 150, 161, 162, 177, 178, 192, 193
Public eating
  as Bangkok habit, 1, 7, 207–10
  as lunchtime phenomenon, 121
  attitudes toward, 87
  health and hygiene, 41, 65, 77, 149, 186, 206
  origins, 6
  private space, 64–65
  social class issues, 86–88
  street *vs. soi*, 64–65, 159–61
Public/private sphere models, 31–33
Pushcarts, 8, 100–02, 117, 118, 121, 126, 127, 130, 132, 146, 154, 156, 176

Ragnam Road Area, 50, 81, 106–07, 120, 129, 149, 161
Rajavitee Road, 47–48, 81, 161
Restaurants
  as gendered space (*see also* Gender relations), 166, 196–97
  definition, 10
  design of, 131, 154–59
  kinds of
  Chinese, 10, 47, 84, 104, 135, 140
  elite (*see* Foodscape, elite)
  family, 84
  fast food, 142, 202–03

285